STANDING ALONE

STORIES OF HEROISM AND HEARTBREAK FROM MANCHESTER CITY'S 2020/21 TITLE-WINNING SEASON

SAM LEE · DANIEL TAYLOR · OLIVER KAY

AND OTHER AWARD-WINNING WRITERS OF

The Athletic

POLARIS
PUBLISHING

BACKPAGE

First published in 2021 by

POLARIS PUBLISHING LTD
and
BACKPAGE PRESS

www.backpagepress.co.uk
www.polarispublishing.com

British Library Cataloguing-in-Publication Data
A catalogue record for this book is available on request from the
British Library.

Designed and typeset by Polaris Publishing, Edinburgh

Printed in Great Britain by MBM Print, East Kilbride

MIX
Paper from
responsible sources
FSC
www.fsc.org   FSC® C117931

CONTENTS

A

INTRODUCTION

When we were launching *The Athletic* in the UK, building on the success that the company had enjoyed in rapidly spreading across America, I often found myself explaining things to our CEO or other executives in terms of US sports.

As we put together the list of writers we wanted to hire for each team in the Premier League, we had what we called a Depth Chart, a nod to how NFL teams map out their rosters. The data showed that writers who can pull off outstanding feature writing that readers will share across the internet would be valuable hires for us in Britain, so we sought out those we considered Home Run hitters. Even our early editorial and business structure was more like a Major League sports franchise, with me acting as General Manager and Alex Kay-Jelski, our editor-in-chief, the head coach that all the writers and editors looked to to lead.

One football reference that I repeatedly made, however, involved Manchester City.

Our ambition from the outset was to build the best football coverage available anywhere on the planet. Having at least one writer dedicated to each team was obviously a great headstart but that doesn't guarantee anything. My conviction from the start was that if we were hiring great writers, we would need great editors to guide them, just as City has sought out the best coaches to support Pep Guardiola's philosophy and improve already world-class talents. The focus on editorial talent at media companies always tends to lean towards writers, but having brilliant people who can guide them, who can counsel them, who can improve them is so important and something that the bean counters always struggle to quantify. Manchester City, I would tell my bosses, should be our model in some ways.

Alex, our editor-in-chief, will no doubt love that he is the Guardiola in all this. They do, in fairness, have some similarities. Both are endlessly passionate about being the best, and making those around them better. Both are endlessly creative, and willing to try new things in the pursuit of greatness. We wanted to surround Alex with people who he could make better and who could make everyone else better.

Last summer, Pep brought in the legendary Juanma Lillo to bolster his already impressive coaching staff. Just when you think Guardiola and his sprawling coaching structure has every detail covered, he moved to add and innovate again. Being beaten to the title by Liverpool was tough to take for a coach who so covets the league title for its recognition of superiority over a significant sample size. This season, City emphasised and reasserted their superiority once again.

It isn't just great coaching at City though. The City Football Group has built a state-of-the-art campus to give its talent the best facilities for learning, recovery and whatever else they need. There is an appreciation of the value of sports science. Data scientists push at the edge of what is known about the analytics of football in pursuit of an edge on the competition while one of the largest scouting networks ever assembled feeds reports into a global database to locate and secure the best young talent wherever it may be.

Our business is nowhere near as big and impressive as CFG yet but those principles of trying to be the best in every area, of providing intelligent and empathetic support to everyone in order to try and maximise their potential, and of aspiring to the impossibility of perfection are good things to strive for as we continue to grow.

I hope that is reflected in our coverage of Manchester City that you have been reading since we launched in 2019, and that you will find in this book. We have laid out the story of their title-winning campaign month by month, including articles that we felt helped to explain how and why it happened.

Sam Lee, who will be familiar to City fans, is obviously featured fairly prominently as our Manchester City correspondent. Sam will always hold a special place in my heart as the first UK writer to say 'yes' when we were building the newsroom. I had been impressed by the way he covered the club in a modern way, providing a level of differentiation between what was already available locally and what was interesting to City's new, global audience.

Alongside Sam there are heavy doses of Oliver Kay and Daniel Taylor, two of the finest football writers in the country and journalists who have covered the Manchester patch for decades. There are a host of other names, including our analytics expert Tom Worville, that bring a different element to our coverage and ensure that, as well as fine storytelling, we were analysing City to explain how they were so impressive. Football's finest newsbreaker David Ornstein was also a valuable contributor, providing behind-the-scenes insight that nobody else can.

It was a sad ending to an otherwise outstanding season for City in Porto, but it ensures Guardiola still has unfinished business and something to strive for. So do we. As proud as I am of what we have achieved in less than two years at *The Athletic* we are going to continue to try and get better, providing the best coverage of football across all platforms. It will take a lot of work, some good decision-making and smart use of our resources but I like our chances, just as I like City's as they go again next year, determined to make history.

Ed Malyon
Managing Director (UK)
The Athletic

JULY

THE STORY OF MANCHESTER CITY'S FIVE MONTHS IN LIMBO

ADAM CRAFTON, DANIEL TAYLOR

ADDITIONAL CONTRIBUTORS: DAVID ORNSTEIN, SAM LEE

JUL 14, 2020

Among the powerful Catalan contingent who bestride the corridors of power at Manchester City, the announcement on Monday morning brought an instant release of euphoria.

On the Instagram page belonging to Manel Estiarte, a long-serving member of Pep Guardiola's backroom staff, a picture rapidly surfaced. In the background, the rolling coverage of Sky Sports News played out and, in front of the screen, the grinning faces of City's leading men beamed out. Guardiola and Estiarte posed alongside the chief executive Ferran Soriano, the sporting director Txiki Begiristain and the chief operating officer Omar Berrada.

Behind the scenes, City's handsomely-paid legal team have worked around the clock to file their ultimately successful submission to the Court of Arbitration for Sport (CAS). This week, all that expense paid lucrative dividends, eliminating a two-year Champions League ban and reducing the fine – for obstructing the original investigation – from £25 million to £9 million. Yet while the legalese secured headline-grabbing success,

City's head coach Guardiola and their Catalan executive staged a careful production of their own, managing the uncertainty pervading the dressing room and keeping a roll call of star turns on board. City's most senior figures only discovered the verdict an hour before its public announcement and the five men pictured are understood to have taken in the news together when the call came in from Switzerland.

In the City boardroom, the news soon went global. At 9.30am, CAS published their statement and, four minutes later, an email dropped into the inboxes of the club's staff not only at their Manchester training base but also to offices in London, Singapore, Japan and Melbourne. Soriano conceded that "these have not been easy times" but praised the "resilience and character" of those employed by City. It carried a triumphant tone, telling staff that the outcome "vindicated the club's decision" to challenge the judgement taken by UEFA's club financial control body in February. The email concluded by describing the episode as an "unwelcome distraction" and said the "club can now push ahead with recovery from COVID-19 and our performance on and off the pitch".

In the City dressing room, confirmation of the reprieve was greeted with similar acclaim. On the outside, City have maintained a stiff upper lip and a brave face over the past five months but even the most ardent supporter may have wondered how some of the squad's most talented players would respond to a potential two-year ban from the continent's elite competition. Sergio Aguero is 32 and Kevin De Bruyne, now 29, would have been 31 by the time Champions League football returned to east Manchester if the worst punishment transpired.

There were red flags. Early in May, for example, De Bruyne said in an interview in his native Belgium that he would consider his future. The midfielder said: "Two years would be long but in the case of one year I might see."

Equally, *The Athletic* reported in February how Bernardo Silva, the Portuguese playmaker, would require some major persuading to remain at the club for the two years preceding the major World Cup of his career without access to Europe's biggest club competition.

Perhaps most curious, however, was the concern that privately gripped City over Raheem Sterling, now 25 and at the peak of his powers. Shortly before City travelled to face Real Madrid in the Champions League, Sterling afforded an interview to the Spanish *AS* newspaper and it is no exaggeration to say that eyebrows were raised internally over the player's decision to pose with a Real Madrid shirt draped over one shoulder and a City shirt over the other. In Madrid, the antennae pricked up and anyone who has witnessed Real's pursuit of star names over the years sensed it may be the beginning of a drawn-out affair. City, at the time, felt that making a big deal out of the affair may only serve to inflame a sensitive situation, although the player's agent, Aidy Ward, had previously said publicly that Sterling would not leave the club.

Despite the Sterling reservations, however, it is also true that not one City player approached the club's executives during this period to state an intention to leave the club due to their fears over the Champions League ban and much of this loyalty is owed to the careful management overseen by Guardiola and Soriano.

The news of a potential two-year ban dropped on City on the evening of Valentine's Day, just as the club returned from their winter break on a Friday night. Guardiola rapidly called his players in for a meeting on the Saturday. In a conference room at the club's training ground, Guardiola reassured his players he would remain at the club next season, regardless of the result of any appeal, and he rallied the troops. The tone was us-against-the-world and, ahead of their Champions League fixture against Real Madrid, he urged his players to show Europe "we are not money, we are talent". Indeed, on the Friday evening that preceded the meeting, City's executives took a proactive approach, reaching out to their players' agents to give reassurances that the club would overturn the punishment upon appeal. While De Bruyne teased an exit in public, his agent did, however, reassure City, while representatives of Phil Foden made it abundantly clear he wished to remain at the club.

City's players were further comforted when, shortly after the club returned to training after lockdown, Guardiola roused his group with a speech. In the address, he told his players that Soriano had reassured him that the club would be successful upon appeal and, in the immediate aftermath, both Sterling and De Bruyne confided in team-mates that they would remain at the club.

During the pandemic, most clubs broached the possibility of wage deferrals or reductions with their playing squad. City advocated a pay cut of around 10 per cent for the playing squad but the players were only willing to take a deferral of roughly five per cent. With neither side inclined to change their stance, the talks reached an impasse and have seemingly been put on the back burner since then. City's hierarchy ultimately agreed to carry on paying the squad's full wages.

Perhaps most interestingly, those most closely familiar with these City players felt the major sticking point in the group could ultimately hinge upon how their successes in recent times would be framed in the event the ban stood. Yet City did fear their players may feel their achievements to be tainted due to the UEFA judgment, or an asterisk placed against the trophies won under Guardiola's guidance.

Not everybody, it should be said, was convinced City would succeed. While the super-agent Jorge Mendes sent a private memo of support, other agents gossiped privately, aware that the Ballon d'Or bonuses in their players' contracts, for instance, would swiftly fade into irrelevance if their clients could not compete at the highest level. Players can receive five-figure windfalls through partnerships and sponsorships linked to European competition and some boot deals will include clauses based on the number of appearances a player makes in the Champions League.

City's future plans, meanwhile, would clearly have been compromised by an absence from the elite. City recorded a £10.1 million profit last season but £77 million of their income came from Champions League participation. In the absence of this cash flow, it is tempting to wonder whether City may have needed to do more to balance the books than simply sell Leroy Sane in his long-trailed move to Bayern Munich.

Now, however, such concerns have dissipated. City are favourites to see off Real Madrid in the Champions League round of 16 and they will return to the competition next season with added sparkle. The club are determined to recruit players at centre-back, left-back, on the wing and up front this summer. At left-back, City are open to selling any of Angelino, Benjamin Mendy or Oleksandr Zinchenko. City conceived a plan to include Bayern Munich's David Alaba in the Sane deal but the Germans could not be persuaded. Juventus' Alex Sandro is a long-standing target who may return to the shortlist, while City have not yet abandoned all hope on Leicester's Ben Chilwell, in a deal which may be revived if Chelsea fail to qualify for the Champions League.

Southampton's experienced full-back Ryan Bertrand, who has excelled of late, is also on the radar after Guardiola first considered a move for him in 2017. At centre-half, Napoli's Kalidou Koulibaly and Bournemouth's Nathan Ake are contenders while Valencia's breakthrough talent Ferran Torres is running down his contract and impressing suitors in the wide position. Bayern's Kingsley Coman and Bayer Leverkusen's Leon Bailey are alternatives.

While the targets are varied, the nub is clear: City want to recruit and Guardiola wants it done with conviction. Previous summers have irritated the City coach, particularly in the way the club were beaten to transfers by Chelsea and Manchester United for Jorginho and Harry Maguire, despite subsequent protestations that the club will not pay over the odds for players.

While City go on the attack, both on and off the field, the reaction elsewhere has been shock and bewilderment. One senior Premier League club executive described himself as "flabbergasted" on Monday. Meanwhile, a WhatsApp group of leading European club directors rapidly exchanged messages to discuss the next steps for financial fair play within an hour of the news breaking. Soon enough, they were consulting external advisers and deliberating whether to lobby UEFA to take City to a Swiss federal court.

Guardiola, for his part, is expected to be robust in his next press appearance and he has privately been unimpressed by the moves made by the European elite to circle on City. Earlier this year, Guardiola turned on his former club Barcelona, telling them not to "talk too loud" after the club's president praised the decision to ban City. Guardiola may take aim at certain clubs, for City have been equally unimpressed by representations made by Juventus and Bayern over the years, as well as what they see as a concerted bid to cut the club's representatives out of key positions on European Club Association and UEFA committees.

There are no shortage of contenders for a Guardiola riposte but, deep down, the coach will be most content to know his City team will now be able to do their talking on the pitch.

SEPTEMBER

WHAT MESSI'S U-TURN MEANS FOR HIM, BARCELONA AND MANCHESTER CITY

DERMOT CORRIGAN, SAM LEE

OTHER CONTRIBUTORS: ED MALYON AND ADAM CRAFTON

SEPT 4, 2020

Ten days after Lionel Messi asked to leave Barcelona, sparking a bitter, public legal row with the club at which he has played for almost two decades and its president Josep Maria Bartomeu, the six-time Ballon d'Or winner has reversed his position, saying that he is to stay.

The move will be seen as a blow to Manchester City, who have strongly distanced themselves from a move but who multiple sources said were making efforts to finally sign the 33-year-old, and to all those who hoped to see him in the Premier League.

In a saga that has dominated the past week, Messi first communicated his desire to leave in a Burofax to the club, who insisted a clause allowing him to depart for free at the end of the season just gone had expired, a stance supported publicly by La Liga.

The player's father and agent, Jorge, then travelled to Barcelona for talks, following which the first formal statement came on Friday afternoon, with Jorge writing to La Liga president Javier

Tebas, criticising the league's position and reaffirming his son's right to leave Barcelona.

Yet within a few hours an interview had been broadcast in which Messi spoke of his decision to stay at the club he "loves" and his commitment to their cause.

So what's really been going on?

What did Messi say?

The most important message from Lionel Messi's interview with Goal.com was that he was taking back his decision to leave Barcelona this summer. "I could never take the club of my life to court, that is why I am going to stay at Barcelona," Messi said.

It was not because he had changed his mind but because he had realised it would be impossible to force his way out without taking the club he loved through a painful court battle. So he was going to stay and play for Ronald Koeman's team next season.

"I told the president I wanted to go, that my time was over at Barca," Messi said. "I always wanted to finish my career at this club, but I suffered a lot through a very difficult year. I wanted to look for new objectives, a new atmosphere, new challenges. The exit from the Champions League hurt a lot, but that did not make up my mind. It came from many things which had been happening. I had been thinking about it all year."

Why has he decided to make this U-turn?

Messi has not changed his mind about wanting out, but has decided that he could not force his exit, as that would have required a damaging and lengthy legal battle. He still believes that he had the legal right to leave for free this summer, but the club were only prepared to let him leave if another club came to pay his €700 million release clause. So that left taking Barca to court, and he said he could not bring himself to do that to the club he has been at since the age of 13.

How long is Messi really likely to stay at Barcelona? Could he stay beyond next season or is he now likely to leave on a free next summer?

Barca sources have maintained to *The Athletic* all through the last fortnight that there is an offer of a two-year contract extension on the table for Messi to sign whenever he wants. Whoever is president next summer will also surely try their hardest to make sure that Messi does not leave then and walk away for free.

The Argentine avoided saying how long he intended to stay at the club during the interview, sticking instead to saying he would fulfil the final 12 months of his current deal, and give his all under new coach Ronald Koeman.

"The truth is I don't know what will happen," he said. "There is a new coach and a new idea. That is good, but then we will have to see how the team responds, and if it is enough for us to compete or not. All I can say is that I am staying, and I will always give everything."

That was far from a ringing endorsement of Koeman's appointment or the team's chances of success in 2020/21. The problems with Barca's 'sporting project' are unlikely to be fixed before next summer, especially given its financial situation. But a year is an eternity in football, and by June 10 next year the club will have a new president, who will likely bring back some of Messi's former team-mates to the Camp Nou, so there would be time then to change his mind again.

How big a blow is this for Manchester City?

When Messi first signalled his intention to leave, City strongly distanced themselves from any deal and that position has not changed but sources told *The Athletic* that the club were interested in bringing him to Manchester. Messi's comments would seem to have ended that prospect but there is one school of thought around City as of Friday evening that this may not be over.

The same sources that confirmed to *The Athletic* that City were firmly in the race to sign Messi last Tuesday have suggested that Bartomeu might still need to sell Messi (to balance the books and leave the club without being personally liable for any losses) and that that may still be an option in the coming weeks.

It's easy to believe that there is an element of clinging to a dream about this, or that it is even something of a conspiracy theory. But if you were to work on the basis that Bartomeu does want to sell Messi after all, and that Messi does want to leave and join City, but that neither of them want to be seen as the bad guys, this interview could simply be Messi putting the ball in Bartomeu's court, calling his bluff and 'threatening' to stay. Of course, it would only be a threat if Bartomeu does indeed need and want to sell Messi, despite his public stance to the opposite.

So is this interview really the end of the saga or just an elaborate negotiating tactic? It would certainly push the limits of credibility to imagine Messi leaving the club after sitting down and giving an interview like this, but there are those at City that believe this chapter is not entirely closed. They always knew it would be extremely difficult to sign him, even after putting themselves in pole position, and few would suggest their chances are any better right now, but it's one to bear in mind, at least.

Did City really believe they could sign him?

Yes. In the two weeks leading up to Messi sending that Burofax informing Barcelona that he would leave, sources told *The Athletic* that City had been in contact with him and his people had worked out the required figures and put themselves into a position where they were ready to sign him if he could get himself out of Barcelona.

As of Sunday, they were content with how things were progressing, and sources have told *The Athletic* that he even reiterated his desire to join the club on Friday morning. If that is indeed the case, given Messi either filmed his interview the same day or even Thursday, then clearly there are legs to the idea that Messi is calling Bartomeu's bluff. But leaving that to one side, City were ready to try and do a deal if Messi could get out of Barca, it's just that he hasn't been able to.

How will this change what they do in the transfer market this summer?

Not a lot. City have been pressing ahead with attempts to sign Kalidou Koulibaly from Napoli even while waiting to see what happened with Messi, and our information was that they would have been able to sign them both, and possibly even another target. Sources also indicated at the start of the week, when City were content with how the Messi saga was playing out, that there was an alternative forward in the plans just in case. If the Messi dream really is over, they can press ahead with those, but there can be no doubt that they are still well placed to strengthen their squad this summer, although now they have to close the deals they have in place.

Is this likely to have any impact on Pep Guardiola's future at the club?

The assumption/hope among fans after City got their Champions League ban overturned was that it would boost the chances of Guardiola signing a new deal. Obviously, it didn't make it any less likely but the main factor in whether he stays or not will be the strength of the squad next season, and whether he sees enough motivation and desire inside the dressing room to keep listening to his messages for another couple of years.

Had Messi arrived, with the boost he would surely have brought to the team, the chances of Guardiola signing a new contract would have only increased. It would be easy to imagine Messi staying for two, maybe three years, and Guardiola staying for that long as well. But even without Messi, City are still working on strengthening the squad so there is still an opportunity to give Guardiola the squad he needs and wants. So although Messi would surely have made it more likely that Guardiola would extend his contract, the fact Messi is probably not signing doesn't really make it any less likely.

GUARDIOLA STEPS INTO THE UNKNOWN

DANIEL TAYLOR AND DERMOT CORRIGAN

SEPT 17, 2020

A lot has changed since *The Complete History of Manchester City*, written by football historian Gary James, was published in 1997. But if you would like a reminder of the differences between today's version of the club and what City used to be like, perhaps the best place to start is by turning to page 390 and a cartoon that sums up the bad old days.

It shows two players peering nervously through an open door into the manager's office. They look uncertain about what they might find and, true to form, the chair is empty. Another manager has just been fired. Mel Machin, in this case. Or possibly Jimmy Frizzell. "I hear they've fitted an ejector seat," says the speech bubble.

It can certainly come as a jolt to realise that Pep Guardiola is now – no kidding – the club's longest-serving manager since Tony Book in the 1970s. Guardiola, to put it another way, has outlasted the previous 19 City managers. Or 23, if caretaker managers are included. And if he stays until the end of March, he will overtake Book, too. Nobody will have managed the club longer since Joe Mercer, from 1965 to 1971. And, hold on a moment, wasn't it said of Guardiola that he rarely stuck around?

This will be his fifth season in England and, to put that in context, it is the longest Guardiola has managed anywhere. OK, it is some distance behind Sir Alex Ferguson's 26-year dynasty at Manchester United, Brian Clough's 18-year reign at Nottingham Forest and Bill Shankly's 15 at Liverpool. But it does make Guardiola the fourth longest-serving member of his profession in the Premier League. Sean Dyche at Burnley, Liverpool's Jurgen Klopp and Chris Wilder of Sheffield United are the only managers to outlast him.

In turn, Guardiola has helped the club to be seen, and to operate, as a superpower. His mere presence has given City a gravitas they never had before. Amazing success was expected and, in a way, that is exactly what he has given them: two Premier League titles, one FA Cup, three League Cups and, as he insists we should count them, two Community Shields. City have never had it so good.

At the same time, Guardiola might also have to understand why, despite everything, he will also be under more pressure this season than perhaps any time before. The bottom line, after all, is that City brought him to the club because they wanted to see their blue ribbons on the Champions League and, failing that, to have a team that either won, or went very close to winning, the Premier League every season.

Last season, City did neither. Their defence of the title ended with them as a speck in Liverpool's wing-mirrors, 18 points behind the champions. At one stage, the gap was 25. Their Champions League quarter-final against Lyon was another ordeal, losing to the seventh-best team in France, and this season could conceivably be the last chance for Guardiola to put it right.

Tactically, Guardiola got it badly wrong against Lyon. His players knew it and so did the people running the club. It was the lowest moment of his reign and, lest it be forgotten, he is now in the final year of his contract.

Ask Brian Marwood to describe what it is like to work alongside Guardiola and it quickly becomes clear that, inside the club, they have never stopped revering the Catalan. "How do you describe one of the best managers, or *the* best manager, in the world?" Marwood says.

Marwood has been a key figure at City since 2009, first as director of football and then in his current role as managing director of global football. He has seen the club win the league previously, with Roberto Mancini and then Manuel Pellegrini as manager, but to hear him talk about Guardiola is to be reminded why City have always thought, unofficially, that Pep was the real Special One.

"Our aim was to create an identity for the club," Marwood tells *The Athletic*. "What we needed was a consistent style and a framework of how we wanted to play. We wanted a certain type of football.

"Manuel was probably the first one who allowed the club to appoint someone who fell into line with that style. But, with no disrespect to anybody, the one person we always thought was the high priest of that style was Pep Guardiola. Appointing him was a critical point for the club because it was style meets the teacher. That was a watershed moment for Manchester City."

Ideally, City would like Guardiola to extend his contract beyond summer 2021 and remain at the club for as long as he can be persuaded. But it is difficult to be certain at this stage whether he is open to that possibility and, in one sense, it might come as a surprise already that he has stayed this long in Manchester.

Guardiola had four seasons as Barcelona's manager and three in charge at Bayern Munich, and something has clearly changed because, by the time he was done at the Camp Nou in 2012, he was openly admitting that he had nothing left to give and needed a clean break. "Four years is an eternity," he said. "That time can wear you out and take its toll. I'm drained. I have to get my passion back. I have always thought that things are best done in the short term."

In Spain, they call it '*desgaste*' – the emotional fatigue and wear that comes from working in an environment where the pressure is unforgiving and unremitting. "When he took over at Barca, he had a lot of hair. When he left, he was bald," says Albert Benaiges, Guardiola's long-time associate. "There is a big toll on you in these jobs. Look at Jose Mourinho, Zinedine Zidane . . . it's just like prime ministers. All the tension and everything involved punishes the body.

"At Barcelona, Pep arrived before eight in the morning and left after eight at night. He is a great worker. He spends all day running things over, making up his mind, how he can improve things, all day thinking about football.

"For sure, there is a *desgaste*. It's the same for the people who work with him and everyone on the team. If you have a meal with him, all the cutlery and glasses on the table become players. He lives for football. I am the same. It is our passion. I can be watching games and following players from eight in the morning until midnight. I stop to eat and nothing more. Since you were small, you have it in your body, in your personality, and in the end, your life is football."

Benaiges spent more than 20 years at Barcelona, initially as a coach and then as a co-ordinator of La Masia, the club's famed academy, developing the philosophy that turned out Lionel Messi, Xavi Hernandez, Andres Iniesta and many more.

Too much, he says, is made of the fact that Guardiola has never gone past the four-year mark in his two previous managerial roles. "The reality is that coaches don't tend to last long. Pep left Barca when he wanted to, he left Bayern when he wanted to and I believe he will leave Manchester City when he wants to. Unless something big changes, he will stay at City. He has it in his head, or his heart, that he has the chance to win the Champions League."

The issue, perhaps, is to understand why Guardiola, four months short of his 50th birthday, no longer seems so susceptible to the mental exhaustion that saw him quit Barcelona and retreat to New York for a year-long sabbatical. If four years is an eternity, why has the same amount of time in Manchester not sapped his energy as it did at the Camp Nou?

"The atmosphere that he has found in Manchester is a big factor," says Marti Perarnau, Guardiola's friend and biographer. "From the first day, he wanted to be close to (director of football) Txiki Begiristain. He and (chief executive) Ferran Soriano understand each other well. He has connected with the president (Khaldoon Al Mubarak). The relationship with the players has been good, even with some who have left, like Leroy Sane.

"Pep has won a lot of trophies. He has an excellent relationship with the fans, whenever he meets them, and he is very comfortable in the city. I don't believe that thinking about how long he will stay is a priority for Pep. He has just added to his squad and is preparing for competition. When he has a free week halfway through the season, he might start to think about it."

Guardiola has an apartment close to Manchester's cathedral. When he started talking to City, he made it a stipulation that he wanted to live centrally, just as he had done in Munich. He wanted to feel part of the city, rather than migrating to the opulent Cheshire villages where most of the north west's football fraternity tend to end up.

The homelessness in Manchester bothers him. The litter, too, because it feels to him and his wife, Cristina, that some people do not take enough care of where they live. Cristina has now moved back to Barcelona, because that is where her business is based and where Valentina, the youngest of their three children, goes to school.

It is not ideal to be away from his family but Guardiola likes Manchester and can happily testify that, contrary to what Carlos Tevez once said, it has more than two restaurants. His own one, for starters. Guardiola is the part-owner of Tast in King Street, along with Soriano and Begiristain, the former Barcelona executives who played such a key role in persuading him to come to England.

Perarnau, who has collaborated with Guardiola on two books (*Pep Confidential* and *Pep Guardiola: The Evolution*), takes the view that his friend is more relaxed, more at ease and essentially happier in Manchester than many people realise.

"Yes, there is a very big *desgaste* at the top level in football. You just have to see the before-and-after photos: Guardiola, Luis Enrique, Mourinho, Klopp. Everyone who coaches with that passion and intensity pays a huge price.

"With Guardiola, though, it is not as bad in Manchester as it was at Barca. First, because when you are managing in your own 'house', as Barca were to him, you always feel extra pressure. Second, the sports press in Barcelona was deeply toxic. And third, the president at Barca, Sandro Rosell, did many things against Pep. The pressure – the *desgaste* – was much higher."

Benaiges makes the point that, at City, there is no internal conflict or divisive politics. Guardiola and his coaches, he says, trust one another completely. The Spanish/Catalan influence is considerable at the club, including office staff, administrators, a press officer and numerous others. They even have a *padel* court – a racket sport popular in Spain – directly next to the main training pitch.

"Pep is working with a team of people he is very close to," Benaiges says. "Txiki played alongside Pep at Barca. (Assistant coaches) Juanma Lillo, Rodolfo Borrell… these are people Pep has known all his life. They all share the same philosophy. They are all his friends. And working with your friends is very easy. That is the privilege he has at Manchester City, to bring together so many people who know each other, almost like a family."

It was September 2, just 10 days after Bayern Munich had beaten Paris Saint-Germain to win their sixth Champions League, when German newspaper *Bild* carried an interview with the club's former player, Lothar Matthaus, and the conversation turned to Guardiola's record in the competition since leaving Barcelona.

"With Pep, I always have the feeling that he wants to do something special in big games," said Matthaus, a former European footballer of the year and World Cup-winning captain. "Barcelona had a DNA, a system that he established. Pep was successful there. With Bayern and City, he tried to change it over and over again, and failed again and again.

"He always wants to show that he can do better. I would like to tell him, 'Pep, you are a great coach – but please, stick to your system.' I would describe it as egocentric. Yes, that's a harsh word, but it is deserved when you look at his decisions. At Bayern, Robert Lewandowski even had to play left wing once. That didn't work at all."

Nobody from City ever responded to those comments but they might be entitled to point out that Guardiola, for both City and Bayern, tends to get it right more often than not.

Lewandowski as a left winger? That was a one-off, against Hamburg, and it didn't end too badly given that Bayern won 8-0. Guardiola converted Philipp Lahm from a full-back to a central midfielder. That worked, too. He also tried Joshua Kimmich and David Alaba as centre-backs and, for City, did the same with Fernandinho. Again, they all showed they could play those new roles with distinction.

However, it is fair to say that his current group of players were nonplussed by the changes he implemented for that Lyon game last month and that there are parts of Matthaus's analysis that contain some element of truth.

One person with close knowledge of City's dressing room noted recently that Guardiola was not inspiring or invigorating the players in the way that he previously did. One criticism, in particular, was that he was not bringing out-of-form players back to their best levels. John Stones, for example. Or Bernardo Silva, to a lesser extent.

Mikel Arteta's absence has been mentioned, too, in the sense that his December departure for the top job at Arsenal, leaving his position as one of Guardiola's assistants, may have hurt City more than people might appreciate.

The common allegation is that Guardiola, to put it bluntly, can be a bit too clever for his own good. Managers, like players, can temporarily lose form and City's deterioration last season has led to criticism that he tends to over-think their tactics for the bigger games.

But is that fair? Did people complain when he put out a team with no orthodox centre-forward in a Carabao Cup semi-final first leg win over Manchester United at Old Trafford last season? Or was it then a tactical masterclass?

"Just because he lost 3-0 against Liverpool (in a 2018 Champions League quarter-final first leg), I don't believe that he overthinks the important games," Perarnau says. "What do we say when he beat Liverpool 5-0? Did he overthink it in July, when he beat Liverpool 4-0?"

As for the allegation of being egocentric, that jars with the people who have seen Guardiola's qualities close-up and understand that the man who led Barcelona to two Champions League final wins, playing some of the most beautiful football that has possibly ever been seen, bases everything on a fierce work ethic passed down to him by his father.

As another of his friends, the writer and film director David

Trueba, says, "Always bear in mind that underneath the elegant suit, the cashmere jumper and the designer tie is the son of a bricklayer. Inside those expensive Italian shoes, there is a heart in espadrilles".

Guardiola's colleagues talk about the way the job consumes him. They tell his story about missing his daughter's school concert in Barcelona one day because he was watching DVDs of their next opponents, humble Getafe. They talk about his human touch and the various acts of kindness – a text message, a hug, a telephone call – when he has heard someone is going through a difficult time.

Sometimes it might not even be someone he knows. The time, for example, Guardiola sought out Harry Arter after a game against Bournemouth because he knew the player had been through a personal tragedy.

"Pep has brought us a huge amount of success," Marwood says. "But the thing we don't tend to talk about enough is the type of guy he is and how he thinks about other people. Not enough is said about Pep in those areas. The behaviours, the values, everything else that makes him the person he is.

"We all talk about the trophies he has won and the type of football he plays, because it's very clear to see. What we don't talk about enough is the way he manages people, his work ethic, his passion, all the 'people ingredients'. I don't think that is given enough air time.

"I see someone who is first in and last out. He's passionate, intense . . . an incredible person as well as an incredible coach. That is critically important when we see the pressure managers are under from all angles. To maintain that respect – that dignity, the humility he has for other people – is a fantastic quality. He has that in bucketloads."

What he is saying, in short, is that Guardiola should not just be measured in terms of trophies. Ultimately, though, there will always be a spotlight on the fact that he was recruited to win the Champions League and, in four attempts, has not managed to reach a semi-final.

His fifth season as City manager begins away to Wolverhampton Wanderers on Monday and, beyond that, nobody can be certain what his intentions are. It doesn't mean he absolutely *has* to win the Champions League. But a club with City's ambitions are entitled to expect better than last season and Guardiola, who has been backed heavily again in the transfer market, will be putting himself under enormous pressure to make sure they do. Everyone will see it because this is his one real flaw: he is incapable of hiding his feelings, the stresses, the strains.

Can he ever feel totally fulfilled unless he wins the Champions League for his current club and gets his hands on the trophy for the third time as a manager? Does it nag away at him, nine years since his most recent triumph in that competition, that he needs to show he can do it without Messi, Xavi and Iniesta?

"I believe he *does* think that inside," Perarnau says. "Though sometimes he denies it."

GLOOM AROUND MAN CITY LOOKS MISPLACED, EVEN IF THEY DO STILL NEED REINFORCEMENTS

SAM LEE

SEPT 22, 2020

Manchester City are . . . good? You might not have thought so heading into their Premier League opener at Wolves on Monday night, had you been following, well, just about every public measure available.

Injuries, illness, a pre-season that was "all over the place", Pep Guardiola's sour mood and, above all else, a lack of progress in the transfer market (certainly compared to other clubs) had combined to put many supporters into a tailspin of negativity as a team that finished 18 points behind Liverpool last season began their attempt to turn things around – and they were already six points worse off than their rivals before kicking a ball.

Had *The Athletic*'s fan positivity poll been conducted over the weekend, rather than when City were bang in the mix for Kalidou Koulibaly and Lionel Messi, things would have looked very different. Sadly, the only positives of late at City have come from COVID tests, with Ilkay Gundogan the third City first-teamer to contract the virus, on the very day of the Wolves game.

He followed Aymeric Laporte and Riyad Mahrez, neither of whom were ready to feature two weeks on from their tests.

Given City lost twice to Wolves last season, exhibiting pretty much all of the flaws that meant they could not get close to Liverpool and exited the Champions League so meekly, the worst was feared. It would be fair to say some fans, having gone from Koulibaly and Messi to sheer uncertainty, were even angry.

So it was not supposed to be like this. With no pre-season friendlies, seven first-teamers out of action, three academy kids on the bench and money still to be spent on reinforcements, City looked pretty good indeed. Very good, in fact, for the majority.

Raheem Sterling fizzed from the off, Kevin De Bruyne did his usual thing but from a left-sided position this time, Phil Foden helped make the midfield trio a quartet while still supporting the attack, John Stones and Nathan Ake looked very sure of themselves at the back, Kyle Walker was good, Ederson decided not to charge off his line. And as a unit, City knocked the ball around at high speed as they do at their best.

Especially given the less-than-ideal preparation, as Ake admitted, you'd be tempted to say they looked like they'd never been away, had their last game (the 3-1 Champions League quarter-final second leg defeat to Lyon on August 15) not been such a crushing reminder of the strides this very good side need to make if they are to become the best again.

City do need another couple of signings and the complaints of supporters are not merely those of spoilt superclub followers. Win, lose or draw on Monday night their transfer market needs would be the same, the reality is somewhere between the pre-match outcry and the post-match glow of a good win. Wolves' late goal was probably a perfectly-sized reality check.

Even if Stones can replicate the form he showed at Molineux across the full season, City can't be fooled into thinking they can get by with what they have at centre-back, because – as much as anything – that's quite a big if.

Ake did very well on his debut, showing that he's not just a handy squad player, but they went into the summer wanting much more than that. They wanted a guaranteed, week-in, week-out starter, a top-class partner for Laporte.

That mantle belonged to Kalidou Koulibaly, the 29-year-old with bags of top-level experience and a lofty reputation. When chairman Khaldoon Al Mubarak spoke of new signings that would be outside of City's usual age profile, Koulibaly was at least one of them.

He is the man they thought could fill the Vincent Kompany-sized hole in the team, and after missing out on Harry Maguire last summer they were determined to get their man, but they were always concerned about negotiating with Napoli (so much so that they conducted all contact via Koulibaly's agent) after the Italian club's president, Aurelio De Laurentiis, reneged on a deal for Jorginho in 2018 that he had personally signed off.

They made it known a fortnight ago that they were ready to walk away rather than meet Napoli's valuation, and while that hardly screams of avoiding another Maguire situation, they have at least been swift in moving onto alternatives, which they did not do when the Leicester man went to Old Trafford.

City's determination to get somebody on board is evident in their pursuit of Sevilla's Jules Kounde, who is an extremely promising defender (perhaps similar to RB Leipzig's Dayot Upamecano but without the reputation) but does not have any of the traits that attracted them to Koulibaly. He is 21, a shade under 6ft tall, and not exactly a name that will immediately set new standards in the City dressing room and tongues wagging around the Premier League.

That's not to say he's a bad option by any means (nor is Ake), he's just not the specific profile they had in mind when they decided to brave talks with Napoli again. He may not immediately improve the defence either, but that's how much they want somebody in and another reminder that their current options are not entirely trusted.

But City fans want more, given reports on these pages that the club could have spent as much as £300 million this summer had everything gone their way, the fleeting dream of signing Messi, and Al Mubarak's public promise of new arrivals beyond Ake and Ferran Torres. He had actually hinted that the signings were at the behest of Guardiola, which may explain his bad mood even after the Wolves game, although the injury situation, amount of games and absence of five substitutes are definitely factors too.

Monday's performance might have started to persuade fans that they don't need a midfielder after all, which has been City's stance all summer. Despite David Silva's exit, they believe they have enough, which is up for debate and something that had annoyed fans who believed that a move for Lyon's Houssem Aouar had been tied up back in August.

Last season suggests City could do with an Aouar but in fairness to them, 12 months ago they were being lined up for criticism had they replaced Silva in the transfer market, as it would have been seen as bad news for Foden. There's an element of 'damned if they do, damned if they don't' about this one, but they could probably do with an incisive No 8, given 1) they've got the money 2) Silva is leaving a big hole and 3) Foden generally plays in the front line now anyway.

Fernandinho and Rodri looked very good in their deep-lying roles on Monday, providing passing options and a protective shield for their defence, although Gundogan and Rodri also looked very good against Liverpool and Real Madrid – not so much against Lyon (and various others). That was another of City's issues last season, that you never knew what you would get from one game to the next, so no sweeping generalisations can possibly be made from one game, perhaps not even from the next 10 or 15.

Guardiola was always going to try to find new ways to replicate Silva's very specific role in the City team this season and with De Bruyne drifting around on the left and Foden dropping in from a right-wing position this first attempt looked like quite a good one. With those two combining with the two men sitting, it screamed 'overload'.

There would be a large element of confirmation bias about it to look at Monday's game and say City need to bring in another striker and left-back, because Gabriel Jesus linked up play well (although his finishing still needs to improve) and Benjamin Mendy was largely good, but City have known they need to strengthen in those areas for about 18 months and there have been times in their transfer planning when they have seriously looked at new options.

They still might do business before the window closes, as they assess their post-Messi needs. Had they signed the world's best player, they need not have worried about missing too many chances any more, and could most likely have coped at left-back as they did in their two title-winning seasons under Guardiola. Without the possibility of adding Messi, they need to focus on more mortal ways to fix their woes, and regardless of this result it would be almost foolish not to bring in a left-back.

But, of course, things are not all bad. Sergio Aguero could well be back sooner than Guardiola suggested on Friday, and Monday's game offered early suggestions that some things have changed, even if the fact that Wolves' goal was from their first shot on target suggested that some things haven't.

Before kick-off, the big screens showed extended highlights of both of Wolves' victories against City last season, a reminder of their individual and collective frailties. Giving the ball away cheaply, conceding on the break, missing penalties, the difficulty in breaking down well-organised defences – none of those were in evidence as the new season kicked off.

There were a few familiar complaints on social media about Guardiola's hesitance to make substitutions, and fears that they would throw the win away after Raul Jimenez's header, but City even managed to banish those, not just seeing out a 2-1 win, but scoring another themselves.

From a City point of view, it was refreshing, and they would have snapped your hand off for that at kick-off.

WHEN WILL MANCHESTER CITY LEARN?

SAM LEE

SEPT 28, 2020

The worst thing about Manchester City's collapse is that they have done all this before. When they were knocked out of the Champions League by Lyon not that long ago, Kevin De Bruyne declared it "different year, same stuff", and it looks like not much has changed since then.

That was a pained yet succinct analysis from De Bruyne, the man who was at his most shouty and perturbed as things fell apart once again on Sunday in the 5-2 defeat by Leicester, but perhaps another famous summary gets to the nub of this City performance better than any other. Back in 2002, the disdain and disappointment were evident in Barry Davies' voice when he announced Italy's exit from the World Cup with the immortal line, "And the Italians are out because they will. Not. Learn."

When will City, as a team and club, learn?

This was the first time a Pep Guardiola team has conceded five goals, but the second time Jamie Vardy has scored a hat-trick against the Catalan's City. The first was in the opening months of the Pep era, on one of those nights when it was clear that the squad wasn't anywhere near ready to do what he asked of them.

Because this is the latest in a long line of similar defeats in the past year, it is tempting to suggest they don't look much better equipped now. They are, of course, which only adds to the exasperation.

We can look at the quality in the squad and on the touchline and wonder how City are still getting into these scrapes since they put together two of the finest seasons ever seen in English football, and we can look at the club, with its money and its admirable footballing structure, and wonder how they are still a few players short – not just despite the players they have already brought to the club, but despite knowing exactly which positions they wanted to strengthen going into the summer.

So, the team. Brendan Rodgers spelt out the blueprint that City's opponents have been trying for the past four seasons, but one that is becoming increasingly more successful. Rodgers, lest we forget, is very much wedded to proactive, attacking football.

"They're such a great team that they want to go into the pockets between your lines," the Leicester manager said. "And obviously the higher you press against them . . . they have an incredible technical ability, sometimes you cannot pressure players like that. The ball is gone and they go and exploit the space that you've left.

"People will not have seen too many of my teams play like that, but I felt for this game, it was important from a tactical perspective to just take the keeper out of it. Ederson could play at centre-half for some Premier League teams, he's that good with the ball, so we just decided to get into a three-quarter to half-pitch shape (to sit deep), just deny the space and then when the counter-press comes, do we have then the quality to pass out of that and be away on the break? And thankfully we were able to do that with real quality this afternoon."

Indeed, they did it time and time again.

Rodgers probably enjoyed spelling that out in fine detail, and perhaps it is something he could go back to if he were to get a call from City's decision-makers later this season. But, in short, they sat off City, used their own quality players to work around the pressure and *voila*: they were in on the defence, as so many others have been before.

How many times have City struggled to break a team down and then compound it by losing the ball high up the pitch, let the opposition run right through the middle of them and then have the defenders crumple? That was the recipe for disaster last season, when Norwich City, Liverpool, Wolverhampton Wanderers, Manchester United, Tottenham Hotspur and Lyon all benefited.

In fairness to City, their pressing looked more energetic and targeted on Sunday than many times last season but Leicester, as Rodgers said, played out of it very well. And once they did, the game was up. City knew Rodri would need time to learn to cope with men running at him but they never expected so many men to be running at him so often. The forwards and midfielders need to pull their weight, as they did in the good times, and the blame cannot sit solely with the defence.

But that defence. There is not a catch-all answer to the question 'how did it get to this?' It hasn't worked out for John Stones; Benjamin Mendy's injuries were unfortunate and have robbed him of his best abilities; Oleksandr Zinchenko's rise to first-teamer was, in hindsight, effectively a bonus and he could yet leave this summer; you can see what they saw in Nicolas Otamendi five years ago (good on the ball, strong, tough) but he has had only one good full season and is now leaving; the jury is still out on Joao Cancelo but he was signed because Danilo, the guy they signed after Dani Alves' U-turn in 2017, wanted out; Angelino was always a cheap stop-gap but they've sent him on loan again before actually filling that gap. It's dizzying.

They've done very well with Kyle Walker and Aymeric Laporte, and it's a good job the Frenchman has been so good because the decision (and it was a decision) not to pay what Southampton wanted for Virgil van Dijk has helped transform Liverpool into what they are today.

What are City today? They are a very good side, but the 'but' is in danger of becoming too large to ignore.

It would be unfair to gloss over the fact that City have started this season with seven or eight injuries to key players, including their two strikers, and that they have not had any kind of pre-season friendlies. They beat Wolves well on Monday night but that doesn't lessen those factors (and Wolves' 4-0 defeat on Sunday may provide a bit more context).

Yet at the same time, these are recurring issues, and the club knew things needed to improve this season because they went into the summer wanting two new centre-backs, a winger, a striker and a left-back (or Lionel Messi).

It is so telling that Eric Garcia, a 19-year-old who wants to leave the club, had to start. They can only blame injuries for that one to a certain point. Laporte was not fit enough after returning from COVID-19 isolation, fair enough, but Stones' muscle problem should not have affected them because they didn't plan to have him in the squad this season anyway.

Maybe the inability to move him on has helped to explain why they wouldn't pay Napoli's asking price for Kalidou Koulibaly, and why Otamendi has had to be included in any deal for an alternative. Had Sevilla wanted Otamendi, then City would've signed Jules Kounde, but they didn't, so the Argentinian is going to the more obliging Benfica, whose financial woes meant they couldn't say no to a deal for Ruben Dias, a player City have looked at extensively in the past 18 months but was not near the top of their list this summer.

Fans should be heartened to know that they are still looking for a left-back, but that does not mean they will necessarily get one, as it is linked to Zinchenko's future. The Ukrainian has several clubs on his trail and if one of them can agree a fee with City, Guardiola may be able to strengthen an area of the squad that has troubled the club ever since Alves' late snub, which meant they couldn't sign a second left-back.

That particular butterfly flapped its wings three summers ago and, on Sunday, three different City defenders gave away penalties. All after the midfield were bypassed too easily, City players flailing after surging runners, usually Harvey Barnes.

Walker, the least of City's defensive worries on the day, gave away the first. Garcia, good in the first half, bad in the second and over-relied upon throughout, got caught out for the second.

Mendy somehow got the wrong side of James Maddison for Leicester's third penalty to make it 5-2. But the thing is, even at 3-1 with 30 minutes to go, there was never a sense the home side would turn the game around. City had only just pulled a goal back to make it 4-2 when Mendy gifted Leicester another.

This was the first time anybody has put five past them but there have certainly been games like this before, when the whole thing implodes. When Leicester didn't rely on penalties, they scored a cheeky backheel and a screamer, while City didn't have much beyond Riyad Mahrez's early thunderbolt. For all the defence's issues, they barely created anything up front.

It was the kind of night when the cameras zoom in on Guardiola's furrowed brow, and it might never have been more furrowed. Somehow, he was happier in his post-match press conference than he has been in any other media appearance this season, even after the two wins.

But he must be wondering what on earth is going on, and he'll be the one charged with coming up with the answers as to why this most talented group of players can look so ragged so regularly.

One of the more interesting elements of the game is that Guardiola made a very un-Guardiola-like substitution. So often reluctant to change the flow of a game, even with his side losing, and so reluctant to throw a youngster into the fray with the game even remotely in the balance, he brought off Fernandinho, the man who was splitting his time between shielding the defence and forming part of it, and throwing on 17-year-old striker Liam Delap.

It's the kind of change most fans would have called out for, certainly in previous games, and City definitely needed a presence in the area given they like to put in so many crosses, so there is an element of 'damned if you do, damned if you don't', but it's fair to say the substitution backfired horribly. The score was still 1-1 when Delap was introduced in the 51st minute.

That can happen to any coach, and this may be heavy defeat talking, but the substitution doesn't bode well, given Guardiola is the one who has to come up with the answers to all these questions.

He could well do that. He's turned it around once, and with lesser resources. City have enough quality players (including those currently injured) to make us all forget that they could do with a few more signings, but even if not, City have enough money and contacts to do that business in the coming week. It could easily come together very quickly.

But as De Bruyne – not entirely blameless himself – spent the second half on Sunday shouting at half his team (Phil Foden about where to position himself in midfield, Rodri about where to stand in the wall and Garcia for his role in Vardy's impudent second) it really did feel like different year, same stuff. And they will not learn.

'HE SPOKE NON-STOP. IT WAS LIKE PLAYING WITH A DICTAPHONE' – WHAT RUBEN DIAS DOES

SAM LEE AND JACK LANG

SEPT 29, 2020

If Manchester City have many more games like Sunday's 5-2 defeat to Leicester, there's only one thing you really need to know about new signing Ruben Dias: how good is he when the opposition have burst through the midfield and he's the last line of defence?

"One of the things I can tell you about Ruben is he is very ready to deal with those situations," Joao Tralhao, former Benfica youth coach, tells *The Athletic*. "Because when you play for Benfica, not only in the first-team level but the youth as well, you are always exposed. You take so many risks in terms of offensive process that the players who are in defensive roles are always exposed.

"So of course he will be the kind of player that will fit perfectly in terms of City's idea, because he's used to playing with so many risks and exposure since he arrived at Benfica."

Dias, with his good eye for a pass, a reputation as Benfica's 'bad cop' and 'assassin' centre-back, and leadership qualities that those close to him rave about perhaps more than anything else, appears to tick a lot of the boxes required of a City defender right now. Although it would be fair to say that while the club had a good look at him last summer, he was not quite first choice this time.

———————————————— **A** ————————————————

Given the sheer amount of options Pep Guardiola has tried over the last year in Aymeric Laporte's absence – John Stones, Nicolas Otamendi, Eric Garcia, Fernandinho and now Nathan Ake – it may be handy to look at Dias' strengths and weaknesses through the prism of those City players who have gone before him.

And don't forget Vincent Kompany, the man Dias is ultimately replacing. The 23-year-old may be closest to the Belgian's profile, or indeed Otamendi's, in that he came through the Benfica ranks as a defender first and foremost but has improved his passing to the extent that he could well be an all-weather option for City. In recent years they might have played Stones against a defensive opponent due to his passing ability and Otamendi against a more direct rival due to his strength in the air, but in Dias they may have found somebody who can do both.

But perhaps what stands out most when talking to those who know him are the more hidden qualities. Coaches still remember the team talks he gave to his colleagues before B team games. He was only a teenager then, but the desire and sheer intensity of his personality bubbled to the fore, to the extent that even watching the videos now elicits a shiver of appreciation.

"Family, let's go!" he says. "We're a good team, we know that much. Good teams win games every now and then, get the odd result. No problem, that's what good teams do. The great teams are consistent. They never stop. They win a big match in the Champions League and then follow it up in the league. Every game in the league is worth three points. You win one with a great performance, scoring a load of goals, then you have to forget about it. By the next match it's gone, meaningless. Three more fucking points on the line.

"We all know where we want to get to. We can't just be on it sometimes. It's about concentrating at every moment, in every game, no matter where we are. And I'll tell you one more thing: if we start playing as individuals – each player trying to score his goal or do his little trick – we're fucked. This whole thing only fucking works if we're together. One team, on the pitch and off it."

On the pitch and off it, indeed. As much as City have needed somebody to stop the goals going in, have they not been crying out for a dressing-room presence like this since Kompany left? Dias' message may have been delivered in completely different circumstances but given it took City until their 37th league game last season to win four matches in a row, it is entirely applicable to his new team-mates.

Kompany, of course, was Mr Manchester City by the time he left the club so it would be unreasonable and unrealistic to expect a 23-year-old new signing from abroad to set standards in the same way but his former coaches are under no illusion that he will waste little time on that front.

"No doubt about it," Tralhao insists. "When he adapts he will push his team-mates. You will see for sure, he is one of those kinds of players. I haven't spoken with him yet but I can imagine he is excited to arrive at City and to impose his style there."

Helder Cristovao, Dias' B team coach, thinks it could happen even sooner: "That leadership is not negotiable; that's just his natural personality. You're going to see that in England. As soon as he arrives, he's going to be the one commanding the defensive line. He'll be bringing the defence out, telling his team-mates when to clear the ball, controlling the space in behind . . . he'll do all of that, and he'll do it perfectly."

Dias was only in Benfica's E team when he joined the club at under-12 level, and was used in midfield as they felt he did not have the physicality to play in defence, but academy staff identified him as somebody who would be a real asset once he hit a growth spurt.

And by under-15 level, he had become a talker. Nelson Feijao, a former team-mate, once said: "He didn't shut up for a second during matches. He spoke for 90 minutes, non-stop. It was like playing with a dictaphone. 'Move up . . . get back . . . close him down . . . move there . . . come here.'"

Youth coaches normally have to encourage players to be more vocal in training, but at Benfica they actually had to tell Dias to tone it down.

"Ruben brought a really comprehensive form of leadership to the team," Cristovao says. "He always felt like a leader in every team he played in. What he said always carried weight with his team-mates. He would make himself heard, make himself respected, and he was very disciplined.

"He doesn't give himself a moment's rest. He wants to develop, wants to learn, wants to be there for the team. That's how he arrived where he is today, and this isn't the end for him. He's still on the launch ramp."

Tralhao concurs: "The first thing to know is the character. He likes to win every time, even in the small exercises. In terms of personality, he's very special and I believe one of the things that impressed the City scouts most when they looked at him was his character."

City's defenders may not be exposed to as many counter-attacks as they were against Leicester on Sunday all season if Guardiola's plans come together, but it is an occupational hazard in an attack-minded team and his commitment to defending could be a breath of fresh air.

"In terms of technical qualities I think it's very simple to describe him: he's a stopper," Tralhao says. "He's a complete defender, he defends very well. Long balls, short balls, in the duels, his anticipation is very strong in terms of defensive qualities.

"And then, in terms of offensive qualities, he's much better than he was three years ago. Now he is at the top level he is getting better and better at building up with short passes to link the game, and I believe at City he will improve a little bit more."

Not everybody in Portugal is completely sold on his passing ability, but that may be a legacy of his first outings in the senior side in 2017, after Victor Lindelof moved to Manchester United and Luisao picked up an injury.

There is an acknowledgement that he had to improve in that respect but at the same time, once he made the step up to first-team level at the age of 20, he never looked back, impressing with his leadership, communication and the confidence to play a high line.

"In technical terms, Ruben was excellent at hitting long passes," Cristovao adds. "He improved his passing between the lines, which he used to struggle with. When you play for big teams in the top league, you need to know how to play those passes and not just long balls. He understood that perfectly and grew very quickly as a player."

The comparison that City fans are probably hoping to hear, in terms of that split between ability in and out of possession, is with Laporte, but there is a sense that he is more Otamendi. The hope, of course, is that he will be the 2017/18 Otamendi that Guardiola called "Superman".

Regular watchers also describe Dias as very strong in the air in both boxes, very aggressive and, at times, capable of an inexplicable error, which may not fill City fans with confidence.

"When you play centre-back for a team like Benfica, you have to be aggressive," said Rui Vitoria, the former Benfica manager who brought Dias into the first team. "You have to have a bit of assassin in you, make your presence felt. A centre-back who doesn't go through his man every now and then isn't a real centre-back. Ruben brings that dose of competitiveness. He oversteps the limits every now and then, but that's part of the job."

"He can be a bit too forceful, physically," Cristovao admits. "But he's going to be in the perfect league, because a lot of the fouls that are given in Portugal won't be given in England. He can still improve. He'll be playing in a team that has a lot of possession, and he'll be getting constant support from Guardiola.

"Ruben will succeed there. He's Portugal's first-choice centre-back, so I don't think he'll have any problems. He's strong in the air despite not being as tall as some centre-backs; his positional sense is very good; he reads the game well; he plays with real desire and concentration."

The reaction to mistakes is something that Guardiola and his staff really scrutinise. They note how the better players, like Laporte, are able to "drink the poison" and move on as if nothing had ever happened, whereas with Stones they have long been concerned that he dwells on things too much and lets it affect his performance.

"Ruben is the kind of player who demands a lot of himself," Tralhao says, "but when he makes mistakes, his emotional control is top-class, he can move on very, very quickly."

Dias' route to City is fairly convoluted. After Harry Maguire proved elusive last summer, City looked elsewhere, but could not bring in a new overseas player – including Dias – before getting rid of Otamendi. The Argentine could not find a new home though and City did not do any business so ended up needing to spend another £100 million on centre-backs this summer. This time around, as well as Ake, they wanted Kalidou Koulibaly but when that wasn't happening, they found that Atletico Madrid's Jose Gimenez was too expensive, and could not persuade Sevilla to part with Jules Kounde.

At fairly short notice they went back to Dias, with Benfica needing to sell a player to balance the books after missing out on Champions League football.

Even so, he appears to be the kind of defender that City have been crying out for, both on and off the pitch, and young enough to improve even further. Yet as well as the usual concerns about new signings needing time to adapt, Dias' defensive abilities will be thoroughly examined if Guardiola's team cannot provide a proper shield for their back line, which was clearly still a problem on their most recent outing.

It's not easy playing in defence for City at the best of times, and the club have found it equally hard to identify the right men, but those who know Dias best are certain that this time they have got it right.

SEPTEMBER RESULTS

Premier League, September 21, 2020
Wolves 1 Man City 3
Man City scorers: De Bruyne 20 (pen), Foden 32, Jesus 95

Carabao Cup, September 24, 2020
Man City 2 Bournemouth 1
Man City scorers: Delap 18, Foden 75

Premier League, September 27, 2020
Man City 2 Leicester 5
Man City scorers: Mahrez 4, Ake 84

Carabao Cup, September 30, 2020
Burnley 0 Man City 3
Man City scorers: Sterling 35, 49, Torres 65

OCTOBER

GUARDIOLA AND BIELSA, THE LOVE STORY

PHIL HAY AND SAM LEE

OCT 3, 2020

Every now and again, a video cassette would drop through the letterbox. The deliveries took time, covering thousands of miles between Europe and South America, but Marcelo Bielsa was prepared to wait. He loved the days when the post arrived, bringing footage and news of Ajax.

Ajax were his case study, the team he liked to pore over, using grainy images and written match files, but the real attraction was Louis van Gaal. The Dutchman's fingerprints were all over Ajax and, driven by his coaching, the Amsterdam club had Europe under their spell. Van Gaal's football hooked Bielsa in. Of all the European managers, Van Gaal was the one to follow. Bielsa sat through 200 of Ajax's matches, watching and learning. He knew the result by the time the videos reached him, so slow were the dispatches, but the tactics were there to be picked apart.

"After game 150, I asked a collaborator – well, I asked my wife – to tell me in which minutes Van Gaal made his substitutions," Bielsa told the Aspire Academy's global summit in 2016. Without reading the reports, he challenged himself to guess how, or with whom, Van Gaal would change his team when he turned to the bench. "I never believed I knew what Van Gaal knew because I don't know how he feels," Bielsa said, "but this was the only piece of his mind I could get hold of." In that small way, Bielsa was able to think like him.

Bielsa's coaching has long had a European streak about it and today, at Leeds United, there are shades of Van Gaal in him still: the pressing, the rotation of players' positions, the insistence on maintaining numerical superiority at the back. Bielsa was the coach who saw no room for Juan Roman Riquelme in the Argentina squad. Van Gaal was the boss who let Wim Jonk, Bryan Roy and Dennis Bergkamp slip away from Ajax, in the interests of promoting collective thinking and tactical balance. They were on the same wavelength and Bielsa made a point of eulogising Van Gaal after the 69-year-old's retirement last year. "My only desire is to say 'thank you' in public for what I learned from him," Bielsa said.

Pep Guardiola had a love affair with 1990s Ajax too. His relationship with Van Gaal was different to Bielsa's; more personal, in as much as he played for Van Gaal at Barcelona and earned the captaincy under him, yet slightly less engaged. Guardiola credited his evolution as a coach to Johan Cruyff and when it came to the stage of deciding if he was made for coaching at all, it was Bielsa he sought out for guidance and advice on a retreat in Argentina (although Van Gaal's name came up in that conversation). But Ajax, to Guardiola, were no less of a phenomenon. "Van Gaal's Ajax gave lessons to those who knew the game perfectly," he wrote in the 2011 book *Mi Gente, Mi Futbol.*

Bielsa and Guardiola aspired to treat football in the same way; to master it, change it and own it. The men who will stand a few yards apart on the touchline at Elland Road this afternoon have been chasing the impossibility of perfection for longer than they can remember, kindred spirits who are as tied to the pursuit of brilliance as Van Gaal was in Amsterdam and as Bielsa and Guardiola were when they first shared a pitch in 2011.

The rain poured that night as Barcelona and Athletic Bilbao fought each other to a standstill in a 2-2 draw. "Your players are beasts," Guardiola whispered into Bielsa ear at full-time. Bielsa chuckled. "And so are yours."

— **A** —

On the way back to Buenos Aires, after a marathon 11-hour conversation on Bielsa's ranch in Rosario, Guardiola called Matias Manna and declared, "I've just been with the man who knows more about football than anybody."

Guardiola had first been intrigued by Bielsa in 1998, when he was still playing at Barcelona and the Argentinian was in the midst of one of his famously short managerial spells, this time at Barcelona club Espanyol.

In much the same way that Guardiola saw Juanma Lillo's Real Oviedo side and thought, "Something is happening here," he regarded Bielsa's team as special. Guardiola asked his team-mate Mauricio Pellegrino, who had played for Bielsa at Velez Sarsfield, what he was like and something of an obsession was born.

Guardiola was told by Gabriel Batistuta during their time together at Roma, "If you want to coach, you have to talk with Bielsa," but the Catalan was already paying close attention. During the 2002 World Cup finals, when Bielsa's Argentina were knocked out at the group stage, Guardiola wrote a passage that is proof that he held his coaching beliefs long before he ever actually became a coach.

"I still like Argentina, although they did not get out of the group, because I think they played very well; although we know that we live in a world in which if you win you are good and if you lose it does not matter what you have tried. It doesn't matter if you've had the ball, if the team was well organised or if you go with a 3-4-3, like Bielsa did. If you lose, they say you failed. I see it in another way."

In that sense, they have always been on the same page and, with Guardiola weighing up his first moves into coaching, he visited Argentina in 2006. He had always had an affinity for the country's footballing heritage, sometimes getting his old Barcelona team-mates to teach him songs from the terraces of El Monumental (River Plate's stadium) and La Bombonera (the home of Boca Juniors) so he could whistle them around the training ground.

On his fact-finding mission, he sat down with Cesar Luis Menotti, the 1978 World Cup winner, Ricardo La Volpe, a renowned tactician, and also Manna, an amateur coach who had written a book on Bielsa and had been blogging about Guardiola and his footballing outlook for several years.

Guardiola quizzed Manna about Bielsa – *El Loco* – although by that stage he too had only observed him from afar, and ran through the subjects he wanted to find out from the man himself from their meeting the next day. Things like how to build a team of backroom staff, the importance of analysts to study the opposition, how to handle the media and, perhaps most of all, the relationship between video analysis and how it can be used to complement a playing style.

Manna gave Guardiola a copy of his book, Guardiola used it as a reference point during the famous sit-down with Bielsa, and a few months later Manna was called to Bielsa's office. "You're Guardiola's friend," he said to the young coach, and made him one of his cherished analysts. They had both made a big impression during that exhausting chat.

The meeting itself has gone down in a particular corner of footballing history, a pow-wow between two of the most intense men ever to set foot in a dugout. Of course, back then Guardiola hadn't set foot in one, but he turned up at Bielsa's ranch well prepared to pick the brains of somebody who did things the way he intended to.

David Trueba, a novelist and director, accompanied his old friend Guardiola on the four-hour car journey from Buenos Aires and in fact spent an hour talking with Bielsa about cinema, until Trueba turned to Guardiola and said, "You haven't come all this way to talk about films, have you?"

Trueba, who ended up getting used as a mannequin in certain demonstrations, described what came next in an article in *El Pais*, once Guardiola had established himself as one of the world's top coaches.

"There were heated discussions, they consulted the computer, reviewed techniques, practised positioning. There were complicated questions; Bielsa asked, 'Why do you, someone who knows all the rubbish that surrounds the world of football, the high degree of dishonesty of certain people, still want to go back there and get into coaching? Do you like blood that much?' Pep didn't think twice. 'I need that blood.'"

In August, for the first time, Guardiola provided a slightly different version of events. For years, the quote "I need that blood" had been attributed to him. "But the story was not like that," Guardiola said in an interview with DAZN. "When we were talking about the media, I was the one who said to him, 'If we complain so much about a world that sometimes doesn't let us live, how come you don't manage a youth team or a more amateur team and forget the professional world?' He was the one who answered me, 'I need that blood.'"

Bielsa also took the chance to enhance his own knowledge and was especially keen to know more about Van Gaal and Ajax, the 1995 Champions League winners who served as a reference point for both men. Bielsa classed Ajax as his favourite overseas team due to their tactical discipline and understanding. Guardiola had spent more time talking to the Dutchman about football than perhaps any other coach, even Cruyff.

"I think I managed to bore him by the eleventh hour," Bielsa said years later, in his inimitable way, "but I thought he was like that from the beginning and he didn't try to leave. That was the only time in our lives that we saw each other. Speaking so many hours about quite a few topics shows we had a pleasant time, but I don't have any knowledge that Guardiola doesn't have."

Indeed, he has always refuted the idea that he taught Guardiola anything, but the younger man came away completely enthused and motivated to begin his coaching career, his ideas on the game and how it should be played reinforced, with additional tips – like avoiding one-on-one media interviews and the importance of video analysis preparation – scribbled in a notebook.

"I respect and admire Bielsa a lot," he has said. "He opened the doors of his home to me when I hadn't even begun to coach. I've been influenced by other coaches, like Cruyff, who I was with for eight years, but I would have liked to have played for Bielsa, or been part of his staff."

They had both been at the 2010 World Cup in South Africa, where Bielsa coached Chile, with Manna on his staff. Interested in Alexis Sanchez, Guardiola solicited Bielsa's advice by telephone and he was assured the forward was 'buena gente' – a good person – and Barcelona duly signed him.

But they didn't see each other again for more than five years, by which time Guardiola had built the best team on the planet, perhaps in history, one that had won everything there was to win, and Bielsa was proving yet again with Athletic Bilbao that trophies are not always the best measure of success.

––––––––––––––– **A** –––––––––––––––

It is no night for football. The heavens have opened, the temperature is dropping towards single figures and a sea of ponchos fills the stands of the San Mames Stadium. Guardiola will lose his voice before the end of the evening and the ball will hold up in puddles of water as the pitch becomes more sodden and treacherous. But somehow, the spectacle is La Liga at its best.

Guardiola and Bielsa had seen the flames in each other's eyes, the whirring of cogs in complex minds as they sat together in Argentina five years earlier, but they had never before thrown themselves against each other as coaches. Bielsa will discover what it is like when Barcelona's tiki-taka toys with you; when you "surround them but the ball gets out anyway," as Bielsa laments with a smile afterwards. Guardiola will feel the weight and ferocity of Athletic Bilbao's press, the sprints, the energy, the batteries which refuse to go flat. The game leaves Barcelona's manager hoarse and a little stunned. "I've never played against a team so intense," he says.

To a point, Guardiola saw an epic game coming. He had spoken beforehand about Bielsa's team "not letting you breathe. They attack the box with seven players. Then they lose the ball and defend with 11."

He understood the theory and the process. But in the flesh and in the Spanish rain, the football is something else. La Liga has its milestones and memories but aficionados say the 2-2 draw between Bilbao and Barcelona on November 6, 2011 would sit comfortably in any tribute to the division. Rodri Errasti, a Spanish journalist, was covering Bilbao for Eurosport at the time. "It's one of the best matches I ever watched," he says.

Claudio Vivas, Bielsa's assistant at Bilbao, recalls how the day before the match – a day on which Spanish players liked to rest – Bielsa put his squad through a hard training session, a last chance to fire them up.

"The most significant thing about that game was that we had more of the ball than them, a team that normally has 70 or 75 per cent of possession," Vivas tells *The Athletic*.

"There's more to winning games than possession, it depends on many things, but in that game in particular Guardiola's team wanted to control it. We didn't let them. It wasn't worth much in the end because we drew but afterwards it was something that everybody praised."

Guardiola goes 4-3-3, with Cesc Fabregas in the middle of a front three. Bilbao are closer to 4-1-4-1, with Fernando Llorente up front and Iturraspe in a holding role. Llorente is not famed for covering the pitch but Guardiola watches with surprise as the forward makes 40-yard runs back and forward, covering defensively whenever Barcelona retrieve possession.

Bielsa realises quickly that even on a pitch so churned and appalling, much of Barcelona's passing will be flawless. Javier Mascherano, his fellow Argentinian, is everywhere from the off. "He goes out to the flanks and is a winger," Bielsa says. "Then he marks Llorente as a central defender. And then moves up the field as a holding or attacking midfielder. Honestly, I'm proud to call Mascherano a compatriot."

The risk to Bilbao is the death by a thousand cuts that Barcelona, under Guardiola, perform in their sleep. The risk to Barcelona is Bilbao's high press and their willingness to commit so many bodies forward.

Bilbao score first when their positioning forces a risky pass from Victor Valdes to the right wing. Mascherano slips and Ander Herrera curls in a shot from the edge of the box. Ironically, it is the only good goal of the night. Fabregas nods in a free header after Bilbao's defence go missing. Nine minutes from the end, Gerard Pique turns a corner into his own net. Barcelona have not lost all season but defeat is on the cards.

And then, in the 91st minute, Ander Iturraspe and his goalkeeper Gorka Iraizoz go for the same ball inside their own box. They collide and deflect it to Lionel Messi, who rolls a shot into an empty net.

Bilbao look shattered. Everyone looks shattered. A drenched Guardiola makes a beeline for Bielsa, to shake his hand and commend him on dragging Barcelona so far out of their comfort zone. "The result is hard to take," Bielsa says, "but it was a lovely game."

Someone asks him why it took until the last five minutes for him to make substitutions. "Because I wanted to take off someone who wasn't playing well," he says.

<hr />

A

<hr />

All these years later, Bielsa is still in awe of the team Bilbao faced. Ask anyone who tangled with Guardiola in that era, he says, and they will tell the same story. "The memories I have are that Barcelona managed to neutralise our efforts to impose ourselves," Bielsa said during his weekly press conference on Thursday. "Everybody would give you this answer – the opinion that they are the best team in the history of football. His teams play like no other team."

Guardiola's time at Barcelona was coming to an end. He would leave at the end of that 2011/12 season, concluding the first stage of the career Bielsa encouraged him to begin. But Bilbao had announced themselves and Bielsa's reputation permeated the game. It is not that Europe knew nothing about him or what he was renowned for but, in plain sight, the composition of his team and his tactics were wonderful. In a matter of months, this side would knock Manchester United out of the Europa League. In May, Bielsa and Guardiola contested the Copa del Rey final, their last skirmish with each other until, eight years later, Leeds meet Manchester City today.

Bilbao's campaign, though, poured fuel on the fire of the Bielsa burnout theory, the perception that the way he cracks the whip with his players causes them to hit a wall. Across La Liga, the Europa League and the Copa del Rey, Bilbao had 63 games to contend with. Incredibly, winger Markel Susaeta played in the lot. "But by the end of the season, the players were so, so tired," Errasti says. Fatigued or not, Bilbao had two big dates to aim at: the Europa League final on May 9 and the Copa del Rey final two weeks later.

Defeat in one blew their chances in the other. Barcelona were heavy favourites to win the Copa del Rey but Bilbao fancied their chances against Atletico Madrid in the Europa League showpiece. There was little between the clubs in the domestic table. They had each beaten the other at home in the league. Bilbao flew to the final in Bucharest with confidence oozing but got soundly beaten 3-0, conceding to Radamel Falcao twice in the first half.

"To play so bad, the impact was big," Errasti says. "If they had beaten Atletico, they would have thought that they might beat Barcelona. But to lose to Atletico like that, there was no chance against Barca. No one really believed. The team looked exhausted and you knew that only Barcelona could win that match."

Barcelona and Bilbao met in Madrid at the old Vicente Calderon and there were no parallels with their November rumble at San Mames. The pitch at Atletico's former home was dry and fast and Barcelona scored three times in the opening 25 minutes.

Bilbao looked passive, second to everything, and there was a telling moment in the 20th minute when Messi rifled Barcelona's second goal into the roof of the net. A jaded Jon Aurtenetxe switched off and gave up on Messi's run, devoid of intensity. At 3-0 down, Bilbao started to play but were already beaten. Bielsa said Bilbao struggled to beat Barcelona's press. Guardiola, for Bielsa's sake, tried not to dwell on the scoreline or the result. "I don't think we are very conscious here of everything this coach is doing for football," he said. "We were facing the best manager on the planet."

Vivas is not convinced that Athletic were mentally or physically shot. "No, no, no," he says. "It was quality above physical aspects. The reality was that Messi was inspired, and Pedro and (Andres) Iniesta. It was Guardiola's best Barca that season. Their opening period destroyed us.

"We tried but, to be honest, we were never close to a result. There was tremendous disappointment because the whole Basque country was looking forward to it and we couldn't live up to those expectations."

Guardiola was finished at the Camp Nou. His time was up and he was speaking as Barcelona manager for the final time. "The loss is huge, because he made this sport shine," Bielsa added. "The title of maestro is justified by his work. The work I have done in football doesn't justify this title. If we were to establish maestro and student, I wouldn't be the maestro."

Bielsa was possibly leaving too. He and Bilbao were about to discuss his future, the way forward for the 2012/13 season, and Bielsa couldn't say with any certainty he would stick around. He told his players as much in a private dressing-room conversation, the audio of which was leaked to the media a few months later (and after Bielsa agreed to stay on as manager).

The recording was made by one of Bilbao's players but nobody has ever taken responsibility for it, or explained how it was that it reached the press. "Actually, in the eyes of the public, it was not bad for him," Errasti says. "What he said (in that conversation), people were thinking." In it, Bielsa accuses his squad of being "premature millionaires". He saw some of them laughing after the Copa del Rey final and their brevity angered him. You don't suffer like ordinary people in Bilbao, he told them. You cannot let them down like this.

"He was disappointed because the whole Basque country were behind us," Vivas says. "So many fans came to the game, even without tickets.

"He didn't complain but it was a speech based on reality. Maybe it could upset some people but for others it could be useful. A player thought the speech could hurt him (Bielsa) but the fans liked Marcelo even more because of it. He was praised by the Basque people. The player betrayed him. He recorded it and published it. We don't know who it was but whoever it was it didn't go very well for him because the fans loved what Marcelo said in that private chat."

In spite of his ire, Bielsa could not deny that the squad's application in the build-up had been exemplary. "You trained like animals for 10 days," Bielsa told his players. "You obeyed, submitted and applied yourselves to everything I asked of you." Bielsa had done likewise, compiling a vast analysis document detailing every aspect of Barcelona's system. Afterwards, he gave it to Guardiola as a gift and a sign of respect for him. "You know more about my team than I do," Guardiola joked. "But it was useless information," Bielsa admitted during his famous Spygate briefing at Leeds last year, "because we conceded three goals."

Vivas was closely involved in the preparation of that document, working for hours to help pull it together. "Before the final (Bielsa) told me to watch every Barcelona game from that season, to cut up every game and split them into different videos – goalscoring opportunities, chances they conceded, how they played out from the back, the different tactical systems Guardiola used in the 64 games, including friendlies," he says.

"The only thing he asked for was to give solutions to the players so they had the knowledge to come up with the answers on the pitch. What happens when you play against a team like Barca is that with everything we planned, some of the things went well and others didn't. They overcame us with their attacking ability. They were very efficient.

"I'm sure Pep loved the scout report. It was a very complete work. Marcelo polished it and made it better. The result wasn't what we wanted but that's how we prepared for it. After the game he sent it to Barca's dressing room as a gift."

The relationship between Guardiola and Bielsa was rare. They were respectful to the point of being reverential and each man preferred the other to be held in higher regard. Their encounters in the heat of battle did not alter their opinion of one another, except for the better. Bielsa could delight in Guardiola's successes. Guardiola played them down when Bielsa's name came up in the conversation. "I don't dare call him," Bielsa once said. "I feel inhibited by what he is."

Even this week, as a long-awaited reunion came around, the phone line stayed quiet.

——————————— **A** ———————————

In England, personal meetings between Guardiola and Bielsa have been relatively few. They are understood to have met for dinner in Leeds and Manchester and their paths crossed in the transfer market when the Yorkshire club first signed Jack Harrison on loan from Manchester City in 2018 but they have their own jobs, their own lives and their own daily stresses.

"I don't see him every week but the pleasure when I spend time with him, it's always so inspirational for me," Guardiola said on Friday. "He is probably the person I admire most in world football. My theory is that, for a manager, it's not about how many titles you win. I have won many titles but my knowledge of things is far away from his." *The Athletic* has been told that City's last training session before their visit to Elland Road was a double session – the first time Guardiola has done that in four years as City's manager.

The two men made beasts of Barcelona and Bilbao. At Elland Road this evening, they will find the same old spirit at work: City's 4-2-3-1 meeting Leeds' 4-1-4-1, Kevin De Bruyne colliding with Kalvin Phillips and Guardiola jousting with an ageless Bielsa. That wet night at San Mames almost eight years ago will feel like yesterday, like a light that never goes out.

In Thursday's pre-match press conference, Bielsa was drawn into speaking about the new and beleaguered handball rule; how to change it, how to fix it, how to make it work for everyone. One sentence in his answer jumped out, unrelated to him or Guardiola but inadvertently describing their respective journeys through management. "In the search for perfection, you know where it starts," Bielsa said. "But you never know where it ends."

INJURIES, TRANSFERS AND ERRORS: WHERE ARE THIS MAN CITY SQUAD AT?

SAM LEE

OCT 4, 2020

What are this Manchester City team? Are they being held back by the injuries in their squad and the lack of pre-season preparation? Are they a team lacking a bit of luck in both boxes? Or are they staring down the barrel of a bleak season, and are the issues that have set them back over the past year rearing their head again already?

Can it be all of the above? Not quite, because even when the squad is back up to full strength, they still have some points to prove. It is easy to imagine the absent players making a difference, though.

Sergio Aguero would have scored that one-on-one that Raheem Sterling missed, surely? Gabriel Jesus might not have, to be honest, but he may have disrupted Leeds so much that City could have sewn up an easy victory in other ways.

"We struggled a bit to make the first pressing when they were able to use the central defenders," Pep Guardiola said afterwards. "We were a little bit back because with the quality of Riyad (Mahrez) and Ferran (Torres) we struggled a little bit in this way.

We did it really well but, for example, the intensity is not like (when we have) Gabriel in this position."

Essentially, Mahrez and Torres bring plenty to this team, but not quite the quality of pressing that the Brazilian does. If Jesus was playing, City might have won the ball in Leeds' half much more often and it would have been a different game.

And with a bit more match sharpness, City's transitions could have flowed much better. Mahrez, Kevin De Bruyne and Phil Foden might have been a bit more decisive with more preparation; Bernardo Silva might have helped a bit more off the bench.

And Marcelo Bielsa may have added a bit of much-needed context to things and provided a reminder that Guardiola is quite good at what he does.

"When Guardiola made an apparently defensive change, when Fernandinho came on, that's when they started to regain control of the match," the Leeds manager said. "It was a very, very intelligent substitution, it had a huge impact on the game, and it is proof that very often if you want to attack better you have to defend well."

Of course, defending well is not something City have been doing too often of late, nor have their midfield been helping. Funnily enough, it was only a week ago that Guardiola took off Fernandinho with 51 minutes on the clock to bring on a 17-year-old striker and everything went to hell in a handcart. But if that was a rare poor substitution, he seemed to have rectified it on Saturday. It's good news for Fernandinho, too, given the concern about his performance levels among senior figures at the club last weekend. Maybe the captain still has a lot to offer as well.

And, don't forget, it was only six days ago that City's defence was getting exposed time after time by Leicester, but you wouldn't really have known it at Elland Road. Even when Bielsa's charges did manage to fly through the middle (until Fernandinho came on), the defence actually coped with it, by and large.

Ruben Dias looked pretty handy with just two days of training behind him, while Aymeric Laporte looked much more solid than any of his stand-ins so far, which suggests that things might already be changing for the better with the return of the team's best players.

And as much as the draw was fair – Bielsa said it would have been "unjust" had Leeds won, and that's surely a fair reflection for City too – the visitors could have had a penalty when Sterling was fouled in the box late on. If Ederson hadn't fumbled a cross, which is rare, Leeds wouldn't have scored.

So things could have been much better.

But . . .

City are five points behind Liverpool already, and in a sense that's the least of their worries. There is potential for the gap to get bigger because Jurgen Klopp's side seem to have settled into an impressive rhythm early, while Guardiola's are still finding their way.

Dias was never going to solve all of City's problems, nor would any centre-back on earth, because that defence is going to have a hell of a lot of work to do if the forwards and midfielders lose the ball and can't win it back, which was effectively the problem all the way through last season, and happened a fair bit on Saturday.

Guardiola tried all sorts to pack his midfield in 2019/20 but it wasn't enough for City to achieve any consistency. They would get things back on track for three or four games and then lose inexplicably. He's got to find an answer this time, but he doesn't have David Silva to help, and because City decided they have everybody they need in that area of the pitch, there is no replacement either.

It was good for fans to see Foden get a rare run-out in Silva's No 8 role, but it won't necessarily be happening again soon. This was one of the few games, due to its unique openness, where Guardiola was willing to forego the control of a passing midfield, and instead put in somebody willing to drive into the gaping spaces in midfield. That's partly why Leeds had more possession.

"As a team it's so difficult to keep possession because, for the way they play, they help you to make transitions," Guardiola explained, "so you can run, they can run, and that's why the possession is more difficult." In short, there's so much space you may as well attack it, rather than pass the ball around. If all of City's opponents played like Leeds, they wouldn't pass it so much.

That's another example of the way Guardiola looks for solutions in a way that's specific to every single opponent. One man's game plan is another man's overthinking. Nobody expected that replacing Silva and Fernandinho would be easy, but perhaps the constant changes do not help City's midfielders and the more they struggle, the more the defence does. As Bielsa handily noted, a leaky defence isn't conducive to fine attacking play. So there's work to be done for sure.

This could be Guardiola's final season, and it could be defined by how he coaches the players he does have at his disposal, rather than the ones he doesn't. As Micah Richards said on Sky Sports after the game, "Guardiola's a great coach, but it can't all be about signings, I want to see him coach his players."

That particular bandwagon will pick up speed in the coming weeks if City do keep dropping points, and the pundits won't all be as friendly as Richards.

City do need a couple of players – a left-back for certain and ideally a striker – but at the same time there are enough good players at Guardiola's disposal to be performing better than they have of late, including last season. None of City's signings are actually likely to stop the opposition counter-attacking anyway: as Guardiola noted, Torres isn't the best presser, and then by the time Dias and Nathan Ake are called into action it might already be too late.

And, for whatever reason, those individual errors – whether Ederson's drop or Sterling's miss – cannot be dismissed as one-offs. No matter how unrelated they may be, they seem to keep happening, and the concern is that they are still happening and cannot easily be fixed.

There are some things that can be sorted with further investment or better coaching, like Benjamin Mendy's lapses or the three penalties conceded last weekend. Get a better left-back, make the forwards press. For the love of God, do something to help Rodri (he was never meant to do so much defending).

Everybody has a role to play if City are to get back on track and reach their previous heights. Guardiola is good enough to get a tune out of this squad, even if it has a couple of holes in it. If the club act decisively in the market to fill in some of those holes it would certainly help. And the players themselves cannot rest on their laurels.

Leeds themselves are a reminder of that. As Guardiola said after the game, "People say only rich clubs can play like this, but you can do it with teams like Leeds, when the players have the mentality to compete against the big clubs."

If Leeds can, why can't City?

FERNANDINHO – FROM MANCHESTER CITY'S MR RELIABLE TO LAST-MINUTE FIREFIGHTER

SAM LEE

OCT 22, 2020

For a man who only spent seven minutes on the pitch, Fernandinho had an eventful evening for Manchester City against Porto. That's been the story of his season.

He has been Mr Reliable since joining the club in the summer of 2013 but it has been hard to know what to expect from him in recent weeks and, for that reason, it's difficult to gauge just how much of a miss he will be now that he faces a significant spell on the sidelines.

The Brazil midfielder didn't touch the ball for the first of his five minutes of action, his initial real contribution coming when he clumped through the back of Evanilson in midfield. Two minutes later, he played his first pass, immediately got the ball back and played his second, then a muscle pinged and he was off again.

Four to six weeks out, perhaps, although the quality of the Zoom connection meant Pep Guardiola's post-match diagnosis was not completely clear. It looks bad, though, the City manager said.

But how bad is that for City? Clearly, missing any first-team player for around 10 games is far from ideal, especially one with as much experience as Fernandinho as this unusual season develops.

They never planned to rely heavily on him this season, though. The process of moving away from his unique all-action approach began over a year ago when they installed new signing Rodri in midfield and circumstances dictated that the 35-year-old was needed in the centre of defence instead.

Part of Rodri's problem is that every interception he doesn't make and every tackle he misses are compared to a memory of how Fernandinho would have done better, so there was something jarring about it when the Brazilian returned to his old midfield position away to Southampton in July and looked so rusty himself. Only in defeats at Anfield and Molineux did he have a lower pass-completion rate last season and he lost possession 22 times, seven more than in any other game.

He's still got something to offer this team, of course he has, but Guardiola is still working out what his midfield actually looks like now and where Fernandinho fits into that.

It looks like the days of a single holding midfielder are over. Guardiola likes a double pivot these days – to protect his defence and to offer more passing options out from the back. It was easy to believe the manager needed to make that change because Fernandinho's apparent heirs couldn't do the job on their own like he could; but maybe even he can't now.

He started alongside Rodri away to Wolves in last month's season opener, partly because there weren't many other ways the City midfield trio could have lined up with only those two and Kevin De Bruyne fit, but perhaps also partly because he can't hold the fort on his own any more. Whatever the reason, it worked. City had the control they wanted, with and without the ball.

But he struggled so much in the next match against Leicester City that Guardiola made perhaps the most un-Guardiola-like substitution ever and took him off after 51 minutes, with the score at 1-1, to bring on a 17-year-old target man in Liam Delap for his Premier League debut. City went on to lose, 5-2, but rather than wonder whether their manager had made a mistake, senior figures were genuinely alarmed at how poorly Fernandinho played.

And yet his introduction away to Leeds United a week later changed the game, the 77th-minute substitution praised by Marcelo Bielsa, the sport's tactical gatekeeper, for helping City wrest back control of a match they had looked like losing.

With barely any regulation time left against Arsenal on Saturday, Guardiola hurriedly called down the touchline for his enforcer to get ready to help see the game out at 1-0. It was almost exactly the same in the Champions League opener on Wednesday, this time with six minutes to go and City holding a two-goal advantage.

Fernandinho had spent the previous 84 minutes sitting on the bench revelling in the chaos that unfolded on the pitch and further along the touchline. It was a curious game and arguably one that didn't really need his steadying hand, because the Portuguese side had barely threatened in the second half.

The visitors *had* caused City problems before the break, highlighting defensive concerns about Rodri, Eric Garcia and Joao Cancelo and tempering the excitement around new centre-back Ruben Dias ever so slightly, but as much as they caused problems on the break, the lack of control to proceedings was largely attributable to the awful refereeing of Andris Treimanis. That was the one thing that the City and Porto benches could agree on all night.

Guardiola turned to his bench early on and said "three zero, guys," in reference to the early decisions going against his side, but it was his opposite number, Sergio Conceicao, and his staff who were really raging when City were awarded a penalty that might have been overturned for a foul in the immediate build-up.

Pre-game, Guardiola had noted that Porto are "alive with the referees, with the staff on the bench," and the cries of disbelief from the away dugout amused Fernandinho so much that he didn't waste an opportunity to bellow some light-hearted expletives in his native tongue during the rest of the half, starting as soon as Sergio Aguero equalised.

City were 3-1 up and coasting towards victory but somehow it was still kicking off by the time the Brazilian entered the fray. Pepe, up to his old tricks, had put his head into Raheem Sterling and added a knee for good measure while the England forward lay on the floor. The two benches had had enough of each other by this point and, as their leaders exchanged words, Fernandinho had no issue getting in the middle and telling former Porto, Lazio and Inter Milan midfielder Conceicao, who has a bit of 'Portuguese Roy Keane' about him, where to go.

For all the talent City have added to their squad in recent years, there is a feeling they miss a bit of that kind of bastardry when things get difficult, and while the captain's armband has been passed around in recent years, from David Silva to De Bruyne to Sterling, it's Fernandinho who feels like the proper leader. And with a game against Liverpool on the horizon in just over a fortnight, it's tempting to think he would have been a very handy option to throw into the heat of the battle.

But at the same time, his actual contribution on the pitch was perhaps a reminder that City are moving on without him, even if the alternatives do not always live up to expectations.

He will surely not be needed at centre-back anymore with Dias and Nathan Ake now on board and, while Rodri and Ilkay Gundogan have their shortcomings, they find it much easier to open a game up against teams that press them. They helped dismantle Liverpool just a few days before Fernandinho's struggles at St Mary's at the end of last season, and undid Real Madrid too.

Perhaps the Brazilian, as he showed at Wolves, could offer a bit more defensive solidity in all those games when City's opponents choose not to press them and sit back instead, but Leicester's quick breaks forward suggested otherwise.

He has been at the heart of everything City have done since Manuel Pellegrini replaced Roberto Mancini, but in recent weeks has seen his role reduced to last-minute firefighter – and even that's not been easy for him.

We are finding out what life for City looks like after Fernandinho.

KYLE WALKER, AN APPRECIATION

SAM LEE

OCT 30, 2020

For anybody who has seen Kyle Walker turn on the afterburners and mop up the danger in behind the Manchester City defence over the past few years, his description of his very first outing at right-back will sound amusingly straightforward.

He used to be a diminutive striker during his days in the Sheffield United academy, in the mould of Jermain Defoe or Kevin Phillips only without the finishing ability, until the youth team's sole right-back got injured before a game against Nottingham Forest.

"I always remember their left winger was probably their best player, his main strength was that he was quick, and I was quick, and I marked him out the game," Walker told *The Athletic* earlier this year. "So I started in the FA Youth Cup after that as a right-back and I've never looked back since."

That recovery pace is especially useful at City these days, where they can sometimes look slower and more vulnerable as they transition away from life with David Silva, Fernandinho and Vincent Kompany.

Walker motors – or sometimes simply jogs – across, leans a shoulder in to wrestle the ball back and gets City on their way again. It's a fairly rudimentary last line of defence but it sure is useful, and the way he talks about shutting down that poor Forest youngster might sound familiar to a few seasoned Premier League and Champions League wingers.

In one game at Selhurst Park a few years ago, Wilfried Zaha got such little joy down his usual flank that he switched to the other side for the last five minutes (and duly won a penalty from those less equipped to deal with him).

There are nights, such as City's win against Real Madrid in August, when Walker looks like a man possessed, a considerably sized bundle of energy charging up (but more often down) the pitch, barging people out of the way, crashing into tackles and winning headers. So while it may be easy to imagine the 30-year-old knocking fellow hopefuls out of the way, that size and power came a little later.

"I was small," he says. "I was like 1.62m (under 5ft 4in) when I signed the scholarship, everyone had grown and I was just a late developer.

"So I had to go to the gym more than everyone else and I never forget Ron Reid, the Sheffield United academy director, said to me, 'Before you go to bed at night, just make sure you eat a big bowl of cereal, and I want you to do that for a couple of weeks and let me see if you fill out'.

"And to be fair . . . it did work but I don't know if it was down to the bowl of cereal, it might have just been that I was growing!"

Walker has said he wants to end his career at Bramall Lane depending on their trajectories at the time, but as he returns there this weekend, the last thing on City's mind will be getting rid of him. On top of the god-given speed and the Kellogg's-given strength that stands out so obviously wherever he plays, Walker has developed into a jack-of-all-trades defender for both club and country. As one source close to the City first team put it this week when discussing the club's transfer business over recent summers, "They keep buying new right-backs but none of them is as good as Kyle Walker!"

Are we now at the stage where he gets credit for all the things he does do, rather than what he doesn't? There's always been a feeling around Walker that he is lacking something. Even after his time at Tottenham Hotspur, where he proved to himself and Harry Redknapp that he could play at the top level, established himself as England's right-back and evolved his game under Mauricio Pochettino, it was believed that he wasn't fit enough to play two games in quick succession.

That was actually propagated by Pochettino and the two of them have had a strange relationship over the years. Walker sent a heartfelt message to the Argentinian when he left for City in 2017, although when showing it to the media on a pre-season tour, the then-Spurs boss quickly added: "But for me, I think we saw the best Kyle with Tottenham."

Walker disagreed with Pochettino's version of how he left White Hart Lane in a book published last year, leading to another public stand-off between them, though they are on better terms now. "He took my game to a new level," Walker says. "On the field, he made me understand the game a lot more. Maybe I was getting a little bit older and the experience was probably shining through but what he did for Tottenham, and for me as a player, speaks volumes for him as a manager."

Walker appreciated the importance of rest and diet under Pochettino, and City may be benefitting from that now, given he has not missed a significant run of games through injury for over five years. At 30 years old, he looks as strong and quick as ever, and there is a very robust argument that he has been City's most reliable defender since he joined the club in 2017, perhaps even one of their best of the Sheikh Mansour era.

That thought may cause some to recoil but, like Matthew McConaughey going from *How to Lose a Guy in 10 Days* to winning an Oscar, Walker deserves his recognition.

When City signed him for £54 million, the reaction from many was that it was the straw that broke the camel's back, the ultimate sign that transfer spending had gone mad.

City were happy to make it known that they believed the market would become distorted that summer, and that their business, also including Bernardo Silva and Ederson, would eventually look like bargains. This was the same year that Neymar moved to Paris Saint-Germain for £220 million.

"Full-back Kyle Walker becomes the world's most expensive defender at £50 million-plus," Gary Lineker tweeted at the time. "Imagine how much he would cost if he could cross the ball."

The funny thing is that City have barely ever asked him to cross it, and that's almost the beauty of him. About once a game, every game, Walker will burst down the right-hand side, leaving everybody in his wake to cause havoc in the opposition half, and it's tempting to suggest he should be allowed to do that more often.

He feels he has that in his locker and that was at the heart of his exclusion from the England squad last year. He felt he could still be his country's rampaging right-back, even after Kieran Trippier's World Cup exploits and Trent Alexander-Arnold's emergence, but they saw him as a centre-back in a back three, a system that Gareth Southgate was moving away from. That system is back now and so is Walker, and you couldn't seriously argue that either club or country looks better without him.

His absence would certainly be felt at City, which is a point that might be easier to make if he actually ever missed a run of games. Imagine how they might look without his pace and strength, given they are not a team blessed with either in many other positions.

No wonder City have struggled with their right-back alternatives. Danilo left after failing to earn regular football (even in one of Walker's fallow periods around his first two Christmases in Manchester), and now Joao Cancelo's struggles go to show how imposing the competition has been.

"My dad had a motto that he'd never let me win," Walker says. "So we could play *Frustration* or a simple card game like snap and he would never let me win. So I've learned the hard way but I feel that that's made me more determined in life, to get to where I want to get to.

"With my kids, I don't let them win, or I'll probably win the first two and then let them win the last one, just so I don't have any tears," he continues, laughing. "I'm not as harsh as my dad; I can tell you that."

This time last year, he was playing through a stomach bug to ensure he didn't lose his place to Cancelo, who is trying to make the left-back berth his own now, having struggled in his first year to grasp the tactical understanding demanded of a City full-back.

The Portuguese offers a traditional threat: run forward and cross it. But, as Walker can tell you, there is far more to it than that in Pep Guardiola's set-up.

Even after refining his rampaging role under Pochettino, he developed his game in one of Guardiola's hybrid roles, building up play on the right, switching it to the left with pinpoint crossfield passes that not every City defender has mastered, and then tucking inside to guard against the counter-attack.

In Walker's final season at Spurs, he spent more time wide on the right in the final third, compared to his time at City where he is used in more central areas. It is hard to overstate the importance of that ability to sprint back and cover for his team-mates at a time when City are working out how to stop teams breaking on them. So much so that his most notable contributions come when running towards his own goal these days, and while that might seem a waste, it is necessary.

There is still a feeling that Walker has a mistake in him, an idea that has been backed up by Gary Neville a couple of times in recent weeks, when the Sky Sports pundit and former England coach has highlighted how he switches off when the ball is on the opposite side of the pitch. That can undermine any arguments in Walker's favour and when suggesting he is City's most reliable defender, it's hard to know if that says more about him or about the club's recruitment.

But even if there may still be a mistake around the corner, he has improved since working with Neville for England in 2016, and since the end of the 2017/18 season, in which City won the title with 100 points but were knocked out of the Champions League by Liverpool.

Guardiola determined that John Stones, Nicolas Otamendi, Gabriel Jesus and Walker would have to up their concentration levels and perform more consistently if the team were to move to the next level, and Walker has far fewer questions surrounding him than the others.

And consider the tactical understanding that made him an important part of the win against Arsenal earlier this month; the part-time centre-back, part-time right-back belied any notion that he has concentration issues.

Walker's purchase certainly looks like a fine bit of business for City, especially when set against the constant upheaval across the rest of their back line. They are once again hoping that their new centre-backs are the right men for the job, and they would pay a fortune for a left-back as consistent as he is.

He has sometimes struggled to win fans over, including at City, and his lockdown activities earlier this year reflected poorly on him. His attempts to explain some of them did little to garner sympathy.

But for somebody who can't play three games in a row, can't cross and has a mistake in him, he does all right. Walker's come a long way.

OCTOBER RESULTS

Premier League, October 3, 2020
Leeds 1 Man City 1
Man City scorers: Sterling 17

Premier League, October 17, 2020
Man City 1 Arsenal 0
Man City scorers: Sterling 23

Champions League, October 21, 2020
Man City 3 Porto 1
Man City scorers: Aguero 20 (pen), Gundogan 65, Torres 73

Premier League, October 24, 2020
West Ham 1 Man City 1
Man City scorers: Foden 51

Champions League, October 27, 2020
Marseille 0 Man City 3
Man City scorers: Torres 18, Gundogan 78, Sterling 81

Premier League, October 31, 2020
Sheffield United 0 Man City 1
Man City scorers: Walker 28

NOVEMBER

IS RIYAD MAHREZ TOO GREEDY?

SAM LEE

NOV 1, 2020

In the visitors' dressing room at the London Stadium last weekend, as Manchester City's players pored over their issues in a disappointing 1-1 draw with West Ham, Kevin De Bruyne admonished Riyad Mahrez for not passing enough.

Frustration had got the better of the Belgian because in the weeks beforehand, fellow senior players Sergio Aguero and Fernandinho had also had a word with Mahrez on the same subject, taking him aside and suggesting he holds onto the ball for too long and dribbles too much.

The verdict among those players, and some others, is that those interventions have done nothing to affect the winger's style of play, that he is still performing the same way. Watching his display against Sheffield United on Saturday, it would be hard to conclude otherwise.

Mahrez is not an unpopular member of the dressing room by any means, though, and it should be noted that since the start of last season only De Bruyne has created more opportunities from open play and provided more assists than the Algerian has for City.

These kinds of gripes with a team-mate can sometimes be blown out of proportion, either in the pressurised confines of the training ground, where minor issues can build up over weeks or months, or simply when reported in the media like this. But while Mahrez has been one of City's most creative outlets over the past year in particular, some of his colleagues have become frustrated with him.

There were two incidents in that West Ham game last week that were referenced by De Bruyne afterwards. In the 88th minute, with City looking for a winning goal, Mahrez had the ball less than a yard from the byline inside the penalty box. Instead of playing a pass back towards his waiting team-mates, he elected to get even closer to the byline and try to dribble around his man, only to run the ball out of play. De Bruyne was arriving from midfield and was frustrated not to get a pass, although Declan Rice would have moved to close him down quickly.

And then, with five seconds left in added time, Mahrez was played in by Ilkay Gundogan on the left and, after advancing towards goal, tried to squeeze in a shot from a narrow angle. It hit the post and City were awarded a corner, and there were plenty of West Ham defenders between him and his three nearest team-mates, but in the dressing room afterwards, it was made known that a cut-back was not just a better option, it was the only option.

Mahrez frustrated again at Bramall Lane yesterday as City ground out a pretty steady 1-0 win that could help them stabilise their early-season form. There were a few aspects of the performance that hinted at better days to come, whether the increasingly solid-looking centre-back partnership of Ruben Dias and Aymeric Laporte, Bernardo Silva's simple new role in midfield or Ferran Torres' smart runs as a No 9.

However, there was also the fact they didn't carve out too many clear openings despite having 64.8 per cent of the possession and how many transitions they managed to generate. De Bruyne unusually struggled to pick his final pass and had it not been for Sheffield United old boy Kyle Walker's fine goal from outside the box City might have been a bit more concerned with their play in the final third.

So Mahrez was not exactly alone in having an off-day, but as the game went on he became more and more guilty of what his team-mates have accused him of, and what some City fans have held against him no matter how much good work he has done.

There were a few occasions across the 90 minutes when De Bruyne looked exasperated with the 29-year-old's decision making, although it should also be pointed out that that tends to be his way of plugging the leadership void left by the departure of countryman Vincent Kompany.

De Bruyne and Walker have been two of the more vocal members of the dressing room since the start of last season and the midfielder isn't always constructive with his criticism. A good example was picked up by the pitchside microphones during the draw away to Leeds United a few weeks ago when he was heard complaining to Phil Foden at a corner: "Phil, you don't listen, huh? You don't fucking listen."

One of De Bruyne's pet hates is when he feels players put themselves above the team. As far back as when he came through at Genk in his homeland before signing for Chelsea at age 20, he had no issues pulling people aside to tell them to do more to bring others into the game.

It's never personal, and he didn't look too annoyed when Mahrez took a second half free-kick rather than leaving it to him. There's no suggestion of a rift of any kind, but there were certainly times when he looked less than happy after he didn't get a pass from the former Leicester City star.

After 24 minutes, Mahrez chested down a cross and shot over the bar, and nine minutes from time De Bruyne played him in on the right and instead of returning the favour or producing a cross, he simply ran the ball off the end of the pitch. On both occasions, De Bruyne threw his arms up in the air and that last one, running the ball out of play, is something that really annoys fans and certain team-mates. In between those two examples, there were another two similar moments when Mahrez tried to dribble his way to the byline but got crowded out and lost possession.

It would be hard to argue at this point that the man voted Player of the Year by his fellow pros in 2016 is not prone to over-dribbling, even when he ends a game with a goal or an assist to his name. Sometimes, Mahrez is not helped by City's set-up but sometimes he does not help himself either, trying to cut inside onto his left foot when he's double marked by opponents who know full well that is what he wants to do.

Sometimes, as in recent weeks, he has been in more promising positions but has chosen the wrong option. It was highlighted during the 2016/17 season, when Leicester were defending their title, that he was no longer passing as regularly to their top goalscorer Jamie Vardy, but much of that was owing to other problems at the defending champions – and their players have always maintained he was a popular member of the dressing room even when he was trying to force a transfer. It should also be said that while De Bruyne looked frustrated at times on Saturday, Mahrez could also have justifiably complained about passes not reaching him in threatening areas.

Manager Pep Guardiola does not have any major concerns with Mahrez. Amateur body language enthusiasts would not be able to detect any hint of simmering frustration from the Catalan when that first-half shot flew over the bar, although he did take him off with five minutes to go, shifting Silva to the right wing and putting Gundogan in the middle. It's easy to believe this was to give his team extra legs in central areas, rather than any kind of punishment, because Guardiola has made Mahrez one of City's most regular contributors, despite the fact his coaches and analysts spend much of their time during games urging him to press opponents or track back.

Guardiola is very keen on his inverted wingers and when City can get Mahrez into space he is, by far, one of their most dangerous players. Often, City's entire game plan will be based around switching the play to the right-hand side to get the 59-cap international, who helped Algeria win the Africa Cup of Nations last year, into one-on-one duels with the left-back. Given he can take the ball in full flight thanks to one of the silkiest first touches in the Premier League, Mahrez can easily breeze into the penalty area and pick out the bottom corner with a shot.

At times like that, he looks unstoppable, and in terms of chances created from open play between the start of last season and the conclusion of Saturday's action, Mahrez is seventh in the league, despite having played the fewest minutes of anybody in the top 10.

From that inside left position, he has turned the ball around the corner and into the path of an overlapping team-mate countless times, including in the build-up to the final goal in the 3-0 Champions League win over Marseille last Tuesday.

Mahrez was pointedly left out of a match-day squad in the January of his debut season in Manchester as Guardiola made his point that anybody unhappy with coming in and out of his team would simply not play at all, but since then there have been no issues with his attitude.

Last season he was probably in City's top three most consistent performers, both before and after the lockdown, so it's no surprise he is a regular fixture in the team. Since the start of last season, his second at City, he has 22 goal involvements (12 goals and 10 assists) in the Premier League, which is bettered by only the very best players in the country.

Last season he registered more Champions League assists than any of his City team-mates, too, but he is similar to colleague Raheem Sterling – who also posts impressive numbers despite sometimes struggling with one-on-one finishes – in that his flaws are more evident and more frustrating because they tend to happen at decisive moments, when expectation is at its highest and games are won and lost.

Mahrez's problem is that while his team-mates don't intend to miss chances or misplace passes, he sometimes *chooses* to attempt a dribble when better options are available, and City's most senior voices have done little to change that habit so far.

IN 55 DAYS, SERGIO AGUERO CAN TALK TO OTHER CLUBS – SO WHERE'S ALL THE FUSS?

DANIEL TAYLOR

NOV 7, 2020

I sometimes wonder whether Sergio Aguero has ever stopped his car on Ashton New Road, somewhere opposite the nostalgically named Maine Road Chippy, and looked up to the part of Manchester City's stadium that is now named after the most important goal he ever scored.

They light it up at night, so you can see straight into the 93:20 Suite. The picture of Aguero is a familiar one. He is on his victory run, twirling his shirt above his head. The words of the television commentary by Martin Tyler are emblazoned on the walls. 'Aguero' has had to be specially adapted, spelt with 19 extra O's.

It is not a bad legacy.

I was in the press box that day, covering the match for *The Guardian*, and it is the only time I can ever remember a football stadium turning into a 48,000-person mosh pit. It was bedlam. And, amid all the flying limbs, I distinctly remember having my laptop open with a hastily deleted match report, composed after 89 minutes, that began: "Manchester City will never forget the day they blew the Premier League title."

I remember the woman who had seen enough and left in floods of tears as City went into three minutes of stoppage time with the almost implausible task of having to score twice. And the bloke who used to sit a few rows in front of me, who would sometimes nod to say hello, with a haunted look on his face as he also made his way, zombie-like, to the exit.

There were loads of them, on that final day of the 2011/12 season, who could not bear to see any more. And loads who sprinted back in when Aguero reminded us, with a swish of his right boot, that there is a difference between a great footballer and a football great. The genuine greats shape the sport.

Drink it in, soak it up. "I swear you will never see anything like this again."

One day, City will immortalise that scene by putting up a statue of Aguero outside their stadium. A sculptor has already been commissioned to create a permanent tribute to Vincent Kompany. David Silva is getting the same treatment. Aguero qualifies too, and not only because of one seminal goal that changed the landscape of English football.

He has also scored 252 others in City colours (or 254 if, as Pep Guardiola says, we should count ones in the Community Shield). Aguero is the club's all-time record scorer. Eric Brook took 11 years, from 1928 to 1939, to put together the previous 178-goal target. Aguero went past that number in his seventh season and, for a long time, maintained an average of 30 goals a year. It has come down to 29.5 now. The poor fella must be in decline. All of which makes it perplexing that so little has been said about the fact it is not just manager Pep Guardiola who is set to be out of contract at City at the end of the season.

You will have heard a lot about this potentially being Guardiola's long goodbye. Just not so much, perhaps, about Aguero being in the same position. Or the growing possibility, the longer it goes on, that he might want to see if there are new adventures to be had elsewhere.

Aguero will be allowed to speak to prospective new overseas employers from January 1 and on the market, potentially, as a summer free transfer. That's 55 days away, to be precise. And, though we can safely assume his wages will be eye-watering, it is also reasonable to expect a long queue of elite clubs fluttering their eyelashes in his direction. Let's put it another way: City are going to have to get their skates on if they want him to stay, as we have to assume they do.

When the chairman, Khaldoon Al-Mubarak, was asked about it before the start of the new season, he made the point that it would be for Aguero, just like it was for Kompany and Silva, to decide what happened next, rather than the club. "Sergio is going to be the same. We will work it out together and it will be very natural. It will play out in a comfortable way, whatever Sergio decides."

That was fair enough. Yet it is also worth bearing in mind that City were increasingly optimistic at that time about their chances of prising Messi away from Barcelona. Messi, City hoped, would change everything. His mere presence would have elevated City to new heights. It would have been the biggest coup there has been in the Premier League. And City were probably entitled to think Messi turning up might influence Aguero's thinking. With Messi on board, who wouldn't want to be a part of it? Guardiola, too.

That, of course, has not happened. Messi announced 10 days later that he was staying at Barcelona, Guardiola's next move remains unclear and, as it stands, the only real certainty when it comes to Aguero is that, if this does turn out to be his final season in Manchester, it is going to be a hell of a job for City to find someone who can take his place.

If that sounds harsh on Gabriel Jesus, it is not intended that way. He has many qualities and a City record of 70 goals from

155 appearances. It would be a stretch, however, to think Jesus can worry opposition defences in the same way that Aguero does. The Brazilian, lest it be forgotten, also tends to miss quite a lot of games because of injuries. So, who else? And if this is the part when your mind starts wandering towards Harry Kane, how much money would it need to make that kind of deal happen?

Some people will point out that Aguero turned 32 in the summer and that tends to be the age at which a bit of insecurity can appear on a footballer's horizon. They might also point out it counts against him that he finished last season, and started the current one, on the treatment table. And, yes, these would all be legitimate points.

At the same time, how do you think City's rivals will feel if it turns out this is the final season when Aguero is lining up against them in a sky blue shirt? This really is the bottom line: Liverpool, Manchester United and all the others will be delighted to see the back of him.

Aguero has already scored 180 times in the Premier League. Eight more will put him above Andy Cole. Only Alan Shearer, with 260, and Wayne Rooney, on 208, will have more. The difference is that Shearer played 14 years in the Premier League (and another four in the top flight before its rebranding). Rooney 16 and Cole 14-and-a-half. Aguero has been in Manchester just over nine years. Nobody has scored more goals in less time, or done more to elevate his team to a new level.

Sir Alex Ferguson mentions in his last autobiography that he, too, had the chance to sign Aguero from Atletico Madrid but decided the agent's fees were too high. What a regret. What a shocker, given some of the sums United have forked out since.

If anything, it feels strange that a player of Aguero's achievement is not revered more. Do we value him enough? Just because he makes the art of goalscoring look so natural, do we forget sometimes that there are actually very few of his type in the modern sport?

Even Guardiola can give out mixed signals sometimes.

When Manuel Pellegrini was City's manager, he used to say there was only Lionel Messi and Cristiano Ronaldo on the list of modern greats who were superior to the wearer of City's No. 10 shirt. You knew why he was doing it: buttering up Aguero, playing on the fact that all footballers, strikers in particular, tend to play better when they are filled with confidence.

With Guardiola, it has always been more difficult to figure out what he makes of the Argentinian. The Aguero-Guardiola dynamic can feel like a puzzle. There is clearly respect. You wouldn't say they were particularly close, though.

Sometimes Guardiola's eyes will light up when he is invited to say nice things. At other times, there isn't the warmth in his voice that might be expected and maybe a line or two that hints at some form of dissatisfaction. Aguero is an important player, Guardiola will say, but then a few sentences later he might chuck in something that can seem incongruous when it was once unprecedented to hear a City manager, even one as hard-to-please as Roberto Mancini, ever question Aguero.

Somehow, though, I don't think the average City supporter needs to be reminded about the contribution that has been made by the club's longest-serving player. Aguero is the only man left from the team their modern-day supporters might always revere the most.

Kompany has gone. Silva, too. The 93:20 team. Joe Hart, Pablo Zabaleta and all the rest.

Aguero will have been there 10 years next summer and, similar to Guardiola, City probably need to find out what is happening sooner rather than later.

MANCHESTER CITY'S ATTACK LET THE DEFENCE DOWN, FOR ONCE

SAM LEE

NOV 9, 2020

Manchester City might have beaten Liverpool. In some ways, it was the same old story for Pep Guardiola's side: they created the better chances but were left lamenting their profligacy. In terms of the more minor details, they did not always do enough to stop the transitions, either.

But something was different. They defended well.

Since City lost 5-2 to Leicester in September, suggesting a season of toil ahead, they have conceded just three goals in eight games in all competitions, keeping five clean sheets. What changed? Well, they signed Ruben Dias, but it could not just be that, could it? Not quite, but he has made a hell of a difference so far.

It is a cardinal sin in football to get carried away with a new signing, especially at City where fans still remember Eliaquim Mangala's fine debut against Chelsea six years ago. And it is always important to remember that City's last three opponents, Marseille, Sheffield United and Olympiakos, were not that threatening. John Stones and Nathan Ake played in midweek and much like Dias and Aymeric Laporte, already the first-choice partnership, whatever they had to do they did well. The big test was always going to be Liverpool.

And after 90 draining minutes against Jurgen Klopp's side, who made it a nightmare to play out from the back and were ready to stream through the middle whenever they got the chance, City's new-look backline emerged with their reputation enhanced further.

OK, Kyle Walker gave away a penalty in similar circumstances to the one he conceded against Leicester, only this time he could not blame those in front of him for leaving him exposed: he was skinned by Sadio Mane and reacted poorly. He has been City's best player this season, though, and on an afternoon when his performance level dipped, his three defensive colleagues stepped up and ensured this was not the same old story.

"He played exceptional," Pep Guardiola said of Joao Cancelo, "with the ball and without the ball." The more he plays like this, the more credit you have to give the club for claiming they can get through the season without buying a left-back. Guardiola did acknowledge that he has to work on the defensive side of his game, and Liverpool did look like they would have some joy down his side, getting the ball in behind him twice in the first nine minutes and forcing Ederson into two dashes from his line, but he got much, much better as the game went on.

It was he who created City's best chance of the second half, scooping a delightful ball over the top for Gabriel Jesus. The Brazilian had drawn his side level with a fine piece of work, but planted his header wide of the post.

Given Kevin De Bruyne had missed from the penalty spot earlier on, City fans would have been thinking, 'Here we go again' – that their punishment for missing good chances would be to concede a sloppy goal at the other end. Especially against these opponents, who usually only need the sniff of a chance to score a goal.

Some of the issues that have plagued City were indeed still evident: Raheem Sterling faded more and more, Ferran Torres struggled at times with the pace of the game, Jesus scored a fine goal but missed the best chance of the second half, Ilkay Gundogan and Rodri could not always get things going in the middle, either stopping attacks or starting them (and again, Liverpool usually do not need much of an invitation). Even De Bruyne was wasteful by the end, perhaps tired out by having to be everywhere and do everything in the breathless first half. Everybody looked tired, in fairness.

But that frustratingly sloppy goal never came. Every time Liverpool broke forward, which admittedly happened less and less as the game went on, City's defenders just dealt with it. There was rarely anything flashy about their defending, nothing remarkable about the statistics. There were not too many shots on goal compared to normal games between these two sides – in fact, one team normally thrashes the other – but there were fewer in January 2019, when City edged a victory that helped them lift the title.

Cancelo made four tackles (more than anybody on the pitch, including an incredibly smooth slide to deny Mohamed Salah towards the end) and a couple of clearances and interceptions, Dias did his fair share and Laporte was on hand to win the odd header. It should be nothing to write home about, nothing City have not done in their title-winning seasons, nothing Liverpool themselves have not managed over the last 18 months or so.

But City have not been able to rely on that for about a year now. They struggled without Laporte last season, no matter who stepped into the breach. At times it was easy to feel sorry for Stones, Nicolas Otamendi, Fernandinho or Eric Garcia, because even if they crumpled under the pressure, somebody else had piled it onto them in the first place.

Whether the forwards did not counter-press properly or the

midfielders did not do enough to stop the runs through the middle, City's centre-backs, as poorly equipped to deal with the danger as they sometimes were, were done no favours.

And, truth be told, they were rarely done any favours on Sunday. Liverpool looked so nimble in midfield, especially when Roberto Firmino was on the pitch and dropped deep to help his team-mates out of sticky situations, setting them off at full speed towards the City goal. Guardiola's side did brilliantly to stay patient and get themselves back into the game, but Liverpool's threat in transition was real, certainly for those first 45 minutes.

And in the second half, when City looked like they might have an extra gear in them, they were undone by a key pass going astray, or a little flick not quite reaching its target. Suddenly, their midfielders and forwards were chasing back again, trying desperately to keep up with Liverpool's incisive forwards. But City's defenders were there, always well placed to just get a foot in, or win a shoulder-to-shoulder, or see the ball out of play. Simple stuff, the type you do not miss until it is no longer there.

And credit too for their use of the ball. Dias has been caught out a couple of times with loose balls into the middle, but did not fall for Liverpool's traps. Laporte looked as dependable as he did in the vast majority of his games before his injury. Although it is still early days, it can be said with a little more certainty now: they have the makings of a fine partnership.

On another day, City might have won it. They might have taken the chances they did have, or pushed harder to create others in the final 15 minutes. Those loose passes let them down and, curiously, Guardiola called for Phil Foden to come on for the final minutes before changing his mind, perhaps indicative that he was ultimately happy with a draw, which seemed to be the same for Jurgen Klopp as well.

The two managers both complained about the Premier League's decision to not allow five substitutes this season, arguing, understandably, that it puts the players at greater risk of injury. But both men only made three substitutions between them anyway (one of Liverpool's enforced by the injury to Alexander-Arnold), perhaps a reminder that while they are very worried about their players' wellbeing, they are also paid to win football matches.

Or in this case, not to lose them. Whether you call it fear, respect, or simply an acceptance that everybody was knackered, nobody was willing to roll the dice and hope for a bit better, lest things get much worse.

Klopp certainly appeared the happier of the two managers, delighting in the fact that his side usually concede far more chances against City at the Etihad. Indeed, his Premier League record there against Guardiola before Sunday is worse than you would probably imagine: one draw, three defeats, two goals scored and 12 conceded.

City, while not always looking entirely convincing, had done enough to win it. In the end they got a point, but they can at least celebrate a much-needed impressive defensive performance, and were it not for that, they might have suffered even more.

EXPLAINED: WHY PEP GUARDIOLA HAS SIGNED A NEW DEAL AT MANCHESTER CITY

DANIEL TAYLOR

NOV 19, 2020

Pep Guardiola is staying at Manchester City. After all the debate about his future, all the uncertainty about this potentially being his final season in the Premier League, Guardiola has signed a new contract and is already talking about winning more trophies. "We have the feeling there is still unfinished business," Guardiola said, having agreed terms until the end of the 2022/23 season.

His decision comes after extensive talks with City's hierarchy in which the people at the top of club made it clear they had always wanted him to stay. He, in turn, informed them he still felt energised and motivated and was convinced that he could re-establish City as the best team in English football.

His new contract means he will be City's longest-serving manager since Les McDowall, who was in charge from 1950 to 1963, and gives him three seasons to put their blue ribbons on the Champions League.

Project Pep, part II, starts here.

97

So, how did City persuade him to stay?

Let's be clear: City *had* started making contingency plans. Any club in that position, with an elite manager in the final year of his contract, would have to start thinking about a succession plan. Yet the club knew right from the beginning that there were not too many candidates who would tick all the relevant boxes. Anybody other than Guardiola, they concluded, would have been a downgrade.

Txiki Begiristain, the director of football, had the task of exploring all the different possibilities and had worked out that there were maybe only half a dozen managers in the world who would have fitted seamlessly into the playing philosophy that Guardiola inherited from Manuel Pellegrini and which runs throughout all the teams in the City Football Group.

This is why City would never have employed Jose Mourinho or Diego Simeone in the past. Begiristain is, however, an admirer of Brendan Rodgers, manager of the Leicester City side that currently top the Premier League table. The clubless Mauricio Pochettino's availability was obviously well-known and City have substantial information on a number of other candidates.

Ultimately, though, that is immaterial now and City have got what they wanted by persuading Guardiola to sign a two-year extension. He is currently in his fifth season in Manchester and a lot is always made about him needing a clean break from football, taking a year-long sabbatical in New York, after his four years as Barcelona head coach. Then again, he finds working at City considerably less stressful than it ever was for him at the Camp Nou.

What has Pep had to say about it?

His interview on the club's website was notable for its eulogy to Khaldoon Al Mubarak and making the point that it was City's chairman, more than anyone, who had influenced his decision.

Al Mubarak, according to Guardiola, was "the main reason why I decided to continue."

That isn't just a case of Guardiola saying all the right things to please his bosses. He genuinely has a huge amount of respect for Al Mubarak and the generally calm manner in which the club is run. It is the polar opposite of what he had at Barcelona when Sandro Rosell was president and, plainly, it has worked to City's advantage that Guardiola and Al Mubarak have developed a relationship based on mutual respect and trust.

Yes, it isn't ideal that Guardiola's wife, Cristina, has moved back to Barcelona because that is where her business is based and where Valentina, the youngest of their three children, goes to school.

At the same time, that was never the biggest stumbling block for Guardiola. The life of a football manager means he is away from his family for long periods anyway and, when the lockdown restrictions are lifted, they will make time to see each other, just as they have done over the last year or so.

For Guardiola, the key issues focused on whether he was happy in Manchester, whether he enjoyed his work and whether he felt he was capable of doing something that very few managers have managed in one spell: rebuilding a championship-winning team. The answer, in every case, was yes.

There is a feeling from those close to Guardiola, who turns 50 in January, that this is something of new territory for him as he enters the 'second phase' of being a club's manager for the first time. At Barcelona and Bayern Munich, he moved on when the first phase came to an end because he did not see a way to renew it. At City, though, it is different – primarily because he trusts in and feels comfortable working with those around him.

"Usually he only stays for a short period of time," said a source close to a member of Guardiola's squad, "but he has made it very clear to the players that the obsession or target is to win the Champions League with City. The players are still learning from him and excited to play for him. He is so experienced that he has been able to adapt how he coaches to give a longer life at one club as manager."

Guardiola and Al Mubarak had the chance to talk when they were in Portugal at the end of last season for the Champions League's knockout mini-tournament. Yet it is difficult to pinpoint an exact time when these contract talks started because, first things first, City's priority was to discover whether Guardiola was feeling happy and enthusiastic in his work. That was a fluid process that took place over many months, involving lots of different conversations.

All the time, there was an understanding that everything should be done privately and without courting publicity. *The Athletic*'s understanding is that there were face-to-face talks abroad – possibly in Abu Dhabi – in the last few weeks.

When it became apparent everyone was on the same wavelength, Guardiola brought in his brother Pere, who is also his agent, to be part of the talks. The international break was an opportunity to work out the precise terms and everything has been nailed down in the last few days.

Again, it was all kept quiet. And when it reached the stage at which City were ready to announce everything there were still only a handful of people inside the club who knew. The news was released on City's website – 'The Journey Continues' – at 12.30pm GMT, which gave Guardiola time to inform all his backroom staff. Senior players were not understood to have been aware of the development until the story broke.

So what's changed? How come his time at Barcelona left him physically drained, with "nothing left to give", but he is looking at chalking up seven years in the Premier League?
You have to understand the difference in the working conditions. In Spain, they call it '*desgaste*' – the physical toll that a high-

pressure job such as football management can have on someone. And, for Guardiola, it was huge in Barcelona. It was his city – and they were his club – and that immediately left him with an enormous weight of responsibility. The sports media in Barcelona could be harsh in the extreme. If Guardiola went out for a meal in the city, the paparazzi would soon arrive. It could feel relentless. And, yes, he was worn down by it.

The difference in Manchester is that he is working in an environment with people he regards as close friends and confidantes and – here's the thing – without the politics and occasional moments of aggro. Yes, City's protracted battle with UEFA and then at the Court of Arbitration for Sport took its toll but he repeatedly said he would accept whatever judgment was handed out and then came out swinging when the club's two-year ban was overturned in July.

His relationship with Begiristain is the closest of all. But these two ex-Barcelona players, with their shared love for Johan Cruyff, really come as a three if you also include the chief executive Ferran Soriano, another of the Catalan club's former executives. Guardiola has bonded with Al Mubarak and, while there are always a few tensions in any club, there simply isn't the toxicity and politics that diminished his time at Barcelona.

Guardiola still keeps an eye on the goings-on at the Camp Nou and makes it his business to be up to speed on what happens behind the scenes at his old club. The same applies to Begiristain and Soriano and, even now, it will often leave them shaking their heads in wonder. Frankly, they are glad to be out of it.

Any chance Lionel Messi will be joining him in Manchester?
Of course, they would love to sign Messi but, then again, we knew that anyway. And, if nothing else, Guardiola's new contract strengthens City's position in all sorts of ways when it comes to their recruitment plans.

"At Real Madrid they put you in a room with 13 European Cups and ask if you want to be part of the family," one City executive told *The Athletic* a while back. "At Barcelona, there's the city, the weather and, 'You want to play with Messi?'"

For Liverpool and Manchester United, there is the history and tradition attached to those red shirts.

City? They have huge financial power, of course. But so do all the elite clubs. The attraction is Guardiola: what it is like to work with him, playing for a man Al Mubarak describes as "a genius".

A genius would, of course, win the Champions League and you have to wonder whether Guardiola would ever be truly satisfied if he cannot get his hands on the Champions League again.

Inside the club, they always argue that too much is made of this point and that Guardiola should not just be judged on his record in one competition. But signing Messi would undoubtedly help and the chances of it happening have to be greater now the six-time Ballon d'Or winner knows Guardiola is staying in Manchester.

Are City's supporters entitled to see this as a big day for their club then?

Absolutely. City always thought they would be downgrading if they had to find a new manager at the end of the season and, though they would never say this publicly, they also feel this is a good day for the Premier League – and English football – as a whole. As Gary Lineker observed: "His football is joyous."

OK, City finished a long way behind champions Liverpool last season and, by their standards, it has been a difficult start to the new campaign. Yet you can imagine Liverpool, United and all of City's other rivals would have been delighted if today's announcement had instead been that Guardiola was moving on next summer.

As it is, all the uncertainty has gone now.

This had to be resolved now rather than dragging on any longer. And this was always the outcome City desperately wanted.

QUALIFYING EARLY GIVES GUARDIOLA A CHANCE TO LET HIS PLAYERS BREATHE

SAM LEE

NOV 26, 2020

Pep Guardiola made a couple of tactical tweaks against Olympiakos as he searched for answers to Manchester City's recent attacking woes, but it was perhaps a simple injection of energy that underpinned their best moments.

Both with and without the ball City looked sharper than they have done in many of their Premier League games this season. Whether closing down the Greek champions to win the ball back or pinging passes around on the edge of the box, best demonstrated by Phil Foden's winner, Guardiola's side looked a bit more like their old selves. For a bit, anyway.

Guardiola acknowledged in the build-up to the game that he had to find the solution to their recent stodgy performances and steps were taken towards that aim even if the second half could be better described as stale domination. The most important thing may well be that they have sealed qualification for the last-16 with two games to spare, which should make their fixture list slightly more palatable.

After all, one of the intangible factors thought to be holding them back this season is fatigue, a lack of sharpness. "We had about seven days of pre-season, I played with my national team after one training session," Kevin De Bruyne said following the 2-0 defeat at Spurs on Saturday. "So, what do people expect of us?"

City, domestically at least, are enduring their worst start to a season since the 2008 takeover, having scored just 10 goals in their eight games, conceding 11. They are not just creating fewer chances but converting a smaller percentage of what they do create, compared to last season.

Fans scrabbling around for assurances that things will soon click into place can cling to the hope that once the players are fully up to speed, they will fire on all cylinders once again.

There are a couple of problems with that, though. One is that Liverpool are coping pretty well with their injury crisis (similar to City's earlier in the season) and Tottenham have come through a frankly ridiculous fixture pile-up, more demanding even than City's. The point is that City have been dealt a bad hand, but so have others and it simply can't just be fatigue.

The other issue, more pertinent to City, is that their fixture list shows no signs of easing up anyway. The only breaks in the calendar up until the middle of February are the days scheduled for cup matches.

If City reach the Carabao Cup semi-final and the FA Cup fifth round, their next clear match day will be either February 16/17 or February 23/24, depending on when their Champions League last-16 tie is. That's three months away. So the importance of sealing qualification should provide some small but very welcome respite.

Guardiola will still want to seal top spot in the group, which will mean getting a result at Porto in five days' time. That should mean City will not yet be afforded the luxury of sending a complete second string to Portugal, but every little helps at this moment in time, when rest and recovery are extremely hard to come by. If even two or three key players can be left behind then that should be a big help, especially because the other five of City's next six games are in Manchester, meaning very limited travel.

And if City clinch top spot before they play Marseille at the Etihad on December 9, Guardiola can make as many changes as he likes ahead of the Manchester derby. With home games against Burnley, Fulham and West Brom before and after that game at Old Trafford, there is an opportunity for City to finally get up to speed.

It has been hard to nail down Guardiola's genuine feelings on the fatigue situation, though. Yes, he has been almost as vocal as Ole Gunnar Solskjaer and Jurgen Klopp in decrying the TV schedules, and perhaps even more vocal in calling for the ability to use five substitutions in the Premier League, but for all that he has very rarely actually used three subs, so what difference would five make?

On only two occasions out of eight has Guardiola used a full complement in the league, which is the biggest suggestion available that despite the unquestionable demands on his players, the most important thing is results.

Even so, there was an element of risk in the decision to leave De Bruyne out of the travelling party, given he has become the team's biggest creator by miles. Even at below his best, the idea of this struggling team without him is pretty bleak. In the event, City passed the test without him and Kyle Walker, and both should be better for the breather.

City have to take the positives where they can get them at the moment and while it wasn't the most sparkling performance by any means (and they played even better in Marseille but failed to take that into their league games), this showing surely signposted a few things that should be kept for coming challenges.

For one thing there were wingers playing on their stronger sides, something fans and even some inside the club have been crying out for in recent weeks. There is nothing wrong with wingers cutting inside onto their stronger foot but the issue for City is that they have not been able to provide enough width or move the ball quickly enough to make it work.

Ironically, Benjamin Mendy, making his first appearance in well over a month, did provide that width and energy from left-back, meaning the left-footed Foden could tuck inside and, indeed, use his weaker foot.

We jest, of course, as it was from an inside position that Foden did score, sweeping home with his stronger left after the best example of City's incisive passing, between Gabriel Jesus and Raheem Sterling following a quick switch of play by Ilkay Gundogan. Those players mentioned, as well as Bernardo Silva, combined for City's most promising attacks.

Perhaps that goes to show that speed and energy were more important on the night than any tactical tweaks, as welcome as they were. After all, this wasn't Guardiola ripping up his rulebook: it was more Guardiola than ever. He retained Gundogan, his vital 'control' midfielder, and put him alongside Rodri, something else fans don't really like.

There was the commitment to controlling the game via passes, of course, giving Olympiakos just two touches in their box, and there were times, particularly in the first half, when the pressing and interplay looked like something from the good old days of 2017-2019.

If they can make that last for 90 minutes then the inverted wingers and double pivots simply won't matter quite so much.

The word 'if' is doing an incredible amount of lifting there, and maybe City's problems run deeper than their truncated pre-season, but perhaps with a 'lighter' fixture list and a clearer idea of his more energetic performers, Guardiola might get closer to finding his answer.

NOVEMBER RESULTS

Champions League, November 3, 2020
Man City 3 Olympiakos 0
Man City scorers: Torres 12, Jesus 81, Cancelo 90

Premier League, November 8, 2020
Man City 1 Liverpool 1
Man City scorers: Jesus 31

Premier League, November 21, 2020
Tottenham 2 Man City 0

Champions League, November 25, 2020
Olympiakos 0 Man City 1
Man City scorers: Foden 36

Premier League, November 28, 2020
Man City 5 Burnley 0
Man City scorers: Mahrez 6, 22, 69, Mendy 41, Torres 66

DECEMBER

GUARDIOLA WANTS FIVE SUBS BUT ONLY USED ONE IN LACKLUSTRE DERBY NEEDING SPARK

SAM LEE

DEC 13, 2020

"My decision," Pep Guardiola said. "I saw the team, the players were there, we were sharp, with Kevin (De Bruyne), with Gabi (Gabriel Jesus), with Raz (Raheem Sterling). In the last minutes we had chances on this side. I decided to maintain it, not to move the structure. It was my decision. The rules are the rules and after that (whether) I use the rules depends on me."

Quite a lot to unpack, then, from Pep Guardiola's explanation of his substitutions in a lacklustre goalless Manchester derby on Saturday.

In short: he was happy with how his side were playing, and he still believes he should be allowed to make five substitutions. He made only one of the permitted three at Old Trafford, bringing on Ferran Torres for Riyad Mahrez with 24 minutes to go, and Sky Sports commentator Gary Neville noted that the like-for-like change showed Guardiola was happy with the flow of the game, and that he didn't want to change too much.

Neville was spot on, and that has been Guardiola's approach in many similar matches over the years, win, lose or draw. It's why his use of substitutions has long been a talking point among City fans and why now is a good opportunity to dig into it.

Against Liverpool in November, he joined opposite number Jurgen Klopp in speaking passionately about how the Premier League was wrong to vote against the use of five substitutions. He had only made one change during the game and had even called Phil Foden to come on with five minutes to go, only to change his mind. Last weekend he made no subs against Fulham, and he made just the one at Old Trafford.

In total, City have made 20 of the available 33 substitutions in the league this season. Against Fulham, it did seem to be about keeping players fresh: half the team played for 90 minutes and then got rested for the next game, while the other half got their rest against the west London outfit. Overall, though, it's hard to explain the desire for the option of five changes when the full complement of three has only been used three times in the 11 games so far.

Tactically, though, it's easier to explain Guardiola's thinking. Like against Liverpool, there was a feeling City could've pushed for more than a point at Old Trafford. "I decided to maintain it, not to move the structure." This is the nub of it.

Guardiola's changes usually go like this: they'll be like-for-like, and usually in the final 20-odd minutes. If a game is in the balance in any way (if City only have a two-goal lead, for example), he might not make any changes at all.

The best example of his decision-making in these situations probably came at Anfield last season. City were 3-0 down with 20 minutes to go and Guardiola brought on Gabriel Jesus for Sergio Aguero. They pulled a goal back soon after but no further changes were made.

Again, Guardiola was happy with how the game was going at that moment in time: Liverpool were not flowing forward on the break, City had most of the possession and were camped on the edge of the home side's box. Klopp was probably much happier with the game at that point, but Guardiola did not feel radical changes would help. Mahrez and Foden were on the bench but that's where they stayed. Perhaps Guardiola did not want to risk making matters worse. If he brings on a forward-thinking player in a big game like that and they're not up to speed, maybe they will misplace a pass and destabilise the team.

That's the same logic that applies itself to games City are winning comfortably, or when fans want to see youngsters come on – usually Foden over the past three or four years. But Guardiola, in certain circumstances, will be concerned that a match could quickly get out of hand: if one mistake lets the other team pull a goal back, maybe they'll get another.

It's very worst-case-scenario, but logic that has helped City win trophies left, right and centre. It's brought Guardiola incomparable success and, ultimately, it's just how he is as a coach and as a person.

The recent examples do hint at a preoccupation with the counter-attack, though, something that seems to have grown over the past year or so. As Guardiola also said on Saturday night: "We know we can show more intensity but when you attack, they can punish on the counter. We would love to have more chances. We have to build from here. Without fans, it looks like it lacks intensity, but from the touchline I see the players fight."

There were things to build from, as he says. Barring some dangerous first-half corners, United barely created anything. United were wounded after recent results and they haven't been playing particularly well, but that was also the case when the sides met last season, and Ole Gunnar Solskjaer's counter-attacking set-up still caused City all sorts of problems and secured three wins out of four.

While City fans may not buy into Guardiola's reminder that the opposition are dangerous – "It's Man United!" – there's something to be said for keeping them locked down. And six clean sheets in a row isn't to be sniffed at, either. (John Stones has been a big part of that).

It would be pretty harsh to have demanded City do better with counter-attacks and sort out the defence in October, and then be complaining when they've achieved it in December (even if they did manage to defend well without sacrificing the attack in the not too distant past).

Maybe it all comes back to Lyon. After watching his team go out of the Champions League in the three previous seasons by conceding too many goals, he closed up in August's quarter-final against the French side, concerned about their counter-attacks, but City went out anyway.

And then there was Leicester's visit to the Etihad in September. Remember, if the game is in the balance, the subs will be like-for-like or nothing, generally. That afternoon, he brought on 17-year-old striker Liam Delap for deep-lying midfielder extraordinaire Fernandinho. Six minutes into the second half. With the score at 1-1. Leicester ended up winning 5-2. It was so incredibly uncharacteristic, and given how it turned out, is it any surprise that Guardiola would be even more determined to stick to how he usually does things?

He has been increasingly worried about counter-attacks in 2020 and both Liverpool and United are particularly good at them, so maybe it was better to keep the game as it was – with City in control – than to risk Mohamed Salah or Marcus Rashford running into space the other way. That's the devil's advocacy out of the way, and perhaps we understand the decisions a bit more if we look at them from his point of view.

But would they not have been better off with Foden's spark in those final 15 minutes, with United pegged back? Or the threat from Bernardo Silva that has seen him score two fine goals at Old Trafford in the past two years?

Foden seems to be paying the price for two sloppy performances in Europe, in the home games against Olympiakos and Marseille, when he surrendered possession easily. That intention to force the issue might be exactly what City need at times like this, but it didn't play well with Guardiola. Bernardo has not been in particularly bright form, but that was the case last season when he helped tear United apart in City's one win out of the four meetings.

City were missing something last night. Neville spent much of the game remarking on how it was so unusual to see them playing so slowly, knocking the ball from side to side but without any real intention. The surprising thing is that Neville, still the best pundit on TV, has commentated on several City games this year alone when they have played *exactly* like this.

Since the start of last season, they have won just one of their seven games away to fellow 'big six' sides. The last time was only three weeks ago, against Tottenham Hotspur. All three defeats by United last season were like this, too.

It does beg the question: Is Guardiola happy with this?

City do seem to have sorted out their defence and there was no guarantee of that just a couple of months ago. The next challenge is to get the attack firing yet again. With the talent at their disposal, surely it will be a matter of time before something clicks at the sharp end?

Then again, after another night when Raheem Sterling struggled to make inroads on the left, when Jesus couldn't impose himself on the game, and with Kevin De Bruyne throwing his arms up in the air in frustration, it's not so easy to believe.

For Guardiola, it could have been worse.

UNLIKE LIVERPOOL LAST SEASON, CITY AREN'T PLAYING LIKE LOSING THE TITLE HURT

DANIEL TAYLOR

DEC 18, 2020

Have the players of Manchester City really forgotten some of the essentials that are needed when it comes to the business of winning league championships? It increasingly appears that, yes, they might need a refresher, judging by how they have reacted to finishing last season as little more than a speck in Liverpool's wing mirrors.

Many of us who saw City being deposed as the Premier League champions with an 18-point deficit might have reasonably expected a response that demonstrated to the football world how a club with their ambitions regarded it as a professional affront. We anticipated a positive reaction because that is the expectation for all the great teams and, despite their various ordeals in the Champions League, most people would argue that City deserve to be recognised as one.

But who could look at Pep Guardiola's team this season and confidently make a case that they are displaying the force of personality that will be required for them to stand any chance of re-establishing themselves as the best in the league?

When Liverpool accumulated 97 points only to finish as runners-up behind City in 2018/19, Jurgen Klopp used the disappointment as the fuel to inspire his men to come back the following season and make sure they put it right.

No matter that they had just won the Champions League, Liverpool's players made it absolutely clear the Premier League was their burning obsession and that the only way they could ever be satisfied was by releasing City's grip, finger by finger, on the championship trophy. Liverpool won their first eight games last season, drew the next one and then went on a freewheeling 18-match winning run. Klopp's team had a 25-point lead by mid-February. It was spectacular. The league became a procession. This was one of Manchester United's strengths, too, back when the Premier League trophy had a habit of returning to Old Trafford like a homing pigeon.

Everyone remembers Sergio Aguero's title-winning kick for City in the final moments of the 2011/12 season and the scenes from Sunderland as Sir Alex Ferguson took in the news, the blood drained from Phil Jones' face and, this being the sport of *schadenfreude*, a gloating home crowd turned their backs to 'Do the Poznan', City fans-style.

What the cameras did not capture that day was Ferguson walking up and down the aisle on the bus journey from Wearside back to Manchester, telling his players never to forget how it felt and to make sure that when they came back the following season, they had the wit and gumption to do something about it.

Michael Carrick was on the bus that day and saw, close-up, why Ferguson used to say the best way to judge any team was how they dealt with adversity. "His message was mainly to the young players," Carrick wrote in his autobiography. "The boss knew the senior ones were smarting and already counting down to next season. 'Don't you ever forget what this feels like,' he repeated. 'Let this motivate you to win the league next year.'

The boss didn't go mad, he didn't shout. He just rammed home the message."

This is the thing about serial champions: the disappointments stay with them longer than the glories. They want to get that losing feeling out of their system. They cannot tolerate the idea they might have to go through the same again. That following season, United moved to the top at the 13-game mark and were never caught. It might not have been Ferguson's most exhilarating group of players but they had a shared purpose and a fierce spirit of togetherness and that, ultimately, gave them powerful momentum.

With City, however, that appears to be missing from the current team. Where is their impetus? Where is the relentless ambition that symbolised the brilliant championship-winning teams constructed by Guardiola and, before him, Roberto Mancini and Manuel Pellegrini? Where is the professional hunger that has taken Liverpool back to the top of the table, despite the debilitating run of injuries that was supposedly going to shipwreck their title defence?

One more question, too, for Guardiola now the huff and puff of their midweek draw against West Bromwich Albion leaves them with only five wins from their opening 12 league fixtures. If this collection of players are hurt to have finished so far behind Liverpool last season, why are we not seeing it in their play?

Instead, it feels like deterioration has set in. City have dropped more points from their first dozen games than they did throughout the entire 2017/18 season. They are five points worse off than the same stage last year and have managed only 18 goals in comparison to 35, 36 and 40 at this point of the previous three seasons.

To put that in context, Brian Horton's 1994/95 City side who ended up two places and four points above the relegation places were more prolific, with 21 goals from their first 12 league fixtures – and don't forget Guardiola's men scored five of their current total in one game against Burnley. In only one other match, the opener against Wolves in September, have they managed more than two goals. In eight of their 12 matches, they have scored either once or not at all.

They look flat, uninspired, strangely subdued. Worse, there doesn't appear to be any competitive anger coursing through their veins. Not like there used to be anyway, whenever there was another team enjoying the view from the top of the league.

Gary Neville made this point after the goalless Manchester derby last weekend and, while City supporters might not be appreciated being lectured by a United man, let's not forget he knows a thing or two about winning league titles. Neville collected eight of them throughout his playing career and his impression of City was that they now seem "bored" where once they were inspired.

"That's a shadow, an absolute shadow, of the team that won the league two years ago," he said. "City could win the league, they could surprise us, but it's the body language – they look like all the juice has been squeezed out of the orange. You look at (Kevin) De Bruyne on the pitch and he looks a bit like he's looking round at his team-mates thinking, 'You're not as good as the ones I used to play with.'

"There's a spirit sometimes in a team that looks like it's going to win the league and, at the moment, they are obviously going to have to develop that. I don't see that at this moment. It could change; it is early."

That last point is worth remembering when there are over two-thirds of the league season to go and, as such, plenty of time for Guardiola and his players to conjure up some form of collective improvement.

There is all the usual mitigation, too, that over the last 18 months, City have lost two players, David Silva and Vincent

Kompany, whose contributions were so significant there will be statues going up outside the stadium. Aguero has missed nine of the 12 games through injury, and only started two. Fernandinho's influence, at age 35, is not what it was. These are changing times and, in fairness to Guardiola, it was never going to be a seamless process.

All the same, it must be troubling for City's supporters when they remember the qualities that brought about the song, first heard on Mancini's watch, to celebrate the way their team "fight to the end".

Yes, they had outstanding individuals but collectively, they also gave the impression they wanted the entire football world to know about their superiority. Every game felt like an occasion. They were quick to the ball, strong in the challenge. They swarmed over opponents. And, boy, it was a lot of fun to watch.

Now, though, is Raheem Sterling troubling opposition defences the same way? Is too much resting on De Bruyne's brilliance? Are the players running as hard? Nobody could ever doubt Aguero's competitive courage but at 32 this could conceivably be his last season in Manchester. And if these are City's best three players, when are the others going to step up?

When Guardiola announced a month ago that he had signed a new contract, the reaction was overwhelmingly favourable because everyone associates him with beautifully constructed football and a trophy count that puts him among the authentic greats.

Yet managers, like players, can lose form and there are legitimate questions to be asked about whether – even if it is just temporary – he has lost a bit of his precious magic.

All the time, we are told that Guardiola's challenge is to win City the Champions League and that he will never feel truly satisfied unless that happens.

Maybe, though, we are approaching the time when we need to reassess that statement. Perhaps it would be fairer now to conclude that his challenge is to achieve something that only a small number of elite managers have ever done before, which is to build a new title-winning team at a club where he has already won the championship.

Ferguson did it with United. Sir Matt Busby, too. Bill Shankly and Bob Paisley both achieved it for Liverpool, as did Stan Cullis with Wolves in the 1950s and Harry Catterick at Everton a decade later. Arsene Wenger did the same for Arsenal and, if you know the history, we could go back over a century to George Ramsay's list of achievements at Aston Villa.

There is nobody else, though, and these are the moments when we are reminded why City remain attracted to the idea of luring Lionel Messi away from Barcelona. Project Messi would be one way of re-energising this team.

Something has to change because, on current evidence, it is starting to feel like something deep and fundamental in City's make-up has been pushed off course.

JOHN STONES: THE RESURRECTION

SAM LEE

DEC 21, 2020

It was only a fleeting moment, easily forgotten about and ultimately inconsequential, but it tells us how John Stones is currently playing, and feeling.

On another day his bad luck may have struck again. Southampton had launched another of their forays down the right-hand side, the ball was chipped into the box, evaded the stretching Che Adams and hit the unsuspecting Stones, inside his own six-yard box, square on the forehead. By the time he processed what had happened the ball had bounced out for a corner. The hands went on to his knees, a "thank God for that" expression showed just how close it came to becoming an own goal. Maybe one that would have derailed his resurgence.

But then a smile. You don't see many footballers smile in the heat of the battle these days, but Stones afforded himself a moment to enjoy his good fortune, sharing it with his good friend Kyle Walker. It might have come back to bite him had the towering Jannick Vestergaard planted his header in, having run off the much smaller Ferran Torres, but this was City's day. Once again, it was Stones' day.

He's had a fair few of them now and the left-sided centre-back spot is his to lose. That's been the case for a few games now, and it's why he started the Manchester derby last weekend. "His attitude was always the same but we see him happier and stronger now because he's fit, he's not injured every two or three weeks, and that helps a lot," Pep Guardiola said on Friday. "He's played really well and that gives you confidence. His personal life, now it's settled, is much better."

It's worth pausing here for a second. There weren't too many affiliated with City who would have been happy with how the derby played out, but Stones would have been. Even in his one indecisive moment he quickly reasserted control, stepped in front of Ederson, brought the ball forward and launched the attack that led to City's best chance.

But his biggest coverage in the Sunday morning media was a very revealing peek into the past year or so of that personal life, via an interview with his ex partner and the mother of his daughter.

Some of the topics raised may have shone a new light on his recent struggles, perhaps making a few realise that his time out of the City team has sometimes been of his own making.

Most of the details, some of which wouldn't look out of place on a series of *Footballers' Wives*, were kept out of the media as they were developing, meaning it was often a mystery why Stones' name did not feature on the City team sheet.

Back in February he was left out of a match day squad because those off-field issues – a matter relating to his split – meant he was deemed by Guardiola to not be in the right frame of mind to play football. Between those moments, poor form and injuries, Guardiola simply felt he couldn't trust him.

That should not come as a surprise to anybody who looked at any City match when the 19-year-old Eric Garcia was in the line-up while Stones sat on the bench, such as the Champions League quarter-final against Lyon in August.

Another sliding doors moment. He would have left this summer but for Garcia's desire to join Barcelona, which caught City on the hop. They decided to cash in on the youngster instead, as his contract expires at the end of the season. Everton thought they were getting Stones back, and how would that transfer have been perceived?

If Guardiola couldn't get a tune out of this elegant but sometimes flawed defender, who could? A move back to the club he left four years ago would have been a failure for both him and for City.

Even in the autumn, after yet another injury ensured he couldn't build on an opening-game appearance against Wolves, it was the wantaway Garcia who kept getting picked, with Stones not able to get a look in.

Yet here we are. City have conceded just one goal in 12 hours of football, a genuinely impressive achievement that has been somewhat lost in the team's underwhelming attacking performances. Guardiola was tasked with tightening his team up and he has done it, and Stones is a big part of that, playing in six of the eight games (missing the game where they conceded, against West Brom). Perhaps most tellingly, he has played in the games that Guardiola deems most important. "He's a guy who is so sensible and that helps to be focused on what we have to do," Guardiola continued.

Guardiola has effectively been running two teams of late, a weekend team and a midweek team. One for the must-win Premier League games and for the Champions League, where there were two or three attempts to grab top spot in the group. That is where Aymeric Laporte's only appearance in the last seven games has come, the dead rubber against Marseille, while Stones rested up for the derby.

The Frenchman did not feature in the matchday squad at Southampton on Saturday, with fans worrying about his continued absence and where that may lead. He has just moved into a new apartment in Manchester, so that should allay some fears, although his reaction to dropping out of the team has not done him too many favours with Guardiola.

City clarified that he missed out on Saturday because he's not fully fit, which plenty of supporters didn't believe, but it must be said that there have been plenty of times in the past few years when players have been dropped for non-footballing reasons and the club haven't been moved to comment, so the official verdict shouldn't be taken as suspicious.

He played well in that game against Marseille and that's all he can do now. Stones has had enough opportunities in the three years since injury derailed his fine start to City's 100-point season. That's how long it's been since he played like this.

As Guardiola said, he is in a better place now. He spent time this summer analysing his own performances, working out where things had gone wrong, but as one close observer put it this week, "John isn't doing anything differently, it's just confidence."

It's hard to argue with that. He just looks calmer, more assured. Even when he got his latest break in the side, as part of the 'midweek' team against Olympiakos at the start of November, he looked right at home, ordering his team-mates around and taking charge of situations. That's a basic requirement for top-level centre-backs, of course, but it was striking to see him so assertive after another difficult time.

Perhaps surprisingly, it's not his famed passing ability that has stood out in recent weeks. How often has Stones looked flustered? He looks commanding and in control, and to use a broad phrase, he hasn't put a foot wrong since he got back in the side.

"My only advice to him is that what he's gained right now, in the way he lives his life and how he takes care of himself – his body, his mind, everything – he's got to keep that for the next 10 years, 12 years, here with me, without me, with other managers," Guardiola cautioned.

"The moment that drops he will not be consistent but if he can avoid injuries he can be the player we've always believed he can be. He's given us a good feeling but it's just two or three games. A defender has to be consistent all season."

Nobody wants to get too carried away. In fact, after his first few games back in the team nobody dared say anything, lest a mistake or injury lurked around the corner, or the tougher games showed up his real level.

But so far, so good. Saturday's game was another tough assignment and one that he glided through, apart from that momentary scare 10 minutes before the break.

Stones is smiling again.

DECEMBER RESULTS

Champions League, December 1, 2020
Porto 0 Man City 0

Premier League, December 5, 2020
Man City 2 Fulham 0
Man City scorers: Sterling 5, De Bruyne 26

Champions League, December 9, 2020
Man City 3 Marseille 0
Man City scorers: Torres 48, Aguero 77, Gonzalez 90 (OG)

Premier League, December 12, 2020
Man United 0 Man City 0

Premier League, December 15, 2020
Man City 1 West Brom 1
Man City scorers: Gundogan 30

Premier League, December 19, 2020
Southampton 0 Man City 1
Man City scorers: Sterling 16

Carabao Cup, December 22, 2020
Arsenal 1 Man City 4
Man City scorers: Jesus 3, Mahrez 54, Foden 59, Laporte 73

Premier League, December 26, 2020
Man City 2 Newcastle 0
Man City scorers: Gundogan 14, Torres 55

JANUARY

CITY'S DESTRUCTION OF CHELSEA HAD BEEN WEEKS IN THE MAKING

SAM LEE

JAN 4, 2021

Pep Guardiola says Manchester City have got their tempo back.

And as he discussed his side's improvement following their dismantling of Chelsea at Stamford Bridge, he name-checked three sides that City cannot emulate in the counter-attacking stakes: Manchester United, Tottenham Hotspur and Liverpool. City can't do what they do, he said, they have to play their own game.

The problem this season is that it has taken quite a while to work out how to do that while times are changing. While City have not looked themselves for one or two glaring reasons this season (such as the absences of Fernandinho, David Silva and Sergio Aguero) they were also trying to play a more circumspect style, to adapt to the defensive shortcomings that were evident throughout 2020.

"We are a team that has to play in a certain rhythm, we can't play when everything is up and down, up and down, up and down," Guardiola said on Sunday evening. "We have to play our rhythm, a thousand passes, passes, passes and at the right moment attack. That's why we won the Premier Leagues, with more patience, more calm, and (recently) we missed a little bit – for many reasons – of this tempo, and today we got it."

It's been a fairly long road to finding the right balance, and they will be hoping it stays, but they are only four points off top with a game in hand, so things may be looking up.

— **A** —

Defensive improvement

Guardiola could have probably added Leicester to his list, given it was Brendan Rodgers' side that laid bare City's problems with fast transitions early in the season, and games against those four teams can act as a roadmap for their season so far.

Leicester exploited City's issues early on (in a game before Ruben Dias was signed), Liverpool flooded through the middle but came up against a stubborn backline, Spurs exploited errors and were ruthless with their breaks, while United just could not get going at all.

That United game, perhaps more than the others, told us plenty about how Guardiola saw his team at that point. While fans felt that the game was there for the taking in the final 20 minutes, as was the case against a tiring Liverpool in November, Guardiola's focus was on not losing.

He did not gamble, he kept the game closed – by choice. It may not have been pretty, but he showed that he knew how to keep City stable. That was exactly what us onlookers demanded of them earlier in the season (and *exactly* what they'll need in the Champions League).

After that Tottenham game, they kept eight clean sheets in 10 games in all competitions. John Stones' good form in the cup competitions earned him a place in Guardiola's most important games: the league ones. Full of confidence and alongside Dias, a natural leader, the City defence found its voice. The games, though, were often cagey, with City generally not exactly at their flowing best, and they didn't come up against especially challenging sides.

That's why the United game was such a good bellwether: this was a side that beat City three times last season by exploiting their weaknesses on the break. So to shut them out, and for Stones to pass another test, was a huge positive.

When Guardiola talks about a thousand passes and avoiding 40-metre transitions, he needs his players to be close together and of course to keep the ball. But perhaps they went too far, becoming too safe in their choices and too slow in their execution. It helped keep things tight, but they stopped creating.

City couldn't play like that forever. Guardiola, the high priest of attacking football, couldn't go on like that. The only way that that new-found defensive solidity would count for anything when the trophies are handed out would be by finding a better balance between defence and attack, to be able to venture forward as regularly as the old days without being terrified of what the opposition might do to you.

Restoring the attack

The stodgy draw against West Brom a few days later was not an ideal reaction, but Guardiola did at least show that he was trying to force the issue (as you would expect against a team in the relegation zone).

The wingers played on their natural sides to preserve a bit of width and when the dreaded double pivot was in place it was because City had pushed both full-backs forward to support what was often a front four including Kevin De Bruyne. As the game went on, Ilkay Gundogan pushed further forward as well. It was a poor team performance, but the intention to take off the shackles was there.

The Southampton game was an important win and also one that spelt out how City's strengths and weaknesses had flipped: they were robust defensively but wasteful in attack.

Indeed, were City more clinical then there would not have been any cause for alarm against United and West Brom, and City would be top of the table by now. If my aunt had wheels she'd be a bicycle, and the problem was that there were not enough of those chances for a team that wastes as many as City do.

At the moment, they need to create a hatful of chances and hope they take enough of them to win the match. Last season it was the same, but because the defence was weaker, they would lose the games that they couldn't kill off. This season, with the stronger defence, they are drawing them, but it still means they need plenty of chances to win.

The indecision and imprecision in front of goal has still been evident in their last two games, but they are creating more and, crucially, Guardiola thinks things are looking up.

"I think our momentum started against Newcastle," he said on Sunday of City's Boxing Day win. "I remember in the press conference I had the feeling that we played the way we have to play, it's not about winning or losing by one action, so I had that feeling."

He hailed the 2-0 win against Steve Bruce's side as their best performance of the season and again there were clear signs that he knew they needed to generate more chances.

He kept men in midfield to protect the defence, but this time it was Nathan Ake who came in from left-back. Joao Cancelo was not only allowed to get forward from right-back, he was pushed on into something like an attacking midfield role, where he combined with De Bruyne and the more advanced Gundogan. The front three switched continuously and it promised better things.

That's why the Chelsea game, given the postponement against Everton, promised to be so key. Were City really improving or did they just beat Southampton and Newcastle?

Well, we got our answer. Chelsea are not in the greatest form and their last-minute goal dents the defensive statistics somewhat, but City very rarely looked troubled and their stand-in keeper, Zack Steffen, barely had anything to do up until Callum Hudson-Odoi's consolation.

Guardiola's side pressed well and blocked off passing lanes into midfield, meaning Chelsea could not play out from the back. When crosses went into the City box, the entire back four stood up to the challenge. And when in possession they were adept at drawing Chelsea in and playing a pass that set them free into space.

So what's changed?

Too often this season City have been cumbersome. The focus on defence has hampered the attack, with not enough men pushed forward. In recent weeks they have attacked in greater numbers and with greater variety.

"Maybe I didn't communicate well to them what we have to do or choose the right way to play to be able to do it," Guardiola admitted, perhaps not seriously. "We need to play with one type of tempo, there are teams who play incredible transitions like United, Liverpool, Tottenham. We cannot play that way. No player is slow, absolutely not, no player is lazy, absolutely not, but we have to play another type of tempo, at the right moment run, at the right moment do it.

"I think our success in the past was done in this way and always we try it. It doesn't matter the set-up, if it's 4-4-2 or five at the back or seven at the back, this is not important, it's the idea – to start from the keeper and arrive to the wingers and strikers always through the passes, and at the right moment punish them. Today we were able to do it."

Guardiola played down the importance of tactical tweaks, but after all this is a man who famously makes them for every game, and Phil Foden, unwittingly, shot down that suggestion anyway.

"He always has great tactics coming into big games like this, he's a genius at things like this," the youngster said afterwards. "We did them by staying high and wide down the flanks so it's something we did well."

There was a big change through the middle, too. De Bruyne dropping off the front line as a false nine created City's second goal, and also allowed Bernardo Silva to be restored to a No 8 role, which is perhaps his best position. He was paired with Gundogan, who has been one of the stars of City's recent revival, his forays forward bringing three goals in his last four league games.

So, is this a new City now?

"No, no, no, it's the same. Same manager, the players are the same and the idea is completely the same," Guardiola insists. "When we won the trophies in the past it was because we played like today. It doesn't matter if a player plays more here or there or a bit more here or there, it's the tempo, the way we have to play. We missed it in the past and today we recovered it."

Can they keep it? Next up, United.

IF MAN CITY KEEP THIS UP, IT MIGHT NOT BE LONG BEFORE THEY REALLY ARE BACK

SAM LEE

JAN 7, 2021

Was it really less than a month ago that Manchester City shut up shop at Old Trafford and were more than happy with their 0-0 draw?

The turnaround in their fortunes since that uninspiring – but very deliberate – performance looks more and more impressive as the games go by. After picking apart Chelsea at the weekend to suggest they have got their season right on track, where better than the scene of that December 12 stalemate to highlight just how much has changed, and so quickly?

You never know in this most unpredictable of seasons what's around the corner, with teams losing form as quickly as they find it, but as City fans look forward to a record-equalling fourth Carabao Cup final in a row, things do seem like they're coming together, even with several players unavailable.

Their loud celebrations at the final whistle, in an eerily empty Old Trafford, showed the kind of togetherness and solidity that has been evident in City's defensive performances over the past couple of months.

They have conceded 13 goals in 15 Premier League games and just three in their last 12 in all competitions. Part of that improvement has been due to manager Pep Guardiola's tactical tweaks, with his concern about opposition counter-attacks convincing him to tighten the team up, playing narrow and taking fewer risks in possession, certainly in that derby just over three weeks ago.

The other part of City's improvement has been, simply, due to fine individual performances. There's a lot to be said for good players playing well, and an example of that came in the 1-1 home draw with Liverpool in November, when City still had all sorts of problems with counter-attacks coming through midfield but saw off the champions' threat by simply defending well when they needed to.

And last night, Guardiola used his post-match press conference to publicly thank sporting director Txiki Begiristain for signing Ruben Dias, the Portuguese centre-back who has played a huge role in City becoming the most robust rearguard in the league.

Dias might be their best player so far this season. The first thing those who worked with him at previous club Benfica pointed out in the summer was that he is a leader whose vocal presence, in the dressing room and on the pitch, would not be cowed by a move to one of England's most ambitious clubs. So far that has been proven true, with the 23-year-old already providing the kind of leadership City were missing last season, barking out orders during matches and trying to rally his team-mates in the dressing room.

He seems to be in his element, which might go to show the benefit of signing defenders who enjoy defending. The concern when Dias arrived was that, with all the problems City were having with counter-attacks and transitions, he would be chewed up and spat out like his predecessors last season. Instead, he seems to relish making all the tackles, blocks and clearances;

the things that are certainly required of City defenders but are often lower down the list of their priorities than things such as progressive passes and ball carries.

And perhaps John Stones has found that balance, too. He has been in imperious form, looking every bit as strong a defender as he is a passer or a creator. He was one of the few City players to come out of that last derby with any real credit. He had played well against Olympiakos, Fulham and Burnley but could he do it in a bigger game? He could, he has done so in the games since then, and he did it again at Old Trafford.

Even on the occasion when Anthony Martial darted in behind him, perhaps his only misstep of the past couple of months, Dias was on hand to bail him out. They look a fine partnership and Aymeric Laporte will find it as incredible as the rest of us that he cannot get into the team at the moment, but there can simply be no argument for it, as good as the Frenchman is.

Yet without taking a solid City defence for granted, that was the part of the team that wasn't in question following the 0-0 at Old Trafford last month. What they had to do after that was to stay solid while committing more men forward and looking a bit more like their old selves.

The really impressive thing is that they did that almost immediately. The draw with West Bromwich Albion was dour, a worse performance than the one against United, but the intention was there in Guardiola's approach. Whereas he closed games off with inverted wingers and safer, slower play, he opened things up and pushed players forward in new ways.

A great example of that is Joao Cancelo, who had quietly been having a pretty impressive season as a stand-in left-back but has really helped make a difference to City in the past three games, while Kyle Walker has been out of action with COVID-19.

Cancelo was one of those who stood up to Liverpool's marauding attacks in November, leading Guardiola to praise the improvement in the defensive side of his game, and he has really shone since being restored to the right-hand side at Christmas.

In recent weeks his attacking play through the middle has stood out, helping provide Guardiola with an extra body on the edge of the opposition box, but at Old Trafford last night he again showed his defensive prowess, winning a series of tackles that thwarted United attacks. Like Laporte, Walker might find himself on the bench soon, despite having done little wrong.

City themselves weren't quite at their attacking best in the 2-0 win, with both of their goals coming from set-pieces, and again they were guilty of wasting great opportunities to burst forward into the huge spaces ahead of them. The midfield and attack were fine, and in stark contrast to last month's derby they really tried to get things going. It just didn't quite happen.

A post did deny Kevin De Bruyne a first-half goal that would have ranked up there with one of City's best of the Guardiola era. Oleksandr Zinchenko, picking up a loose ball inside his own box following an early United attack, saw he had few options on and knew that he and the closest player to him were being put under pressure, but he resisted any temptation to just lump it down the pitch and instead launched a superb counter that ended with De Bruyne's shot from outside the box striking the upright.

Had that gone in, it really would have been vintage City.

If they keep this up, and get a little bit sharper up front, it might not be long before they really are back.

ADVANTAGE MANCHESTER CITY . . .

SAM LEE

JAN 18, 2021

After all the dust had settled on Sunday's football, it was not Manchester United or Liverpool grabbing the attention, it was Manchester City.

You can bet your bottom dollar that the City players paid no special attention to the game at Anfield, either.

When Pep Guardiola emphasised that he was solely focused on "Cryyystal Palace", he wasn't joking, no matter how comical his pronunciation may have been. City had only taken one point from their last two home games against Roy Hodgson's men and knew exactly what they would come up against at the Etihad Stadium.

And it's just too early to be worrying about what other teams are doing. The odd eyebrow may have been raised as the City players trotted out to warm up after the final whistle had been blown on the goalless draw on Merseyside, but not much more than that.

This title race is far too open, this season is far too unpredictable, and we're only at the halfway stage anyway. But . . . it's no wonder that everybody is suddenly talking about Guardiola's men.

Their emphatic 4-0 victory over Palace was their eighth win in a row in all competitions, the first time they've done that since the back end of the 2018/19 season. Now that was a nervy title race. That was when City and Liverpool players would have been keeping a very close eye on what was going on in other games, sneaking a look at their phones while on coaches or in hotel rooms. Every single goal mattered.

It's unlikely that the relentless level both teams showed back then will be – or even could be – replicated this season, but City are doing everything that could be expected of them right now.

And you know things are going well when John Stones is scoring twice, one of them from a Ruben Dias assist (albeit a tenuous one). Guardiola's first-choice centre-backs played a major role in shoring up the defence at the end of 2020, helping the team rack up wins when the attack was not quite firing, and now they're making things happen at the other end too.

Everybody is talking about those two now. They've played 10 games together in all competitions this season and City have won nine of them, drawn the other, and conceded just once. City have tightened up all over the pitch but when those two are called into action they can certainly be relied on to do the basics.

The goals are an added bonus and Stones' first, in particular, was certainly needed on Sunday, because City got exactly what they expected from Palace. The Londoners stayed extremely compact, and the home side's cross-field passes were not played quickly and accurately enough to move the visitors around the pitch and cause them too many problems early on.

City have had a few performances like that this season, when inverted wingers and double pivots were the trending topics and the play wasn't exactly fluid; and with Raheem Sterling and Kyle Walker coming into the team for Phil Foden and Joao Cancelo, two of the brightest performers in recent weeks, this game could have gone the same way. That's when Kevin De Bruyne comes in handy.

When City struggled against Palace in the past two seasons, they resorted to chucking crosses into the box and hoping to generate something. When they lost at Christmas two seasons ago, City made 30 crosses from open play (their most that year), and in the 2-2 draw last season they made 46 (the second most).

It actually provided them with their two goals last season, but you'd do well to find any cross, in any game, in any league, better than De Bruyne's on Sunday. It wasn't just the cross, but the touch before it, too.

He killed the ball stone dead from Sterling's cross-field pass, and within a split second wrapped his right foot around it, caressing it – with the outside of his boot – into the air, curling and dipping onto Stones' head. The centre-back hadn't scored in the Premier League for City before but with service like that he could hardly miss. The Belgian now has 10 league assists this season from 16 league games and all of a sudden people are talking about him again, too.

This wasn't a night when City carved open their opponents with crisp, fast passing, like they did at Chelsea a fortnight ago, but the nature of the goals, the performance overall and the results elsewhere mean that will not matter one bit.

As City fans remember from Vincent Kompany's thunderbolt against Leicester, sometimes you just need to put the ball in the top corner – and they did that not once but twice.

Ilkay Gundogan has come into his own since Guardiola started pushing more men forward following the Manchester derby, and his curling effort killed this game off as a contest. Palace were already hamstrung by Wilfried Zaha's injury and City weren't in the mood to make things any easier for them.

Stones kept up the feel-good factor by firing in after Dias' towering header was saved, and Sterling really rammed the message home with a late free-kick that had echoes of his last-gasp winner against Southampton in November 2017, a win that fuelled City's 100-point season.

It is too soon to be getting carried away, but it's understandable that fans across the country are starting to talk about City again. This doesn't just feel like a fleeting run of form, either. They just look so solid defensively that even if the forwards miss their chances, which is certainly possible, they don't look likely to compound matters at the other end with silly mistakes, which set them back so much last season.

Then, they had too many flaws to win the title, but they were only outdone by the imperious Liverpool. This season, they look much more assured, and there hasn't been an outstanding candidate for the title either. Until now, perhaps.

City can go top, for a while at least, if they beat Aston Villa on Wednesday. That game always appeared to be the toughest in this six-game run that could establish them as league leaders. After Villa it's West Brom, Sheffield United and Burnley, three of the current bottom four.

After then it's Liverpool at Anfield at the start of February. Maybe then we'll have a proper title decider.

THE IMPORTANCE OF ILKAY GUNDOGAN

SAM LEE

JAN 20, 2021

"Someone said to me once, I perhaps don't shine but I allow others to shine, and that's how I see myself," Ilkay Gundogan said recently.

It was actually Mikel Arteta, the former Manchester City assistant, who told him that, and it sums up a part of his game brilliantly.

Only a part, though. Gundogan possesses that special ability that is integral to all of Pep Guardiola's teams, the ability to keep the ball moving quickly, setting the tempo, organising his own team-mates while destabilising the opposition; the *'pausa'* to wait for the right pass, and that's why he's so cherished.

It's rarely the most obvious thing happening in a football match and it can be hard to appreciate from the outside, but think of any of City's biggest games in the past couple of years – if Gundogan hasn't been playing, then it's because he was unavailable, especially since David Silva began to feature less.

"There are players who think about what the team needs, about what's best for the group, players who think about the whole team as they're playing," Guardiola said during his time in Germany. "This type of footballer is intelligent and tends to have the global vision of the game that we need. That's why you have some players who control the game."

In fact, there's even been a bit of consternation around the squad on Gundogan's behalf because he hasn't always featured in the predicted starting XIs picked by fans and media, even though Guardiola needs him to keep City ticking.

"You cannot just build a team of 11 players playing the same type of football and the same type of characters and players," Gundogan added, almost defending his style. "In the end, there has to be one harmony – one great picture that fits."

A lot of his work does go unnoticed, but he won't have to spell out the beauty of his performances in recent weeks, when he has reminded people that he can shine just as brightly as anybody else.

---------------------- **A** ----------------------

The basic numbers certainly suggest he has been a crucial member of the team since the very start of the season. After missing the opening games with COVID-19, and needing to take naps after training due to after-effects of the virus, he has missed only six Premier League and Champions League matches this season.

City only won once without him in those games (the season-opening win at Wolverhampton Wanderers). The only time they dropped points in Europe? He didn't play. The 5-2 defeat against Leicester City? Didn't play. Defeat at Tottenham Hotspur and the goalless draw at Old Trafford? Didn't play in those either.

They've won 13 of the 16 games he has started in all competitions, so that's a good indication of his importance. That said, John Stones would be able to boast similar stats and, in a team as complex as City's, it's always important to remember that things are rarely quite so simple. But they have looked back to their old selves recently and Gundogan has been a central – and very obvious – part of that.

Quite simply, he has been playing higher up the pitch. He has played 12 league games this season and, handily, six of them were in a deep-lying role before the Manchester derby on December 12, and the other six have been further forward since that game. He has been using the ball in more advanced areas in his most recent appearances, most notably in the half-space that David Silva used to occupy regularly and inside the penalty area.

Earlier in the season, City were playing a much more compact, narrow style, with wingers cutting inside and Gundogan sitting deep and keeping the play ticking over alongside Rodri. Since the game at Old Trafford, Guardiola has committed more men forward, and that includes Gundogan.

By putting him in more advanced areas within a more attack-minded team, Gundogan's attacking output has understandably increased. He's much more of a goal threat, in terms of creating chances and finishing them.

Guardiola said in 2019 that "when Gundogan is close to the box, he arrives at the right tempo and the right moment to score a goal," and that's exactly how three of his recent goals have come: arriving in the box at the right time. The first two, against West Bromwich Albion and Newcastle United, were almost identical, bursting into the box to convert a Raheem Sterling cut-back.

"Now he's playing as an attacking midfielder he's a guy who always has one or two chances to score a goal," Guardiola says, acknowledging his changed role. "Not just that, it's the quality that he provides with the passes and understanding what to do in every action, and one day when he has to play false nine he will be able to play this position, I'm pretty sure of it."

Sources close to Gundogan insist it is not the tactical change that has led to the improved performances, he just feels good in himself at the moment, and over the COVID-19 complications.

Part of it, too, will be that he knows his role in the team, and knows he was doing it even when his performances were a bit more low-key. "Maybe with the numbers, people think I am better now, but I am honest, numbers are never really important for me in football," he said at the start of January. "When I leave the pitch after the final whistle, if I feel I have played as good as I could, when I am happy and proud of what I have done on the pitch, that's the point I feel comfortable – not if I score one, two goals or whatever."

It raises the question: what is his best position? According to sources close to him, he believes he is a better holding midfielder, which looked more believable earlier in the season when he wasn't asked to stray too far forward and, as a result, his attacking instincts weren't so obvious.

Gundogan said in his recent interview that he believes his best run of form came in the final weeks of the 2018/19 season, when he stood in for Fernandinho as City's sole holding midfielder.

"The year we won the second Premier League, he played as a holding midfielder and he was incredible," Guardiola said on Sunday. "I had the feeling that without his quality, the cleverness, the vision, the league would not have been possible.

"But he's a guy who I knew from Dortmund when he played with Jurgen Klopp and when he plays close to the box he has a sense of goal. It's not easy to find a player who can play as a holding midfielder and also like a No 10."

It's probably fair to say that the kind of hybrid role he has played a lot in the last 18 months does not get the best out of him quite so obviously. He shone in the Fernandinho role and he is shining now in something more like the David Silva role, but asking him to do a bit of both was never quite as eye-catching.

He did his job, as always, but it wasn't the best Gundogan and it wasn't the best City, either. Given the upturn in City's performances since Guardiola's change of approach in the last month, and the fact that the manager's mood has improved as well, the dreaded 'double pivot' may be a thing of the past.

Whatever City go on to achieve this season, Gundogan – as long as he is fit and available – will be a huge part of it. "He's one of the most unselfish players I ever had in my career, and you cannot imagine how grateful, how pleased and how important it is for me, for all of us to have this type of player," the Catalan said of Gundogan this month. "He's so intelligent, he's so clever, he understands the game perfectly, he knows in every action what he has to do, always thinking what is best for the team."

VICTORY OVER VILLA HAD ALL THE INGREDIENTS OF A PIVOTAL NIGHT IN THE TITLE RACE

SAM LEE

JAN 21, 2021

This felt like a big win. There may be a long way to go, there may be many other teams in the race, and there may not have been fans in the stadium to really revel in it, but Manchester City's 2-0 defeat of Aston Villa had all the ingredients of a pivotal night.

Maybe it's just because City don't find themselves having to chase a late goal at the Etihad too often, but when Bernardo Silva finally broke the deadlock with 11 minutes to go, there were echoes of that Vincent Kompany goal against Leicester when they won the title in 2019.

Of course, it can't be too similar, because that was City's penultimate game of the season. It was also in front of a full house of 60,000 fans who will never forget the moment their captain thought, "Sod it. Why not?"

Maybe it's because it would've been a big blow if they hadn't won against Villa. Had they not found the breakthrough, had they not kept up their recent winning run, doubts could've crept in.

There would have been too long to go in the race to write them off, just as it's too soon to declare them this season's champions,

From left, Manel Estiarte, Txiki Begiristain, Guardiola, Omar Berrada and Ferran Soriano celebrate the decision by the Court of Arbitration for Sport to overturn Manchester City's two-year Champions League ban for a serious breach of Uefa's financial fair play rules. The decision in July 2020 had a huge impact on City's season, with the club able to progress to their first Champions League final. © *Manel Estiarte Instagram*

The signing of Ruben Dias from Benfica in September was a huge factor in City's title win. Nelson Feijao, a former team-mate at under-15 level, recalled: "He didn't shut up for a second during matches. He spoke for 90 minutes, non-stop. It was like playing with a dictaphone." *Getty Images*

Leicester midfielder Youri Tielemans (above) celebrates with team-mates after scoring his side's fifth goal from the penalty spot during the 5-2 destruction of Manchester City at the Etihad in September 2020. It was the first time a Pep Guardiola side had shipped five goals in a game and highlighted their inability to deal with counter-attacks. *Getty Images*

However, the huge defensive improvement Guardiola's side subsequently made was reflected in their 2-0 away victory against the same opposition in April 2021, in which Benjamin Mendy (below) opened the scoring for City. *Getty Images*

The first time Pep Guardiola and Marcela Bielsa faced each other in the dugout turned out to be a classic La Liga encounter at Athletic Bilbao's San Mames stadium on November 6, 2011 (above). On a rain-lashed evening, Barcelona and Athletic served up a memorable display of attacking football which ended 2-2. Rodri Errasti, a Spanish journalist covering Bilbao for Eurosport, said: "It's one of the best matches I ever watched." *Getty Images*

The two men's football friendship started when Guardiola visited Bielsa in Argentina in 2006. The pair kept in touch and were reunited in the Premier League in season 2020/21. Leeds and Man City drew 1-1 in October 2020 and then Bielsa's Leeds recorded a memorable victory in April, with a late goal from Stuart Dallas. *Getty Images*

Kyle Walker has been a consistent performer for City in recent seasons, where his ability to play a variety of roles has made him a key part of Pep Guardiola's plans. He came through the Sheffield United academy – initially as a diminutive striker – before making the full-back position his own. Walker (above) scored the only goal of the game when City beat his old club 1-0 on October 31, 2020. *Getty Images*

Amid rumours that he was considering his future at the club, Pep Guardiola – below, with City chief executive Ferran Soriano (left) and director of football Txiki Begiristain (right) – signed a new contract in November 2020, tying him to the club until the end of the 2022/23 season. "We have the feeling there is still unfinished business," Guardiola said. *Getty Images*

Manchester City's 0-0 draw with rivals United at Old Trafford in December (above) drew criticism for their failure to push for victory in the closing stages. If that derby draw – and the lack of late substitutions to take the game to a wounded United – was uncharacteristic of Pep Guardiola's team, then the nadir for the City boss came three days later against West Brom (below). City attacked Slaven Bilic's side but could only manage a 1-1 draw. "It was the day after the draw with West Brom. We could have won but after the game, I went to my staff and friends and said, 'The results don't matter . . . I don't recognise my team and the way we play . . . I don't like at all what I'm watching." *Getty Images*

Season 2020/21 was one of personal redemption for John Stones, who worked his way from the periphery of the Manchester City squad to become first-choice centre-half. The Englishman's partnership with Ruben Dias was a huge part of his renaissance. The pair helped eradicate the defensive frailties of the previous campaign and drive City to the league title. *Getty Images*

Manchester City's 2-0 win over Aston Villa on January 20 marked a pivotal night in the title race. Bernardo Silva's breakthrough strike (above) with 11 minutes to go – on a rain-soaked night at the Etihad – was City's 25th shot of the match and sparked wild celebrations. Ilkay Gundogan's 89th-minute penalty sealed the three points and proved that they had the character to turn a damaging draw into an important win. *Getty Images*

As Brazilian midfielder Fernandinho's on-pitch influence faded in season 2020/21, so he grew into the role of captain. He successfully rallied the dressing room after a string of poor performances before the turn of the year and was praised by Phil Foden. "If the manager misses something, if a player is upset, he'll see that in a player and he'll come and see how they're doing. That's why he's the captain this year: because he's a great player and a great person." *Getty Images*

Manchester City's 4-1 win over Liverpool on February 7 moved them five points ahead of second-placed Manchester United. Ilkay Gundogan missed a first-half penalty, but made amends in the second half when he scored the opener (above). The German midfielder – who revelled in a more advanced midfield role during the second half of the season – added a second soon after, before Raheem Sterling and an inspired Phil Foden completed the scoring. *Getty Images*

Kevin De Bruyne has been a huge part of the success of Pep Guardiola's Manchester City team in recent seasons and signed a new five-year deal with the club in April 2021. Before negotiations began, De Bruyne and his representatives hired a number of leading football analytics service providers to help quantify his value to the team. *Getty Images*

Sergio Aguero signed off his Manchester City career in style by scoring two goals in 25 minutes and picking up the man-of-the-match award in a 5-0 win over Everton in May, after which his team-mates threw him in the air. He picked up 15 major trophies during his 10-year spell at the club. *Getty Images*

Phil Foden runs to celebrate with manager Pep Guardiola after his brilliant strike sealed City's passage to the Champions League semi-final, at the expense of Borussia Dortmund. City came of age in the two-legged quarter-final tie against the Germans, showing the right combination of ambition and control in a 4-2 aggregate win. *Getty Images*

Riyad Mahrez's second-half free-kick gave City a 2-1 Champions League semi-final first-leg advantage over Paris Saint-Germain. Regular free-kick taker Kevin De Bruyne selflessly allowed Mahrez to hit the deadball. *Getty Images*

Pep Guardiola and Thomas Tuchel first talked football together over champagne and wine spritzers in Schumann's Bar in central Munich in 2015, after being introduced by Michael Reschke, then Bayern Munich's sporting director. "It was like watching two grandmasters of chess, Fischer vs Spassky, locked in a battle of wits," recalls Reschke (above left).

Guardiola's Bayern Munich had beaten Tuchel's Mainz 4-1 and 2-0 in the 2013/14 campaign, but the Catalan was impressed by the young German coach's attack-minded style and even encouraged the club to appoint him as his successor in Munich. *Getty Images*

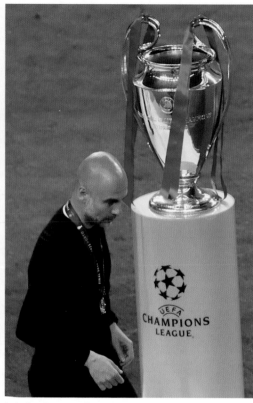

Pep Guardiola embraces Chelsea boss Thomas Tuchel after the 2021 Champions League final. Tuchel delivered a tactical masterclass in his Chelsea side's 1-0 victory over Manchester City in Oporto, denying Guardiola his third Champions League title. *Getty Images*

Fernandinho leads the celebrations as City raise the 2020/21 Premier League trophy at the Etihad Stadium. *Getty Images*

but a 0-0 (or worse) would have been far too similar to results last season when chances were missed and then punished at the other end.

Dropped points would've meant a loss of momentum and perhaps a loss of belief. And belief can go a long way. City might start to believe now. Maybe a more accurate comparison to Bernardo's goal last night is the one Raheem Sterling curled home against Southampton in November 2017. There was plenty of the season to go then, too, but it just felt huge.

OK, this is the second time in two matches we've evoked memories of those Kompany and Sterling goals, but this is the second game in a row when City have conjured up something when they really needed it. Too many times last season, and quite a bit earlier this season too, they couldn't do that.

Against Crystal Palace on Sunday, they scored from set-pieces and from outside the box. The xG champions were not creating great chances, but were scoring anyway. And you need that to win titles.

On Wednesday, as wet a night as you'll ever get at a football match, it was reasonably similar. This time they created a hatful of chances but contrived, for 79 minutes, to keep the ball out of the Villa net when it was often easier to put it in.

Had Bernardo scored from a matter of yards after just four minutes, it may not have felt the same. Had Ilkay Gundogan scored from a matter of inches a few minutes before Bernardo finally did then maybe the result wouldn't have had the same gravity. Because after the German – who was imperious with everything he did outside the six-yard box – missed that, and after City managed to miss another two great opportunities, and after Ruben Dias somehow didn't score an own goal at the other end, it just felt like 'one of those nights'.

There were still more than 30 minutes left when a feeling of desperation set in. Not among the players, crucially, but those watching at home and quite possibly the man in the nice clothes in the technical area may have started to fear the worst.

Pep Guardiola had said recently that his City team are not built for 50-metre counter-attacks or to run up and down into huge spaces, yet that's how last night's game turned with a third of it left. Jack Grealish started to exert even more influence, Bertrand Traore lurked on the other side, waiting to pounce.

Andros Townsend, who faced City for Palace at the weekend, said on BBC Radio 5 Live afterwards that although Guardiola's men are a world-class team, "they do give you chances". "When the centre-backs have the ball," he added, "the full-backs are effectively midfielders, so if you can intercept that first pass, you can get at them."

But City did what they have been doing recently. They stayed solid at the back (at one point, Dias wellied the ball from his own penalty spot into the Villa half and bellowed at his team-mates to squeeze up the pitch, like a grizzled Sunday morning defender) and they now have 10 clean sheets from 18 games (most in the league, above Villa and Southampton, who are both on eight).

They kept attacking, kept creating. One day their profligacy will cost them, but it was not this one. For a team as talented as they are, so good at creating high-quality chances, the finishing is often shambolic, even comical.

At least they stuck at it. For 30 minutes, the game was open, and City continued to waste huge opportunities, but they didn't panic. Bernardo's strike was City's 25th shot of the match. Only two teams have made more blocks in a single game this season than Villa's 10 at the Etihad. It's not easy to generate tension in an empty stadium but this game had it, and the celebrations down in the corner showed just how much it meant to the players. It will have felt big to them, too.

On the subject of feeling, it feels like there is a large whiff of controversy about City's breakthrough because the majority of us have grown up with an understanding of offside that would never have let that stand. The current laws of the game, though, are on City's side. It looks unnatural, and City fans would surely be livid if it happens to them one day, but these days things like that are onside – a bit like the ever-changing handball laws that have cost City dearly in the past but benefitted them last night.

Injuries to Kyle Walker and Kevin De Bruyne mean not everything went their way, but Bernardo managed to do the unthinkable and replace the sidelined Belgian in 2018/19. And in recent weeks, he has been returning to something like the form he showed then. Considering their finishing, though, somebody will have to shoulder the creative burden, because without De Bruyne they will need to create three or four big chances a game. Perhaps it'll be Phil Foden, who was superb and created six chances by himself.

Maybe further injury news will change the perspective in the coming days but even the sight of De Bruyne going off could not spoil the celebrations at full-time.

Paul Pogba's goal at Fulham later in the evening may have Manchester United feeling good, too, but City managed – briefly – to get back to the top for the first time since that day down in Brighton when they built on Kompany's goal to seal another title. If they keep this up, they might get another.

"The most important thing is the fact that we are back, since the Newcastle game, playing the game we have to play to be contenders," Guardiola said afterwards. "Everyone wants to win, wants to be champions, but you have to show why you are champions.

"Today, I had the feeling that we controlled many aspects, we had the right tempo of the game. We concede few, create a lot. We have to be more clinical in the final third, especially in the 18-yard box and penalty spot, but we'll improve."

The more they feel it, the more they believe it, the better they will be.

JANUARY RESULTS

Premier League, January 3, 2021
Chelsea 1 Manchester City 3
Manchester City scorers: Gundogan 18, Foden 21, De Bruyne 34

Carabao Cup semi-final, January 6, 2021
Manchester United 0 Manchester City 2
Manchester City scorers: Stones 50, Fernandinho 83

FA Cup third round, January 10, 2021
Manchester City 3 Birmingham City 0
Manchester City scorers: Bernardo Silva 8, 15, Foden 33

Premier League, January 13, 2021
Manchester City 1 Brighton & Hove Albion 0
Manchester City scorers: Foden 44

Premier League, January 17 2021
Manchester City 4 Crystal Palace 0
Manchester City scorers: Stones 26, 68, Gundogan 56, Sterling 88

Premier League, January 20 2021
Manchester City 2 Aston Villa 0
Manchester City scorers: Bernardo Silva 79, Gundogan 89 pen

FA Cup fourth round, January 23, 2021
Cheltenham Town 1 Manchester City 3
Manchester City scorers: Foden 81, Jesus 84, Torres 90+4

Premier League, January 26, 2021
West Bromwich Albion 0 Man City 5
Manchester City scorers: Gundogan 6, 30, Cancelo 20, Mahrez 45+2, Sterling 57

Premier League, January 30, 2021
Manchester City 1 Sheffield United 0
Manchester City scorers: Jesus 9

FEBRUARY

NO DE BRUYNE, AGUERO, OR STARTING NO. 9 – IT SHOWS HOW SPECIAL CITY CAN BE

SAM LEE

FEB 8, 2021

So Manchester City did miss a penalty, and Ruben Dias did make a mistake, and at half-time it looked as if Pep Guardiola's men needed something special to avoid another one of those days at Anfield. And something special is exactly what they got. City did to Liverpool what Liverpool have done to them on too many occasions to remember.

By the end, City were toying with their opponents, kicking the ball off full-backs to win throw-ins down in the corner just like they have done at Old Trafford. They've had the run of the Theatre of Dreams over the past few years but they have very, very rarely got close to any feeling of superiority at Anfield. Until Sunday and their 4-1 victory.

When Riyad Mahrez blazed a late penalty over the bar a couple of seasons ago it felt like their last win there, in 2003, might never be repeated. More so when Ilkay Gundogan, one of many City star men in the last six weeks, blazed another one over the bar this time around.

But that's enough looking back. No more need to talk about 2003, about Nicolas Anelka's goals, no more curses or hoodoos. It's done now, because this group of players have set a new standard.

This would feel like a breakthrough night for Phil Foden if he hadn't had so many of them already. After his 103rd appearance for his boyhood club, the 20-year-old was being praised by everybody from Carles Puyol to Liam Gallagher to Alex Caruso of the LA Lakers. Even a downcast Graeme Souness managed to call him England's best youngster. He is truly special.

Perhaps a better mark of his performance is that he managed to overshadow Gundogan. The German bounced back from that penalty miss to put City 1-0 up, then 2-1 up, and he now has eight goals in nine league games. But like Foden, this was not a performance you can boil down to statistics, no matter how impressive they are.

Collectively and individually, it was a performance that made fans feel something. Whether it was Foden slamming the ball into the top corner or forcing Fabinho into conceding a yellow card by nipping around him and darting in on goal, so much of what he did was genuinely exciting. He's not mastered everything, according to his manager, but it's a good start.

Gundogan's always done his job, getting on the ball, keeping the game moving with the right pass at the right time, but now his remit includes getting into the box and it turns out he's fantastic at it. There's something stirring about seeing a central midfielder pop up in the penalty area with important goals and Gundogan has to be in the conversation for the league's player of the year. He's not the only one.

Most of City's players put in stand-out performances. Bernardo Silva didn't have the goals to show for it but his energy and quick thinking helped set the pace in the second half, as he did against Liverpool at the Etihad in January 2019. Of course, the assist for Raheem Sterling's goal, City's third, was pitch-perfect.

OK, Alisson made his second mistake of the night, but that can happen when City's players have covered off your passing options and how many times have Guardiola's forwards been presented with a perfect chance to score only to somehow fluff it? If ever they were going to waste a chance like this, it was at Anfield. Yet Bernardo kept his composure to pick exactly the right option, even if Gundogan would have been dreaming of a pull-back to complete a hat-trick.

Sterling, too, was impressive. "Phenomenal," Guardiola called him. He won the penalty, played a huge role in the first goal and fully justified his manager's protection beforehand. The Catalan was asked about the winger's poor record at Anfield down the years but quickly pointed out his resilient performance last season, giving Trent Alexander-Arnold a rough ride even as City slumped to the usual convincing defeat.

Sterling has had his struggles in front of goal this season but he is only the third player to have scored 100 goals for a Guardiola team, after Sergio Aguero and Lionel Messi. He has four in the last five games, too, and the fact he is always in the right place ensured he was completely unmarked to head home from about four inches after Bernardo's fine work.

These players ensured the only post-match comment on Guardiola's decision to line-up without a recognised striker was to ask whether he should do it more often. These are the games the City boss is accused of overthinking but when everything goes to plan, nobody is asking any questions.

Certainly not of the defence. At the start of the season, not even Guardiola would have expected to line up with Joao Cancelo, Dias, John Stones and Oleksandr Zinchenko at Anfield, certainly not by choice, but they had all justified their inclusions before kick-off, and doubly so afterwards.

Dias might have made that uncharacteristic mistake but was imposing otherwise. He and Stones were probably City's best players in a first half that didn't have the gleam of the second. They are another two player of the year candidates, or at least prime options for the PFA's team of the year.

Fears about Zinchenko being caught out by Mohamed Salah, or Cancelo by Sadio Mane, were completely unfounded. In the first few minutes, the Ukrainian showed exactly why he was selected several times, refusing to panic when pressed into a corner, instead picking the right pass.

Cancelo, another player of the year contender, has stood out for his attacking play recently but he was more circumspect here. No doubt, he would have been told to pick his moments a bit better when it comes to his adventurous through balls, given how quickly Liverpool can get up the field on the break after a turnover. Instead of forcing the issue, he fulfilled his brief by offering his team-mates passing options in midfield, and ensuring he was not beaten defensively. That's not to say he didn't just pop it through somebody's legs to get a City attack started a couple of times, though. It was a really mature performance.

And what about the man in the middle of it all? Rodri has been looking better of late, which is no huge surprise. He struggled when City were leaving him exposed and having to do the defensive work that he had not yet mastered. Now they are much more cohesive, offering him much more protection, so he looks more comfortable. And of course, there is a glut of options ahead of him. Earlier in the season, the plan was 'give it to Kevin De Bruyne'. Now he can take his pick of attacking midfielders.

One handy way to appreciate his talents is to watch how he receives the ball from Ederson on the half-turn. Then watch basically any other Premier League holding midfielder do the same – it's just not as slick. No wonder Guardiola is a huge admirer, even if some critics haven't always felt the same.

This is very much a time for appreciation. City were, for the second 45 minutes, wonderful. Their disappointment at half-time makes everything that came afterwards even more admirable.

In fact, what's perhaps most impressive is that there was no disappointment at all. "It was tough for us mentally but at half-time, we didn't even speak for one second about this," Guardiola said.

Talk about the title can wait, but City are looking ominous. And when Guardiola's reaction to Foden's performance is to remind us of how much better he can be, you know they're in the right frame of mind. He praised the youngster, of course, and he genuinely believes in his ability (Foden's mother once thanked Guardiola for everything he had done for her son and he looked confused, insisting it was all down to the player). But the manager is having a say.

"In the first half, we struggled a lot to find him, he was not in the position he should be," he said. "When he plays in the middle sometimes, he has some difficulty understanding what he has to do and the places he has to move.

"Right now, he's moving perfectly as a winger, and of course, the second and fourth goals were outstanding, phenomenal, because the quality is there. But we cannot forget he is just 20 years old, he has an incredible, huge margin to improve. If he stays in the position, he has to stay . . . he is a guy who loves to play football and I'm pretty sure he will improve. Still, I have the feeling he has a margin to understand the game a little bit better, and the rhythm he plays as a winger is the rhythm he has to play when he plays in the middle, and he has a little bit of time to improve it."

Imagine how good he'll be when he starts to get that right. Imagine City winning at Anfield without De Bruyne, without Aguero, without a striker at all, without Aymeric Laporte, with that back four, after missing a penalty.

Guardiola did acknowledge that things could have been different after Salah equalised had there been a full crowd at

Anfield, and Liverpool will surely be making that case this time next season when, hopefully, fans will be allowed back in up and down the country.

But City have nothing to fear any more.

ZOOMS WITH THE UNDER-8S AND BEATING KLOPP'S PRESS – ZINCHENKO IS VITAL AT CITY

SAM LEE

FEB 17, 2021

Before COVID-19, the Manchester City players used to train next to the academy pitches, so the club's young hopefuls would often get to meet their heroes from Pep Guardiola's first team.

The youngest age groups would line up and wait for high fives from all the players, and of course, there was always huge excitement when the biggest names like Sergio Aguero, Kevin De Bruyne and Raheem Sterling came past.

But there was one player that always seemed to generate even more of a buzz, who was welcomed more like a favourite teacher than megastar to be in awe of: Oleksandr Zinchenko. His senior team-mates are always friendly and helpful, but nobody shows more of an interest than the Ukrainian, something that is genuinely appreciated among academy staff. He has been known to join in with sessions and matches and in lockdown last May, he even did a Q&A session over Zoom with the club's under-eights to help keep spirits high.

Like Phil Foden, another who cannot walk past a football without kicking it, he has a genuine love for football. It explains why he was recently training on his own in a south Manchester park, and when he spotted two teenagers having a kickabout between themselves, he went over and joined in, exchanging long passes at a social distance.

That was probably the furthest he's kicked a ball all year. Back in the City left-back spot once again, he has played a crucial role in the team that has racked up 16 wins in a row by coming into midfield and linking up play with his short passes.

There's a bit more to it than that, namely positional awareness and improved defensive output, but to put it simply, he is back in that specialised inverted role that all of Guardiola's best City sides have needed, the one that he made his own in the final months of the 2018/19 season.

Full-backs going into midfield has been a hallmark of City's title-winning sides under Guardiola but for around 18 months between the start of last season and the middle of this, Guardiola tried other systems to attempt to cover for the absences of Vincent Kompany, Fernandinho, Aymeric Laporte, Leroy Sane and David Silva.

City weren't bad by any means, but they weren't quite the City that we've come to know and appreciate. The set-up did not suit some players, something that is becoming more and more clear as City's run goes on. Ilkay Gundogan's attacking influence and Rodri's increasing confidence is proof that the team is playing more to their strengths at the moment, and the same goes for Zinchenko.

That run in the team at the end of 2018/19 earned him a new contract (he was earning less than some of the club's 18- and 19-year-olds) and the No. 11 shirt, but last season went badly enough for City to be prepared to sell him in the summer transfer window.

In fact, in four of his five seasons at the club, he could have moved elsewhere, either on loan or permanently. In 2016, after signing from FC Ufa, he moved on loan to PSV Eindhoven. In 2017, he nearly moved to Napoli for the season but the deal fell through on deadline day. In 2018, City sporting director Txiki Begiristain was effectively packing his bags for him, having agreed to a £15 million deal with Wolves. But despite starting just five league games as City won the title with 100 points, Zinchenko didn't want to go, insisting he was good enough to earn a place.

He was right (eventually) and became a regular, starting in February 2019. That summer was the only one where his immediate future was guaranteed. As City looked for a new left-back in September and October 2020, they would have moved Zinchenko on had a buyer come forward.

The City back four at Anfield for the 4-1 win – perhaps Guardiola's first-choice back four at the moment – might not have been at the club at all had things gone differently.

Guardiola hinted recently that there was some truth to the rumours linking Joao Cancelo with a move away last spring. "He arrived at a moment last season when he decided he wanted to stay here for a long time," the Catalan said on Friday.

Ruben Dias was not City's first- or even second-choice signing, and offers for John Stones would have been entertained had Eric Garcia not asked to leave. Sometimes, things just work out for the best.

That's certainly the case for Zinchenko, whose route to the first team is incredibly convoluted and goes all the way back to Dani Alves pulling out of a free transfer to City at the last minute in 2017, meaning the club could no longer afford to buy two left-backs. Even so, Guardiola used Fabian Delph and Danilo before Zinchenko, and had he not been so determined that he could make it at City, he would have been sold before proving how good he can be.

He even needed a bit of luck to get back in this season: Guardiola picked Nathan Ake against Newcastle on Boxing Day, a game that had a big say in City's season. Guardiola liked what he saw that night but Ake got injured, so a door opened for Zinchenko. Once again, he has grasped his opportunity. He had played only 12 minutes of Premier League football up until starting away at Chelsea on January 3. Since then, he has played the full 90 minutes in seven of City's last nine league games.

He came off the bench against Burnley, but returned to the starting XI four days later to face Liverpool. Within 10 seconds at Anfield, he showed why. It perhaps isn't the best example of his composure, given he miscontrolled Dias' pass, but with Mohamed Salah bearing down on him, he quickly rolled the ball under his studs and flicked it back to Dias, eschewing a panicked hoof or sloppy ball into the midfield to be snapped up by Jurgen Klopp's press. It allowed City to keep possession and, crucially, control.

There was perhaps a better example of his cool head at Old Trafford in January, when he was put under pressure down in the corner. It looked as if he gave serious thought to a hoof forward, but instead, he played a short pass to Foden. When he got it back, he was even further into the corner, but he looked up and played a composed pass to Fernandinho, which opened up the whole pitch. A one-two in midfield, a searching De Bruyne pass and a Sterling dribble later, City were up the other end and De Bruyne's fierce strike was cannoning off the post. It was classic City and it was all possible because Zinchenko kept a cool head. If you look closely, even Gundogan is saying 'send it long'. Even Gundogan.

That kind of composure couldn't be further from his first showing at left-back in the 2017/18 season, an incredibly nervy performance in and out of possession against Wolves in the Carabao Cup. He has worked hard to improve. No wonder he told Begiristain he wasn't going anywhere.

"From the keeper to the striker, we have to put the ball on the grass, make 1,000 passes and pick the right moment," Guardiola remarked after City's 3-1 win at Chelsea.

He attracted criticism after that game for not getting close enough to Callum Hudson-Odoi for the late consolation goal.

There are still some question marks about his defending, but in recent weeks he has looked at home. He was impressive against Liverpool and Tottenham.

In City's current set-up, Zinchenko is the yin to Cancelo's yang. When City have the ball in defence, Zinchenko will be one of the three defenders that split across the pitch, while Cancelo will go into midfield next to Rodri to offer passing options.

Once the ball progresses up the pitch, Cancelo will join the attack and force the issue by playing through balls, while Zinchenko stays back in a more withdrawn role to provide support and take up positions that help to reduce the chances of a counter-attack.

Zinchenko's use of the ball is extremely important to City, though. Only 4.4 per cent of his passes are played long (more than 32 metres) and there are 11 City players who play more long passes. He also carries the ball a lot, but over short distances. He has the seventh-most carries in the squad per 90 minutes, but is 18th for average distance carried (3.2 metres). Laporte, Stones and Dias carry the ball the most and for longer distances.

At the risk of doing him a disservice, he keeps things simple. Short passes, short carries – keep City moving. A thousand passes at the right tempo, as Guardiola says. He plays in central midfield for Ukraine and although he might not be as expressive as he is with his country, his left-back role is similar to a midfield brief, considering how much he sees of the ball.

And as with Cancelo and everybody else in this team, he has to hold up his end of the bargain without the ball. He is certainly doing that. His tackle success rate is 39 per cent, which is the seventh-best in the squad.

It is the same for 'true' tackles, which is considered a better metric for judging a player's ability to win a challenge, by taking into account challenges lost and fouls committed. Only Stones has won a higher percentage, but he has attempted far fewer.

Those who have attempted more than Zinchenko have not won as many as he has. And again, this has been consistent over his three seasons as a regular in the first team.

Perhaps that's no surprise considering he did a lot of extra defensive training with Vincent Kompany – including how to win more aerial duels despite his small frame – and Mikel Arteta.

He has been described as a 'sponge' for his capacity to take in and retain information, and has been praised by Guardiola for his cheerful attitude even when not in the team, something he learned during his loan spell at PSV, which didn't go according to plan.

When trying to break into the City team a couple of years ago, he was one of the players, like Stones, who learned some Spanish phrases to help. This week, his wife revealed that he is studying Guardiola's methods closely.

"He is taking notes on Guardiola," she said. "He outlines changes in tactics, moments during training, innovations. He notes all this and shares it with me. We have a big notebook at home, a big folder where he writes everything down. Sometimes he explains things to me. I do not manage to understand everything at once, sometimes he has to explain it three times."

It is hard to think of a better fit for what City need from a left-back. He certainly gets forward to support attacks, but they don't need him to swing balls into the box and, despite being signed as an attacking midfielder, he is disciplined in his positioning.

It is interesting to think where he would play if he ever did move clubs. Would other managers use him as a left-back in the same way? Perhaps his previous suitors have been impressed by his midfield performances for his country.

But he just seems so perfect for the quirky left-back role that is so important to City. And you get the feeling he wouldn't want it any other way.

MANCHESTER CITY: THE GREAT CONTAINERS

SAM LEE

FEB 25, 2021

This was a game that provided proof of the old Pep Guardiola mantra that the best way to stop your opponents from scoring is by keeping them as far away from your goal as possible.

Manchester City can already start thinking about the quarter-finals after smothering Borussia Monchengladbach in Budapest – not that they will.

In all honesty, it was never a tie to set the pulses racing, a clash that would not have attracted too much attention around Europe had the two teams been drawn against each other in the group stages. There are very few teams on the continent that can live with City at the moment and Gladbach are not among them.

Yet Guardiola's men have been scarred by inferior-looking German sides before, from Hoffenheim to Schalke, and if this match looked like a 'walk in the park' or a 'stroll' as television commentators put it, it wasn't quite so straightforward.

The first half, in particular, was an example of highly organised, intense pressing. If Gladbach looked short of ideas (they didn't touch the ball inside the City penalty area in the first 45 minutes), it was because City swarmed all over them and gave them no options. Look at the number of tackles and interceptions in dangerous areas.

Perhaps a better side than Gladbach would have been able to mix it up, to try something else. On Sunday, when Arsenal made it difficult for City to play through them, Guardiola got Ederson to pump long balls towards the strikers, which is what they did against Real Madrid last August, too.

That probably highlights the gulf in class between the two sides and two coaches but there's a reason City have won 19 matches in a row, and a reason so many of their games look easy. Yes, they have lots of top players, but it's the top-level coaching that sets them apart, that gives them all the answers.

Gladbach did pose a few questions, too. They play out from the back because they are good at it. Marco Rose is a highly rated coach who will be heading to Borussia Dortmund at the end of the season because he gives his players solutions on the pitch, he enables them to play out from the goalkeeper.

It's not new to them to be put under pressure in their own third. They are confident with the ball at their feet and they know not to panic, but the beauty of this City performance was that they didn't just block off the options initially – they blocked off all the others as well.

"It was our idea to be courageous," Rose said afterwards, "to not give away balls so easily and to press them off the ball, just to maybe have a little bit of control.

"My lads did a good job of that but Manchester City are a team that close down the free spaces, and the spaces in general. I'm not talking about the last third but even the spaces in midfield because they defended very high."

That's a very underrated element of the performance: City didn't fall for Gladbach's attempts to mix things up, to pull a body out of position. In his early seasons, Guardiola talked about his players needing to come up with better in-game solutions themselves, without his input, and it certainly looks like they have got there over the years.

They did it against Real Madrid at the Etihad in August and they did it again on Wednesday. If teams are patient in the face of pressure, they will move things around to try to find a spare man. What City have done, in these two games particularly, is move intelligently.

To try to outwit City, Gladbach brought more men closer to their own goal, trying to increase their options, but City's players knew to keep their shape, to not get sucked in. Let them find the centre-back on the other side, for example, because as long as you stay back and block off his options, it makes no difference. If you move in, you'll vacate the space behind you and top teams will exploit it.

City didn't allow them to open up too many spaces, and when they did, Rose admitted that Gladbach weren't good enough to take advantage.

It is why, for the vast majority of the game, they barely got out of their own half. There was no relief, no let-up. When Gladbach had the ball, City kept coming at them. When City had it, they looked after it, making Gladbach chase their tails. They played not to lose easy balls.

It was a classic Guardiola performance in that sense. His players were controlled, the others run ragged. No wonder it *looked* so easy.

"If we concede just one shot on target, you need to learn that we made an incredible effort up front, with Raz (Raheem Sterling), Phil (Foden), Gabriel (Jesus), Bernardo (Silva) and Gundo (Ilkay Gundogan) and everyone," Guardiola replied when asked about his defenders. "That's why the opponents gave us problems only a few times, and that's why we defended well."

Still, there were flashes of the problems that have haunted them in the past, and reasons not to get carried away just yet (even if it's incredibly tempting, with a 20th consecutive win up for grabs against West Ham on Saturday).

Guardiola was keen to point out that his side were not clinical enough for the required level of tougher matches down the line. He raged on the touchline as Jesus dithered over one chance to make it 2-0 before he did indeed score their second goal with a much more instinctive finish.

Jesus will probably always be favoured for a game like this but when Sergio Aguero finally returned late on, he played a big part in what might have been City's best attacking move. A little backheel in midfield set free Gundogan, showing how Aguero added fluidity to City's attacking play that hadn't always been there on the night.

There was an uncharacteristic misplaced pass from Rodri right at the death, though, played blindly into the path of Hannes Wolf, which could have made things needlessly uncomfortable. Ederson made a smart save and then screamed at his team-mate.

A reminder, perhaps, that errors like that are all it takes to go out of this competition. Not that City need any after the last few seasons: it's impossible to remember the good work against Madrid without remembering that Lyon came next. But barring that late aberration, this was total dominance and it did not come easily.

FEBRUARY RESULTS

Premier League February 3, 2021
Burnley 0 Manchester City 2
Manchester City scorers: Jesus 3, Sterling 38

Premier League February 7, 2021
Liverpool 1 Manchester City 4
Manchester City scorers: Gundogan 49, 73, Sterling 76, Foden 83

FA Cup fifth round, February 10, 2021
Swansea 1 Manchester City 3
Manchester City scorers: Walker 30, Sterling 47, Jesus 50

Premier League February 13, 2021
Manchester City 3 Tottenham Hotspur 0
Manchester City scorers: Rodri 23 pen, Gundogan 50, 66

Premier League February 17, 2021
Everton 1 Manchester City 3
Manchester City scorers: Foden 32, Mahrez 63, Bernardo Silva 77

Premier League February 21, 2021
Arsenal 0 Manchester City 1
Manchester City scorer: Sterling 2

Champions League, Round of 16, first leg, February 24 2021
Borussia Monchengladbach 0 Manchester City 2
Manchester City scorers: Bernardo Silva 29, Jesus 65

Premier League, February 27, 2021
Manchester City West Ham 1
Manchester City scorers: Dias 30, Stones 68

MARCH

RELENTLESS MAN CITY ARE A TEAM ON A MISSION

OLIVER KAY

MAR 3, 2021

When the time comes to tell the story of Manchester City's third Premier League title in four seasons, there will be an overwhelming temptation to use words like 'procession'.

They are 15 points clear now, having won their past 15 Premier League matches and their past 21 games in all competitions. But a procession, it is not. Such a term would do Pep Guardiola and his players an injustice.

The noises that echoed around the empty stands of the Etihad Stadium on Tuesday evening spoke of a relentless pursuit. Bernardo Silva was insatiable in his desire to win the ball back, earning loud acclaim from the coaches on the touchline and the various staff dotted around the lower tier of the Colin Bell Stand. He and his team-mates simply wouldn't allow Wolverhampton Wanderers – or themselves – to rest.

A 4-1 victory did not flatter City. Neither does their growing lead at the top of the table. It took them much longer to find their rhythm and their cohesion this season, but they now look like champions-in-waiting – except, no . . . that term doesn't do them justice either. Procession, champions-in-waiting, cruise control . . . the language all sounds too passive. This City team are nothing of the sort.

On Tuesday afternoon, *fivethirtyeight.com*, which has a strong track record for projecting sporting outcomes as well as elections, estimated City's chances of winning this Premier League title at greater than 99 per cent.

Another data-driven projection came from Stats Perform, which put City's chances at 99.9 per cent.

Those projections will have to be revised if Manchester United win away to Crystal Palace this evening and then the derby at the Etihad on Sunday, but, with City in this mood, that doesn't seem likely.

A 99.9 per cent certainty sounds like a hard sell for the Premier League broadcasters over the weeks ahead, particularly when this difficult season continues to unfold without the backdrop, soundtrack and all-round intensity supporters bring. There have been many games this season when teams have appeared to be going through the motions. There was a time earlier in the campaign when wildly unpredictable results had us wondering whether there could be a wildly unpredictable outcome in the title race. City had other ideas.

The point is that City are not playing like a team who are content to enjoy a procession to the title. They are a team on a mission, as Guardiola underlined on Tuesday evening by reminding his players that "Liverpool are still the champions and they have the crown." City are, quite clearly, desperate to take that crown back.

Inspiration did not come easily at home against West Ham United on Saturday lunchtime, but City dug deep to get a 2-1 win. Three days later, after six changes to the weekend's starting line-up, they looked refreshed, reinvigorated and raring to go. The right-hand side of the team, with Kyle Walker at full-back,

Bernardo roaming in a loose No 8 position and Riyad Mahrez on the wing, was as impressive as it has looked all season.

Guardiola was effusive in his post-match Zoom call with journalists, jumping from one subject to another, praising Bernardo ("always he performs well with desire", "he's skinny and not tall, but so strong"), Mahrez ("outstanding", "he has a special quality, a guy who dances on the pitch"), Gabriel Jesus ("you cannot imagine how happy we are when he scores", "we know the stats and he's not in the highlights, but what he does is amazing") and others.

There were so many strong individual contributions, but what delighted Guardiola was the way it all came together from the opening moments of the game when Joao Cancelo threaded a typical pass through to Raheem Sterling, who was denied by goalkeeper Rui Patricio. "I had a feeling we would be good this morning, and I saw it in the warm-up," Guardiola said, a glint in his eye. "We could lose or draw – on the counter-attacks, we can lose – but we played so well for 95 minutes and I'm so pleased. It's what we like the most: solidarity, friendship, run for the others and they run for you."

The breakthrough came when Rodri, who was excellent in the first half, played a diagonal ball to pick out Mahrez, whose superb first touch, taking him to the byline, was followed by a cross that Leander Dendoncker could only divert into his own net under pressure from Sterling. It could have been 2-0 just before half-time, but the tightest of offside calls against Aymeric Laporte was upheld by the VAR when, to the naked eye, it was hard to see an infringement.

The quality was dauntingly high at times, notably when Kevin De Bruyne went close early in the second half after a lovely flick from Sterling, but what delighted Guardiola most was the way his team responded to the setback of Conor Coady's equaliser on the hour.

For five minutes or so, the game seemed to be in the balance, with Adama Traore threatening to get away from the home defence, but City found another gear, applying more and more pressure. Faced with defiance from the Wolves back line, they managed to crank it up again before the floodgates opened in the last 10 minutes, bringing goals for Jesus, Mahrez and Jesus again, the final one in stoppage time (this time City benefited from the VAR correcting an earlier offside call against the forward).

"How we overcame (was) the best," Guardiola said afterwards. "In football, you have to handle these minutes. The players felt it was unfair after what had happened, but it's a good lesson for the knockout games as good players can punish you. The response was good. We reacted well – not immediately, as (Wolves) were better for a few minutes, but in knockout games you have to be stable in these moments, not concede more, and then get the game back in your hands."

Clearly, the Champions League is playing on his mind. In Guardiola's first four seasons in Manchester, City have paid a heavy price for conceding goals in quick succession in its knockout stage – against Monaco, against Liverpool, against Tottenham, against Lyon – but this season, with summer signing Ruben Dias in central defence, they seem better equipped to handle those moments of instability. They look more resilient and more composed, as they will need to be.

And the wins just keep coming. To win 21 consecutive matches in all competitions is remarkable – especially, Guardiola said, through the winter months of English football, which he described as "hell". "Twenty-eight games unbeaten is incredible," he added. "We analyse this and then the next one."

The next one just happens to be against Manchester United and, while Ole Gunnar Solskjaer might well point out that his team will have had less recovery time having played their midweek match a day later, the reality with City right now is that Guardiola – in stark contrast to the opening months of the season – can make six changes from one game to the next in the expectation that fluency, rhythm and intensity will still be there. His starting line-up for the derby? That is a discussion for another day.

Five weeks ago, it was possible to imagine United going to the Etihad on Sunday as league leaders, but it will take something special from Solskjaer's team over the next few days if they are to have any chance of overturning what that one particular data-based projection is calling a 99.9 per cent certainty.

From a distance, yes, it has begun to look like a procession, but take a closer look and you see it is more than that and far more than, as some would have it, the inevitable result of having the biggest budget and the best squad.

It is not just individual quality. It is rhythm, cohesion, fluency and quality. And right now, that slow start is a distant memory.

It is relentless.

STERLING? BERNARDO? FODEN? WHAT DOES MANCHESTER CITY'S BEST XI LOOK LIKE?

SAM LEE

MAR 17, 2021

What is Manchester City's strongest XI? It's a question that has been asked regularly since Pep Guardiola rocked up in 2016, and it is one we are no closer to answering.

How would you measure it? One way of trying is to ask, "What would the team be if the Champions League final were this weekend?" – but the answer is simple: who are they playing against?

Guardiola is always going to change things around whether the occasion is big or small, but were he to select something like the team that beat Borussia Monchengladbach on Tuesday night you would not find too many complaints, no matter the opposition. Ruben Dias and John Stones at the back. Ilkay Gundogan, Kevin De Bruyne and Bernardo Silva in the same side. The in-form Riyad Mahrez. Phil Foden!

On Tuesday night there was none of the usual concern about Guardiola's starting line-up among fans and media, as has become customary. It was a line-up that just felt right. After cramming several players short of game time into a wing-back system at Fulham on Saturday it was back to something much more familiar, much more comfortable, and as they ripped through Gladbach early on there was no sign that the weekend's changes had thrown them off their stride.

That is why Guardiola keeps saying he needs all of his players to think about the team rather than themselves, so they can all get minutes and all stay sharp. Benjamin Mendy and Eric Garcia are the only two outfield players to have barely kicked a ball in the Premier League this year, until last Saturday anyway, meaning there are still another 20 outfield players competing for just 10 places.

Just look at the players on the bench at the Puskas Arena. Gabriel Jesus is more than capable of doing a job, either as a false nine or a proper nine; his good mate Fernandinho still knows his way around midfield; Oleksandr Zinchenko has proven his worth again at left-back, Ferran Torres has got a goal in him and so has Sergio Aguero, although he did leave the pitch complaining, according to South American lip-readers, that his team-mates "don't pass me the ball".

And then there is Aymeric Laporte and Raheem Sterling. At the start of the season, they would both have been shoo-ins for a City strongest XI but they have lost a little of their shine over the course of the campaign. They have also lost their status as near-guaranteed starters and their reactions have angered Guardiola. That is why he has felt the need to send a couple of coded messages out via the press this season, seemingly unprompted. Each time he has jumped on perfectly inoffensive questions from reporters, about things such as rotation and fitness, to make his point – even if the full details are intended to be kept private.

In the 70th minute on Tuesday night, Laporte and Sterling were brought into the action alongside each other, demonstrating not just how strong City's options are, but perhaps more importantly that even those who have fallen foul of the boss will be needed for the run-in.

Laporte is perhaps the example for Sterling right now, because while it was the Frenchman who prompted the first Guardiola reality check in November, he has turned his situation around.

"Any players who believe they deserve to start because they have been here for three or four years, they have made a big mistake," the City head coach said after being asked if he had the luxury of resting his players in a Champions League dead rubber – at a time when he regularly bemoaned the demands of the schedule. "It doesn't matter if you win a lot of titles in the past or you score a lot of goals, you have to show it on the pitch."

Behind the scenes, Laporte had not reacted well to losing his place and there was even some doubt cast on his future at the club but he was brought back into the team after an injury and has, despite the Stones and Dias partnership continuing to impress, started seven of the last 11 league matches.

"Ayme now is back again," Guardiola said after the match in Budapest. He meant his form and, most likely, his mentality.

There was another reminder for Sterling on Tuesday, though. "When everybody is generous and everybody is in a good mood, thinking about the team, about the club, they are more than welcome and they will have their minutes."

When discussing the winger's absence at Craven Cottage on Saturday, Guardiola said: "To win the titles, especially the Premier League, we need everyone, everyone, everyone wanting the best for the club and the best for the team."

It should be said that Sterling and Guardiola have denied rumours of a rift in the past few days, but multiple sources close to the squad have confirmed to *The Athletic* that the two did indeed exchange words ahead of last Wednesday's win against Southampton.

Sterling was angered by being left on the bench and took his complaint to Guardiola, which is the exact opposite of what the City boss expects. As a rule, he does not explain his decisions to his players and expects them to get on with the job without any dissent, with the goal of forging a competitive and consistent squad.

That is a cornerstone of his management, and although it does not please everybody (other players have kept their complaints away from the manager in recent weeks) it has helped City to win 24 of their last 25 games.

Sterling was left out of the game against Fulham as punishment, *The Athletic* understands, and the situation was considered serious enough for senior players to ask the England man to apologise on Sunday when they returned to the training ground.

Guardiola was never going to admit the full story in public and while his and Sterling's denials will always carry the most weight, his comments after the games against Southampton, Fulham and Gladbach are telling in their own way.

"Now we arrive in the right time of the season with not many games, the players who help me a lot in the season, the players who think about the club and the team, I will rotate less," he said last Wednesday, when asked about the joys of having a fully fit squad at his disposal. "The rest will be on the bench."

Guardiola brought Sterling back into the fold alongside Laporte and in the coming weeks the winger will have to get his head down and re-establish himself as the go-to guy for the vast majority of games, as he has been since Guardiola arrived.

Like Laporte, the only thing you can do when others in your position are impressing every week is put on a brave face and play well. Perhaps even join in with the fist pumps after successful tackles.

Sterling's task will not be easy: the forward line was well stocked before Guardiola put De Bruyne or Bernardo, sometimes both of them, in there to ensure his best players are always on the pitch.

Then there is Foden, who is generally involved when City are at their slickest, and Mahrez, who is in his best form for the club and, in fact, is another player that has come back after complaining about a lack of minutes, on two occasions.

That is the mentality you need to thrive in this team, and it is the mentality the team needs to thrive. Another example: Kyle Walker, Joao Cancelo and Zinchenko all deserve to start, too, but three into two does not go at full-back either. Cancelo is so threatening from either flank it is hard to work out where he should play, and who should play on the other side. Walker looked like losing his place in January, but, as Guardiola said on Tuesday, "Kyle is back in his best moment."

Most of them are. No wonder it is so hard to work out their best XI.

SERGIO AGUERO'S EXIT IS EMOTIONAL – BUT IT'S BUSINESS. MANCHESTER CITY WILL LOOK TO FUTURE WITH ERLING HAALAND

SAM LEE

MAR 30, 2021

It's hard to sum up just how much Sergio Aguero means to Manchester City but perhaps his 18-minute cameo against Southampton three weeks ago works just as well as some of the more obvious examples.

When you've scored perhaps the most famous goal in English football history, become the top-scoring overseas player in the Premier League and cemented your place as City's all-time leading scorer, your status as a legend pretty much speaks for itself.

But the desperation among the City fanbase when he stepped out onto the Etihad Stadium pitch against Southampton was a timely reminder of just how much affection there is for Aguero around the club.

They just wanted him to score. There were no fans in the ground, of course, but the anguished tweets spelled it out loud and clear. They were *desperate* for him to score. Every touch, every half possibility that the ball might fall in his general direction was greeted as an opportunity to prove that he had put his injury struggles behind him and was back to his best.

189

You could have been mistaken for thinking he was playing his last match for the club. Soon, he will be.

On Monday night, slap bang in the middle of an international break, City broke the news, completely out of the blue. The club's fans have had plenty of practice in recent years: it is almost as if their departing legends have got bigger and bigger – from Pablo Zabaleta to Yaya Toure to Vincent Kompany to David Silva in consecutive years. Now this.

Kompany called time on his City career after he had played his final game for the club and Silva left without any fans in the stadium, but even those circumstances could do little to prepare anybody for Aguero's exit. When he goes, he will be the last member of the 2011/12 title-winning squad to leave the club. It is the end of a cycle, as Aguero's statement put it, in many ways.

News of this magnitude – which will be talked about just as much by non-City fans – will always come as a shock but it is fair to say the writing had been on the wall, certainly behind the scenes, where people close to him had been talking about his likely exit as far back as January.

At that point, Aguero had just overcome COVID-19, which did not affect him greatly but did leave him fatigued for a short period, which was the last thing he needed as he tried to prove his fitness after a string of setbacks at the back end of 2020. City told him that he would be much more likely to get a new contract if he was fully fit by the end of last year and, clearly, that did not happen.

A move to Italy is thought to be an attractive proposition for Aguero and his family, not least as his girlfriend Sofia Calzetti, would welcome the lifestyle. It is hard to imagine them rejecting a move to Barcelona if Joan Laporta's new board follows through on their interest, though, and it is fair to say that Aguero has been weighing up options for a while, with hope of a new deal at City slipping away.

He would have stayed if given the opportunity but City

confirmed the news to him on Monday, with Pep Guardiola explaining the club's decision at the training ground. Chairman Khaldoon Al Mubarak immediately followed up with a phone call to convey his gratitude and confirm that he will have a statue in his honour, to go alongside ones for Silva and Kompany. While some of his team-mates had been expecting this news, many of them only knew for sure when the club released their statement.

For the fans, it is probably easier to look back in hindsight now and realise that things were hardly shaping up for a new deal for Aguero. Some have argued over the past 24 hours that he should have been given an extra year come what may given all he has done for the club and the fact that he does not deserve to say his goodbyes in empty stadiums.

Emotionally, they are strong cases but clearly, this has been a business decision. As well as City have looked after Aguero over the years, and in the way they have tried to handle this departure, they have made a difficult decision swiftly and with one eye on the future.

The timing is interesting. Is it beyond the realms of possibility that come the end of the season, City regret their decision? Possibly, but concerns about his fitness – more specifically the condition of his knee – have not been dispelled as the season has progressed and they do not believe that things will change dramatically. There has been talk of a rift with Guardiola but the City boss has nothing but admiration for the striker after adapting his game in their first 18 months together.

Then, there is the question of his eventual replacement. City's best laid transfer plans do not always come off (see Alexis Sanchez, Jorginho, Harry Maguire and Frenkie de Jong, among others) but they do act swiftly when it comes to ascertaining their targets' intentions. Things usually pick up in March and April.

For all of those misses, they have wrapped up agreements and then swift confirmations for Ilkay Gundogan, Bernardo Silva,

Ederson, Nathan Ake and Ferran Torres in recent years, and even those deals that took a little longer, like Kyle Walker and Benjamin Mendy, were set up months in advance.

City have made contact with Erling Haaland's father, Alf-Inge, who played for the club between 2000 and 2003. Their domestic rivals believe City have the edge in the race for the Dortmund striker and while Spanish clubs are bound to find money from somewhere, Guardiola and his club's board realise the importance of moving on from Aguero. Getting his replacement right is key.

That's if Aguero could ever be replaced. Haaland, at 20, might just have a big enough reputation to mean that he will not quite be viewed as the Argentinian's replacement but others might find it harder to escape his shadow. Spare a thought for Gabriel Jesus, who has been – rightly or wrongly – held to his team-mate's standard for the past four years.

And yet, as tempting as it is to look at what lies beyond the summer for all parties, Aguero still has plenty of opportunities to make his mark in the short-term future. In April alone, City play Leicester, Dortmund, Leeds, Dortmund (again), face an FA Cup semi-final against Chelsea, the Carabao Cup final and a potential Champions League semi-final, as well as a league game against Aston Villa to be rescheduled.

Beyond that, there are potentially even bigger games.

Imagine, then, an Aguero goal when it really matters. He's done it before, after all.

MARCH RESULTS

Premier League, March 2, 2021
Manchester City 4 Wolverhampton Wanderers 1
Manchester City scorers: Dendoncker 15 og, Jesus 80, 90+3, Mahrez 90

Premier League, March 7, 2021
Manchester City 0 Manchester Utd 2

Premier League, March 10, 2021
Manchester City 5 Southampton 2
Manchester City scorers: De Bruyne 15, 59, Mahrez 40, 55, Gundogan 45+3

Premier League March 13, 2021
Fulham 0 Manchester City 3
Manchester City scorers: Stones 47, Jesus 56, Aguero 60 pen

Champions League, Round of 16, second leg, March 16, 2021
Manchester City 2 Borussia Monchengladbach 0
Manchester City scorers: De Bruyne 12, Gundogan 18

FA Cup, sixth round March 20, 2021
Everton 0 Manchester City 2
Manchester City scorers: Gundogan 84, De Bruyne 90

APRIL

INSIDE DE BRUYNE'S DATA REPORT: SANCHO COMPARISON AND IMPACT OF PLAYMAKER'S POSSIBLE CITY EXIT CRUCIAL TO NEW DEAL

TOM WORVILLE

APR 12, 2021

You probably didn't sense it, but the tectonic plates upon which the foundations of how transfers and contract negotiations within football take place shifted slightly this week.

It's rare the news of a player signing a new contract or moving to a new team will cause such a disturbance. The sheer volume of moves made and contracts signed in any given season means most deviations from the norm in how those transactions take place largely avoid the limelight.

That wasn't the case with Kevin De Bruyne's new contract. The Belgian signed a new five-year deal with Manchester City on Wednesday which will keep him at the club until 2025. There's nothing groundbreaking about this deal per se – most of the headlines read along the lines of 'very good player commits to very good team' – but the manner in which the deal was finalised was notable.

The initial offer tabled by City to De Bruyne would have meant he earned less over the course of the new deal than he does at the moment. City was always the right club for De Bruyne, just the economics of the initial offer didn't match his status as one of the best players in the Premier League. His new wage represents a notable increase on his previous one.

Before any negotiations began between the player and club, De Bruyne and his representatives turned to data and the field of football analytics to get a better idea of the value he brings to the team, purely in terms of his on-field contributions. Through his lawyers, Daan Buylaert and Sven Demeulemeester of Atfield, De Bruyne retained a number of leading football analytics service providers to crunch his numbers.

One of the companies retained was Analytics FC, a football data analytics company that works with clubs in the Premier League, Serie A, Belgian Pro League and in other countries and competitions further afield.

It's not uncommon for agencies to work with these sorts of companies to help them use data to find a team for their clients which suits their style of play. Memphis Depay is one such example of a 'laptop transfer'. He and his agent worked with another analytics company – SciSports – who flagged Lyon as an ideal destination after his time at Manchester United.

By all accounts, that's a move that has worked out very well for the player, who's scored a goal every other game (0.52 per 90) and an assist every three games (0.33 per 90) in his time with Lyon since joining in January 2017.

Analytics FC themselves have also worked in the past with agencies, providing data to First Access Sport on one of their clients, Chelsea's Callum Hudson-Odoi. The request was made around the time that a move to Bayern Munich was heavily speculated upon by the media.

Agencies working with data is part and parcel of how the game functions now. What is uncommon is for a player *themselves* to commission a third party to prove their worth in contract renegotiations with a club, especially one of De Bruyne's calibre, and to also be open in doing so.

It represents another clear case of how players are becoming more aware of, interested in and looking to improve upon their own performance data, adding to a string of examples from this season alone. Leicester City's James Maddison openly gave credit to "Jack, the analyst" for helping him improve his goalscoring form when speaking to Sky Sports after his side beat Chelsea 2-0. Aston Villa's Jack Grealish mentioned in a recent interview how he identified needing to improve his expected assist and big chance creation numbers to take his game to the next level. It was only a matter of time, then, before a player mentioned the use of data in their contract talks.

Speaking about how the opportunity to work with De Bruyne came about, Analytics FC's CEO and co-founder, Jeremy Steele, tells *The Athletic:* "De Bruyne and his team were very knowledgeable about companies in the data industry and the specific questions they wanted to look into. After discussing the scope of the work, De Bruyne commissioned us to create a report studying almost every aspect of his contribution to the club."

The Athletic can exclusively reveal some of the details of that report. For a start, the headline reads that "De Bruyne's output is amongst the best in the Premier League, particularly for chance creation metrics."

In the report, comparisons to other top talents in Europe were made too. De Bruyne's output places him as the best in Europe by Analytics FC's bespoke attacking contribution metric, which considers the positive or negative impact made by every single touch by a player in a given match, in the past 12 months. Notably former Manchester City winger Jadon Sancho was second on the list, showing the young winger's prowess and perhaps how the 21-year-old's performances have gone under the radar a little.

When comparing that output alongside the wages of other players, De Bruyne appeared underpaid compared to some of

Europe's top attacking players, who earned more than the Belgian but contributed far less according to Analytics FC's metrics.

The other notable aspect of the report was that it showed – despite the considerable strength of the squad at Pep Guardiola's disposal – how integral De Bruyne is to City's chances of winning the Champions League. The report noted the double-sided impact for City if De Bruyne were to leave in the near future.

The first is the impact on City themselves, which would be a not-insignificant drop-off in their odds of winning the competition. The second is the positive bump in chances of winning the competition that any European rival would receive if De Bruyne were to sign for them. Combined, those two effects will have a great impact on City's ability to win the one trophy that has so far eluded them during Guardiola's tenure.

In the eyes of Steele, the report served its purpose. "Kevin was already convinced that he is integral to the team and that City was best placed for him to continue his career. Despite the quality of his performances on the pitch being clear for all to see, he wanted to see this clearly by the metrics."

All of this is a far cry from how things used to work in football. In his autobiography, Tony Cascarino talks about how he'd always dye his hair when it came to contract renegotiations. "Present yourself to the chairman in your naturally greying state and you're asking for trouble . . . add a bit of colour to your roots and the contract is in the bag."

This is football in 2021 though, and clubs are run more and more like the multi-million-pound businesses that they are. Or they should be, because the players are now getting wise to their own value and how data can help prove that.

RELIEF, EMOTION AND FLAIR OF PHIL FODEN – MANCHESTER CITY 'BROKE THE BRIDGE' IN CHAMPIONS LEAGUE

SAM LEE

APR 15, 2021

It's hard to work out which little moment best sums up Manchester City's huge Champions League victory over Borussia Dortmund. Was it Kevin De Bruyne literally biting his thumbnail as he awaited Riyad Mahrez's 55th-minute penalty to make it 3-2 on aggregate, or scorer Phil Foden, Pep Guardiola and everybody else in City gear hugging on the touchline in an unprecedented display of unity after the clinching goal with 15 minutes to go?

Both certainly prove just how much last night's game in Germany meant to the club. "Today we broke this bridge, from quarter-finals to semi-finals, mentally for all the club," Guardiola said, an acknowledgement that this really meant something. "It was a big relief and it's so important."

For so long, it looked as if it would be another of those Champions League nights. Even as City rallied after Dortmund's opening goal, the ball just would not go in. De Bruyne hit the bar, Mahrez had an effort blocked from three yards out.

Suddenly it was half-time and they were heading out of another quarter-final, this time on away goals. They looked like scoring, but would they? They have played this game before.

The wait for the penalty decision, referred to the VAR, was nigh-on traumatic. Not just to see if it would be overturned or not, but to see who might miss it if it was given. City have struggled from the spot for a while now and the sight of Mahrez standing there with the ball in his hands was only going to conjure memories of him blazing one over at Anfield in 2018. In the past two seasons alone, they had missed nine of their 25 penalties – more than one in three.

To Mahrez's immense credit, given the weight of the occasion and the sheer amount of spot-kicks he and his team-mates have missed, he buried it to equalise on the night and put the tie firmly back into City's hands. And then Foden struck, just as he did in the first game. He let fly with one of those low, powerful shots of his and Marwin Hitz could do nothing about it.

The celebrations the goal sparked told their own story. For all the dedication to Guardiola's footballing ideals over the past five years, can you ever remember his players rushing to him for a moment like this?

Foden has had a tough time recently following the death of his adviser, Richard Green. He celebrated his late winner last week with a sombre tribute to the Liverpudlian's memory, pointing solemnly to the sky. Those scenes on the touchline in Dortmund represented a much more raw outpouring of emotions, for everybody concerned.

It had the feel of a special night, and not just for what did happen, but what didn't. For more than two years now, City have been working on how to avoid the chaotic periods in games that have seen their Champions League hopes go up in smoke in a matter of minutes. From Monaco to Liverpool to Tottenham to Lyon (and scares against Schalke, Hoffenheim and Lyon, again, in between) City have left themselves open and been punished for it. They concede one, push forward to try to put things right and then concede again. In this competition, that is a killer.

How would City stop it happening again, less than a year on from their flawed attempts to thwart Lyon at this stage last season, with that "mental bridge" very much a factor? Would they shut up shop, as they did at Spurs two years ago and again in that Lisbon one-off in August?

Not at all. This time they found the control. As Guardiola reflected on a good night's work, he repeatedly mentioned how he had stressed to his team the importance of scoring a goal, that even losing this game 2-1 would be enough for extra-time. They just had to score.

But did they look like a team desperate to do so? When Jude Bellingham scored after 15 minutes, no doubt causing a few of those old doubts to resurface, did City lose their patience and put themselves in a bigger mess? They did not.

"The reaction after 1-1, when you can become crazy, we didn't concede one chance and created corners and free-kicks at the other end," Guardiola said after last week's first leg, which saw City bounce back to win 2-1 after Dortmund equalised on 84 minutes. And in Germany, they were even more impressive.

After Bellingham's goal, Dortmund only had one more effort on target the whole night – a header from a corner three minutes on from that opener.

Things did look a bit rocky for City at that point, it must be said. Guardiola admitted that their high pressing wasn't working in the first quarter of an hour, that they had to bring their wingers inside at that point to control things a little better, to use the ball better. And that was the key to the game.

"When we select this kind of player today, it's players that have the ability to not lose the ball," Guardiola explained when asked how his team kept pushing for a goal without leaving the back door open.

"A team like Dortmund, waiting to run on the counter-attack, if you lose the ball in easy situations always it's a problem. We spoke many times, we have to try to 'make' high pressing, we have to try to regain the ball as quickly as possible and as high as possible, but sometimes it's not possible. In that moment, you defend: medium block or deep, no stress, defend well. Compact."

After Mahrez's penalty, City knocked the ball about with freedom and flair. But while they stayed on the front foot they were also careful, to say the least. There were chances for the players to open up their bodies and move forward, but they checked back. There were chances to dart in behind, but they wanted it to feet.

It felt different, but that is what Guardiola would scoff at. He might point out that they did this sort of thing against Lyon last year but because they missed their chances and made mistakes, the whole thing was branded a disaster, whereas because they scored a penalty and a long-range shot in Dortmund everything was rosy. But they just seemed to find the right balance this time.

"You cannot expect teams in Europe not to create chances or run but the important thing is the way we defend, because the possession that we have, we control and be organised through the passes, because what makes the team balanced is the ball," said Guardiola.

"It's not three incredibly huge holding midfielders or physicality. What makes the team have good balance, compact, is what we do. With. The. Ball. Extra passes help everyone be in the right position and when you lose the ball always you are organised, and that is what we have done since day one we arrived but sometimes you need more time to get it."

Perhaps they have got it now.

Over the two legs, Erling Haaland only had four touches in the City box. Three of those came in the first leg. He had 25 touches on Wednesday, two fewer than City goalkeeper Ederson. That should not play down Haaland's ability, but spells out City's impressive handling of him. And they have their own 20-year-old sensation one who summed up the entire team's approach.

"He's a guy who never hides," Guardiola said of Foden. "He always creates something. He's dynamic offensively, defensively and in small spaces." Perfect for these games, then. "Good, but not perfect," was Guardiola's verdict of last night's performance.

And with a semi-final against Paris Saint-Germain looming, those concerns will come to the fore again soon enough. With Kylian Mbappe, Neymar and Angel Di Maria, the French side will be far more potent on the counter-attack than Dortmund were. They will be far harder to contain than Haaland alone (and while he struggled for chances, he did play a big role in Marco Reus and Bellingham's goals).

City will surely not be able to get away with missing the number of chances that they did across both quarter-final games, either. But now they have finally reached the last four under Guardiola, it might just be time to focus on the things that City do well.

The list is growing.

GUARDIOLA KNOWS HE HAS A STERLING PROBLEM

SAM LEE

APR 18, 2021

Raheem Sterling is not the only reason Manchester City lost to Chelsea on Sunday. The finger of blame could be pointed at any number of individuals, and as a result it was a collective failing at Wembley.

Pep Guardiola is under fire again for rotating his squad, this time in a legitimately big game, although in mitigation he surely has to believe, if his team were to win all four competitions/go on to win three, that players like Sterling, Gabriel Jesus, Ferran Torres, Joao Cancelo and Benjamin Mendy will be more than capable of stepping into the breach when others need a rest.

Those players were a big let-down on the day, but had Guardiola stuck with his Dortmund conquerors then fatigue could catch up with them down the line. We will never know. Kevin De Bruyne, one of the stalwarts, started on Saturday and went off injured anyway. It's not easy to go this far into a season with everything still up for grabs.

"When you lose the game the decisions are bad, but it's a poor argument, my friends. It's a poor argument," Guardiola contested afterwards, and he was not happy at all with the suggestion he took the game for granted.

He pointed out that City had two and a half days to recover from the Dortmund game, including delayed travel back, and that the players he did pick deserved to play. "Listen, do you think Sterling, or Ferran or Gabriel, they don't deserve to play the game?" he asked as he rounded on one reporter, before asking him to name the people who felt he rotated his team too much.

Torres started his first season in promising form and was City's top scorer heading into December, but he didn't really link up with his team-mates even then and since their New Year resurgence he has struggled to fit in, although he will surely be better in his second season and beyond.

Jesus is the constant enigma. And now Sterling. It could justifiably be argued that, as much as he has been a huge player for City over the years and surely will be again, he has struggled of late and, no, he didn't deserve to start.

There would be thousands of fans, and this writer, who would have at least suggested he be substituted against Chelsea as his evening fizzled out.

Guardiola knows, as well, that there is a problem. Saturday was just Sterling's third start in nine games. The three he has started are the FA Cup games against Everton and Chelsea and last week's defeat against Leeds, when Guardiola was clearly keeping his Dortmund selection back. The run stretches back to when City beat Southampton 5-2 at the start of March.

Sterling and Guardiola have denied that there was any sort of row following rumours on the internet (the most popular of which was dramatically embellished) but it is quite clear that something went on and, in any case, several different sources close to the team have told *The Athletic* that words were exchanged after the City coach named his team to face Southampton and Sterling was not best pleased that he wasn't in it.

Whoever you believe, Guardiola's comments at the time suggested that something was up. "Now we arrive in the right time of the season with not many games, the players who help me a lot this season I will rotate less," Guardiola said after City won the match. "The rest will be on the bench."

The next game, Sterling wasn't in the squad at all and Guardiola's response to questions about the winger amounted initially to a couple of short sentences – "Yeah he's OK", "Tomorrow we have training, we will see" – to eventually saying that Eric Garcia "deserves to be here too". Hardly a ringing endorsement of somebody who has been, up until the last few weeks, a staple in Guardiola's team.

Sterling is not in the highest of spirits at the moment, according to sources close to the squad, which is in part understandable and inevitable given he isn't playing, but it is also thought to be due to the events around the Southampton game.

That leads to other questions. His contract expires in two years' time and now would be the ideal time for City to tie him down and secure his value, both as a player and an asset.

If Sterling were to consider his future – and it must be stressed that that is purely hypothetical at this point – he might not find it so easy to move this summer due to Europe's top clubs struggling financially. He does not have an agent currently, either, and to give an example of how that can affect things, his previous representative had been keeping Real Madrid on a back burner.

A very good solution for all parties, of course, is for Sterling to put pen to paper at City and regain his best form. Of course, Sterling had to have given Guardiola a reason to leave him out of the squad in the first place and he has been lacking an end product of late, something that was painfully apparent on Saturday.

Sterling has always been a high-risk player, like De Bruyne, in the sense that he gives the ball away a lot but that is the price to pay for constantly probing for openings. While De Bruyne passes, Sterling dribbles, and if you force the issue that much you're going to give up possession.

As long as you make up for it elsewhere, nobody really cares.

This season, Sterling has been dispossessed 73 times in the Premier League, which is 43 times more than De Bruyne in second. That's a staggering little statistic that hints at a major problem, but Sterling was also dispossessed more than any of his team-mates last season and the season before that, too. Sterling's problem now is that he's not offering anything to draw the eye away from the times he loses the ball. On Saturday it looked like that was all he did.

Part of the problem is that City are not creating the kind of chances that he usually finishes. Last season, the trademark goal where they worked it to the byline on the left-hand side stopped happening, partly because David Silva was out of the team and partly because teams had worked out what City were going to do, and packed the spaces they liked to exploit. Sterling scored many of these goals arriving late at the back post when he played on the right wing.

It didn't matter too much for Sterling personally because when he moved to the left he could at least rely on De Bruyne swinging balls to his wing where he would again be there to finish, showing his superb ability to understand exactly what was asked of him.

But De Bruyne hasn't really played those crosses this season. So not only is Sterling finding all the spaces he likes to run into blocked by extra defenders and midfielders, making it harder for him to dribble inside and shoot, he doesn't have that steady supply line of chances no matter where he plays.

The issue here is that he's not a strong enough finisher in other situations to make up for it. He has scored many one-on-one chances, of course, but there is little confidence when he goes through on goal that he will find the back of the net, and the latest evidence of that was late on against Dortmund when he came on late, burst through, but ended up getting tackled before he could even shoot.

His big-chance conversion rates have dipped over the years, suggesting that either the chances were so good in City's previous title-winning seasons that he couldn't miss, or that he was simply playing better (or with more confidence).

Sterling's big chance conversion rate:

SEASON	BIG CHANCE CONVERSION RATE
2020-21	33%
2019-20	42%
2018-19	60%
2017-18	54%

This season in the league he has scored six of his big chances and missed 12. His conversion rate of 33 per cent is better than only eight players to have had more than 10 big chances, and their identities tell the story: Timo Werner, Chris Wood, Che Adams, Roberto Firmino, Patrick Bamford, Sadio Mane, Anthony Martial and Danny Welbeck. Bar Bamford, they've not had the most prolific seasons.

It must be said, though, that he is City's joint-second-highest league scorer, alongside Riyad Mahrez. He has nine in the league and 13 in all competitions. He has six league assists, which is the second-most in the squad. But it is very hard to make a case that he is playing well at the moment.

Halfway through last season he went through a similar dip in goalscoring output, but he kept his place in the team for a couple of reasons: firstly, he was doing everything Guardiola needed him to do in terms of getting into the right positions and he was also doing an incredible amount of work off the ball, either offensively or defensively.

Secondly, he was the only real option who could play on that side, so even if Guardiola wanted to change things up, there wasn't anywhere else to turn. Now there's Phil Foden. Foden was the brightest spark for City on Saturday and he is now surely first choice, and he plays on the left wing. Mahrez, who has himself been left out of squads due to complaining about lack of game time in the past, is also flying high and showing his worth on a consistent basis.

These are players that, unquestionably, deserve to play. The problem at the moment is that the others have not made their cases quite as strongly when given the opportunity, and this is when Guardiola needs them most.

The City boss insists that without rotating his team the hunt for so many trophies is "unsustainable", and he points out that the players have mental and physical limits that cannot be ascertained by watching from afar.

In the next 10 days, City have Aston Villa away in the league, Tottenham in the Carabao Cup final and then Paris Saint-Germain in the Champions League semis, perhaps the biggest game of Guardiola's reign.

Sterling has been given opportunities to get back into the team since missing out at Fulham, as was the case when Aymeric Laporte complained about being dropped at the end of last year. The Frenchman is not quite first choice yet but he is certainly back in good form and there are few worries when he is put into the team these days.

That is the challenge that Sterling now faces.

EUROPEAN SUPER LEAGUE: MANCHESTER CITY HAVE SWAPPED SIDES, THEY ARE BETRAYING THEIR FANS

SAM LEE

APR 19, 2021

Manchester City fans have come to think of themselves as outsiders. That is something the club have embraced, too.

Over the past couple of years, as City's war against UEFA and its financial fair play (FFP) regulations came to a head, the arguments were spelt out. Namely, that FFP was cooked up by a cabal of elite clubs desperately trying to protect their status at the top of world football, to the exclusion of the likes of City, Paris Saint-Germain and, those clubs argued, others who may now have the backing and wherewithal to break up the game's old hegemony.

There was understandable outrage as clubs including Bayern Munich and Juventus were allowed to enter into cosy deals with sponsors who have very close ties to board members (Juventus' auto-giant partners Fiat are controlled by the Agnelli family, who are the Turin side's majority owners), and only last month the European Union found that Spain's big two of Barcelona and Real Madrid have benefited from state aid for three decades. City wondered why there was so much attention and fury focused on them while all this was going on.

The club were stunned when nine of their domestic rivals wrote to the Court of Arbitration for Sport (CAS) to argue City should be banned from European competition while they were investigated for alleged financial irregularities. Those clubs were Arsenal, Manchester United, Liverpool, Tottenham, Chelsea, Leicester, Wolves, Newcastle and Burnley, and Pep Guardiola took his opportunity to round on them when City had their ban overturned.

City fans loved that, of course, just as they put their faith in chief executive Ferran Soriano and chairman Khaldoon Al Mubarak when they stood up for the club during UEFA's proceedings.

And even in the autumn, with the CAS verdict in the past, fans were disgusted yet delighted with leaked plans for a new breakaway league. Disgusted because it was from the same playbook as FFP's introduction, the brainchild of increasingly irrelevant clubs fighting to cling to power. Delighted, though, that they were not involved in talks. It was the Americans. It was United and Liverpool up to their old tricks.

The idea was met with universal disapproval, went away quite quickly and City fans were happy to have been well away from it, with rumours that they weren't even invited anyway. That was perfect.

But now the European Super League is firmly on the agenda once again. Even when Champions League reforms looked a shoo-in (and they still might be), the movers and shakers behind this most controversial of plans were biding their time, doing their market research, putting the money in place, getting support.

Andrea Agnelli, of Juventus and Fiat, is one of the brains behind it. He was driving those Champions League reforms, but on the night of the Super League's belated announcement, he quit his role as president of the European Club Association, the only recognised body representing clubs that UEFA recognises. He's been described as a "snake" by those on the other side.

Florentino Perez, the Real Madrid supremo, is the League's chairman. As well as Agnelli, Manchester United's co-chairman Joel Glazer is a vice-president. It's been reported that Liverpool's John W Henry and Arsenal's Stan Kroenke have the same positions.

No wonder, then, that City fans feel so betrayed. It must be said that so many supporters of all the clubs involved are against the idea, united in their revulsion that these clubs now get to decide who can enter their new league, certain that endless matches between Europe's top sides will soon become dull, and that the huge financial benefits will further skew competition in domestic leagues anyway.

It's just that City's fans have something else to consider now: their decision-makers have thrown in their lot with all of the predators that wanted to close them out in the first place.

So much for the club's stance against the so-called 'Hateful Eight' which became a 'Nasty Nine' when Newcastle joined in, or the idea that they have been fighting inequalities in European football.

Now City are big enough and attractive enough to be part of the elite, they are only too willing to pull up the drawbridge on everybody else. They are, until we hear otherwise at least, hypocrites.

We haven't heard from them, though, because nobody involved in any of this has yet come forward to explain what they aim to achieve. The rest of us are piecing things together as best we can.

Title-bound City were not closely involved in those talks last year, and it is understood that they only became involved in this latest plan after discussions over the past few days. It has been reported that they and Chelsea were effectively backed into a corner at the end of last week, effectively offered the opportunity to jump on board or be left behind. Their desire to avoid the latter, to cling to the power they have accrued over the past decade, seems to have outweighed their previous arguments about the might of the 'established elite'. We don't know for sure though, because City haven't shed any light on it yet.

After the story broke in the afternoon, the clubs involved, and those who had been building websites and social media accounts for months, were in breathless talks about when best to launch, if at all, at their central London HQ in Millbank, on the River Thames. The English clubs were the most cautious.

A statement was finally published late on Sunday night and the clubs followed suit. What sums up the outrage for City fans in this case is that their statement was effectively a copy-and-paste job, featuring quotes from Manchester United's Joel Glazer but no City representative.

Soriano emailed staff before midnight on Sunday pointing them in the direction of the statement and said that the "objective is to improve the quality and intensity of competition". He also invited them to raise any questions they have at the next company meeting.

There must be a reason why none of the clubs or other people associated with the league are talking yet. That's one question. There is a long list of others. What about the domestic leagues? What about the Champions League? When will this start? Will it ever actually start? Is this all a game?

But perhaps most importantly, and particularly for the City fans who felt that their club was different, they just want to know why.

THIS WAS CITY AT THEIR DOMINANT BEST: 'THE REASON WE DO IT IS FOR THEM'

SAM LEE

APR 26, 2021

"We qualified for the Champions League semi-final but we had no time to celebrate, only to focus on Chelsea," Pep Guardiola said on Friday, the latest lament that he and his players have barely had time to think this season.

And even if Manchester City could hardly let their hair down on Sunday night as they celebrated winning their fourth consecutive Carabao Cup, surely those 20-or-so minutes on the Wembley pitch afterwards in front of 2,000 of their fans will be a reminder, if needed, that all of their efforts behind closed doors are not for nothing.

They are on the verge of another Premier League title after Manchester United's draw with Leeds earlier in the day and they could do something extra special if they get past Paris Saint-Germain in Europe. And it is the first leg of that semi-final in France on Wednesday that means the players won't be able to dwell for too long on their champagne-drenched celebrations.

But what a send-off. What a day for those in the stands.

It hardly needs spelling out that after over a year of lockdowns and restrictions, but that was a special afternoon for those City supporters inside Wembley, who got the chance to cheer, clap and chant. It was clear from the reactions of the players and managers on both sides that they were appreciated.

The feeling was certainly mutual. As substitute Bernardo Silva trotted out late for the warm-up the City fans applauded him heartily, and his team-mates joined in. When Fernandinho trotted off to be replaced after Aymeric Laporte's late headed winner, they applauded him and Guardiola looked over and applauded them. In between it all, the team did their followers proud.

It had not been an easy week for City but their fans have far greater respect for the owners' contribution to the club than those at their Big Six rivals, and it's amazing what two wins – in a big Premier League game at Aston Villa and here in a cup final – can do for unity after the dalliance with the Super League.

Those two victories showed us City at something like their best form of the season, the type of football they played in the early months of 2021 when they got back into their groove and passed teams to death, establishing their insurmountable lead at the top of the table after those shaky autumn months. There had been some concerns of late after defeats to Leeds and, in the FA Cup semi-final, Chelsea, but what a time for things to come together again.

A 1-0 win thanks to a centre-half's header from a set-piece hardly screams dominance but City were, in the first half in particular, magnificent. Tottenham did have a 29-year-old rookie manager, Ryan Mason, in the dugout, of course, and their former boss Mauricio Pochettino will put out a far more intimidating side in Paris in midweek, but it's a good time to remember that Guardiola's team are pretty handy, too.

They swarmed Tottenham, who carried such little threat that the xG collators had to add an extra decimal place to register the few efforts they did muster in Sunday's showpiece – two shots from outside the box, although one did draw a good save from Zack Steffen.

But that was it, and City could have had a hatful. The fact that they miss so many chances could become more of an issue as their European campaign comes to its climax but if they can't enjoy a cup final with fans in the stadium after this past year, when can they?

As Guardiola put it after the game, "I was thinking, 'What would I say to my players if we didn't win this game, playing like that?'"

He pointed out, yet again, that in any other sport, a team as dominant as his would always win the game, but in football, there is always that risk that something could go wrong.

There are games, like their last two, when City can remove any jeopardy thanks to their organisation, efforts and intelligence, but that's always easier to say after the event and the celebrations when Laporte headed in Kevin De Bruyne's free-kick eight minutes from time represented a swirl of emotions, but chief among those was relief – relief that they had got their goal and that, at last, things are starting to look brighter.

Nobody was rushing out of the ground for their trains – even the biosecure ones laid on by the club – as the City players set up camp in front of the supporters to start the celebrations. Guardiola's men would have toasted the significance of yet another trophy even if they had been the only ones inside Wembley, given the drive they have shown over the years, but after months of getting straight back on the bus and going home after winning matches, they would have enjoyed this just as much as those who were asked to pay £50 for the privilege.

"I think everybody at the club has missed the fans and for me, the fans give the players energy as well," said Brian Kidd, the beloved City coach making a surprise appearance at the post-match press conference.

"We miss them," Guardiola added. "It was not full but they represent all the people, in this situation. Sharing with them sounds better with good noise, the reason we do it is for them."

During the match they sang about Istanbul, venue for next month's Champions League final, and after the players had cleared off the pitch and the fans finally headed for the exits, one or two confided that flights have been booked, too. Even if they are refundable.

"We cannot deny one eye is always on the Champions League," Guardiola admitted. "It's only the second time we arrived in the semi-finals, and one eye is always there. Every game we take seriously, and now we just rest and prepare (for) the semi-final against PSG. After that, we are two games away from winning again the most important title of the season: the Premier League is the nicest one and we are so close. Marcelo Bielsa's team made a nice draw against United and we now need two victories.

"Hats off to the players for what they have done all season. We are close to the second (trophy) and we are going to Paris to try to win the next one."

There was not much champagne on Sunday night after all, then, but how sweet those few drops will have tasted.

LANDMARK VICTORY FOR GUARDIOLA AS MANCHESTER CITY FORCE THE ISSUE ... BY REMAINING PATIENT

SAM LEE

APR 29, 2021

"The first half was . . ." Pep Guardiola trailed off and sighed. "It's normal," he continued, "it's 180 minutes . . . you don't want to lose the ball, you don't play free."

To rally from that position of inhibition, to rescue a Champions League semi-final that looked to be in Paris Saint-Germain's hands, is the latest step in Manchester City's evolution.

We've seen games like this before. The team who are happy to sit back and play on the counter-attack score the first goal, then wait for the spaces to open up, exploit them and that's that. With Kylian Mbappe and Neymar, nobody in world football is more dangerous in that situation than PSG.

And while those two will be plotting their revenge at the Etihad Stadium on Tuesday, where were they in the second half last night? City controlled them the only way they know how – by controlling the ball, and thus controlling the game.

It would be a stretch to say the first half in Paris was a masterclass. In fact, it would be wrong. City were far from perfect and PSG were the better side, looking far more likely to score a second goal than their visitors to get an equaliser.

City clearly set out to dominate the game with short passes but they never really carried any threat, except when forcing two errors from high pressing. "In the first 45 minutes, we played to not lose the ball but without any intention to be aggressive or break the lines with the passes," Guardiola admitted, after composing his thoughts.

But their safe passing did at least allow them to stay in the game at 1-0, to provide a platform for what came later. "When you play knockout stages, in the first leg you are thinking about the next game and 'don't lose'," the City boss added. "You cannot win in the first leg, but you can lose it."

We should know by now that Guardiola wants to keep things tight in these big European games: the seeds of this were sown in that quarter-final first leg away to Tottenham two years ago. Such was Guardiola's determination that his team should not push too far forward and leave too many spaces behind them for Mauricio Pochettino's Spurs to counter into, he kept Kevin De Bruyne and Leroy Sane on the bench until the 89th minute. He was concerned that had he brought them on sooner, their team-mates would've thought, "Oh aye. We're going for this then, are we?" and left themselves open to conceding a second. Taking a 1-0 deficit back to Manchester, he felt, was not too bad.

If that didn't teach us anything, then Lyon at the same stage last season would have, when Guardiola arguably went too far in reacting to the opposition's threat on the break. This season, he has seemed to find the right balance.

"The closer you are to who you are, the more chance you have of going through," Guardiola said in the build-up to this rematch with now-PSG boss Pochettino. "Not when you are thinking about the opponent. It's about what you do. I want to be ourselves. That is my wish."

We saw that in the last eight against Borussia Dortmund, when City set out to keep things tight. "When we select this kind of player today, it's players that have the ability to not lose the ball," Guardiola said after City had completed their second 2-1 win of the tie. In both legs, they conceded goals that could have rocked them but they stuck to their task. When they equalised in the decider in Germany, they knocked the ball around patiently – no need to force things, just be patient – and the winning goal came anyway.

It was the same in Paris. It is only fair to say that had City conceded the goals they scored last night, they could lament that they were unlucky.

In the same way that conceding from a set-piece is not the gravest problem, PSG conceded from a cross that went straight in and a through-the-wall free-kick that was branded "terrible" defending by BT Sport pundit Owen Hargreaves. They were not vintage City goals by any means and the margins, yet again, were very fine. This time, they went City's way and all you can say is that they forced the issue . . . by remaining patient.

De Bruyne usually gets to the nub of these things and afterwards he explained what changed at half-time. "Just play a little more with the ball. We were too rushed, we wanted to go forward too quickly and that's not the way we set up as a team," he said, still red-cheeked from his efforts. "I think, in the second half, we did really well. We tried to find the spaces more patiently, and we did that."

As he often does, De Bruyne echoed his manager's message. "Be patient and attack in the right moments. We cannot win this game in 10 minutes. It needs 90, 95 minutes." That's what the Catalan said earlier this month after his side beat Leicester City in the Premier League.

Patience is what he has preached all season, ever since Leicester put five past them in their opening home league game on September 27. It looked like it was going to be a long season then, with Guardiola lamenting how his players, at 1-0 up, attacked too quickly, lost their patience and left themselves exposed.

The season since has been an exercise in eradicating those issues and now City stand on the verge of their first Champions League final, although not a single person connected to the club will be getting ahead of themselves.

This was a truly impressive victory for City, though. Perhaps a landmark victory. Their ability to turn the game around, thanks to their organisation and mentality, speaks volumes about where they are as a team. Imagine they hadn't. Had the second half panned out like the first, they would have been accused of being bottlers: the tag now being levelled, once again, at PSG.

"Sometimes you need time to be more relaxed, to be ourselves," Guardiola said of the half-time changes, but they were something more than even the City team that stormed to the top of the Premier League at the start of the year. They are improving.

Rewind just a fortnight and City's record at coming from behind in matches was worryingly poor. In their last 10 matches when going a goal down, they had drawn two and lost eight.

Since then, they have recovered from going a goal down to beat Dortmund, Aston Villa and PSG. In just two weeks. They perhaps gave too much respect to a team that ran riot at the Camp Nou in Barcelona and Bayern Munich's Allianz Arena, but they can be surer of themselves now.

"That's why when you start the game, you are a little bit cautious," Guardiola said of his side's inhibited start last night. "I'm not complaining. At half-time, I said, 'I'm not complaining. I understand you feel the responsibility because you want to get to the final.'

"It's just to understand how to handle this and be ourselves; don't be shy. If we lose, we lose. If we don't get to the final, we will try again next season but try to play our game, like we spoke about. What is our identity with the ball and without the ball? Go out there and try to do it – and they were fantastic.

"I admire them, from being not good to how they changed to do well. That means a lot to me about these players. Normally, when you are not good and are not good over 90 minutes, you lose 2-0 or 3-0, it's over. It was completely the opposite."

By the end, City could have had more than their two away goals. Ilkay Gundogan was gliding around the pitch, Phil Foden looked like he was just getting started, De Bruyne was ready to burst into spaces on the left had Rodri's passing been better, and Riyad Mahrez, "a guy who does not feel pressure", according to his manager, would have been right there with him. Mbappe and Neymar were nowhere to be seen.

It's not quite 'job done', but nobody can deny that City are getting better and better. If they have another night like this, they will be in the Champions League final and Guardiola really might be lost for words.

DEFERRING TO MAHREZ HIGHLIGHTED DE BRUYNE'S OTHER SPECIAL QUALITY – HE IS A SELFLESS SUPERSTAR

DANIEL TAYLOR

APR 29, 2021

Perhaps the most revealing moment came a short while after the final whistle at the Parc des Princes when Kevin De Bruyne – pink cheeks, flushed forehead, magic in his feet – was asked to talk us through the moment that had put his team on the cusp of a Champions League final.

What had been going through his mind when the referee blew for a foul just outside Paris Saint-Germain's penalty area and the opportunity presented itself to be the hero? The free-kick was 25 yards from goal. It was prime territory for a player with De Bruyne's accuracy and, if you assumed the Belgian was going to let fly with his right boot, don't worry about getting it wrong. You weren't alone.

Maybe we ought to have remembered one important fact about De Bruyne: he has never allowed his priorities to be blurred by a streak of self-indulgence. It is one of his more attractive traits, one of the qualities that makes him so special. It is why you do not have to be a Manchester City supporter to realise he is everything you could possibly want from an elite footballer.

Riyad Mahrez wanted to try his luck. He was feeling confident, having a fine game. The two players conferred. De Bruyne listened, took it in and whispered his instructions: go for it.

"He asked me if he could take it and I said: 'If you believe in yourself, take it,'" De Bruyne later explained. "I have full confidence in my team, and he scored the goal, so who am I to say something about that?"

And that, in a nutshell, sums up the way De Bruyne operates, his team ethos, his understanding of the bigger picture and the way, even now, he manages to be a category-A footballer while retaining an unassuming, boy-next-door demeanour. If the boy next door also happens to be capable of playing football that takes the sport to its absolute peak.

It helped, of course, that PSG's defensive wall parted so obligingly when, in ordinary circumstances, Mahrez's shot would have been blocked and everyone would have moved on.

But history will tell us this was the moment when City moved closer than ever before to a Champions League final and, at the heart of it, De Bruyne had enough about him to recognise that he did not need to pull rank as the team's free-kick specialist. Mahrez was telling him that he fancied his chances. And it tells us so much about De Bruyne that, in these critical moments, he made the ego-free decision to place his trust in his colleague.

Perhaps it might seem strange to some people to praise the player who decided not to take the decisive free-kick. What those people might not understand is that De Bruyne, by choosing to step away, was absolutely taking responsibility. In the process, he was also demonstrating why he had the captain's armband on his sleeve.

Maybe this act of selflessness stood out more because it took place during a second half in which Neymar had ceased to have any telling influence and seemed to regard it as a personal affront that the Premier League's champions-elect were playing the more coherent football.

But the thought also occurred that not many superstar footballers would have been persuaded to stand to one side in the position that De Bruyne found himself, with the score 1-1, standing over the ball as City's usual go-to guy whenever there is a free-kick to be aimed at the opposition goal.

Would Cristiano Ronaldo have left the ball to a team-mate if he had the chance to put his team in sight of a Champions League final and enhance his already considerable reputation in front of a global audience?

Some people might argue that it is Ronaldo's ridiculous self-belief that has helped him to become a serial champion and an automatic entry on any list of the sport's all-time greats. They might have a point, too, judging by his record of achievement and all the occasions for Manchester United, Real Madrid and Juventus when he has provided match-winning contributions.

It doesn't change the fact, however, that sometimes there is something to be said for a player who knows when it is time to stand aside.

Ronaldo has had long stretches when his accuracy from free-kicks has deserted him. Lionel Messi has, too. Ronaldo has scored only two of his last 81 attempts, going back to the start of the 2016/17 season, whereas Messi's free-kick statistics have also dropped off. These are giants of the sport, with 11 Ballons d'Or between them, but it is difficult to think either of them would hand over the responsibility to let somebody else have a go – or even entertain the kind of conversation that took place between De Bruyne and Mahrez in the 70th minute of Tuesday's game.

We already knew, of course, about De Bruyne's uncommon ability to shape football matches to his will. We knew about his ability to visualise the perfect pass, then have the skill to execute it. We ran out of new superlatives a long time ago and, if you were watching the League Cup final on Sunday, you might have seen him making his point, yet again, that a pass can be the most beautiful part of his profession.

Not many footballers would have had the audacity to try to float the ball on to Raheem Sterling's boot, 40 yards away, as his team-mate ran into Tottenham Hotspur's penalty area. Even fewer would have been able to pull it off bearing in mind Eric Dier, standing over six feet tall, was positioned to head away any pass that was not centimetre-perfect. Even Sterling, who wasted the chance, seemed taken aback to find out that such a pass was on.

These are the moments when it is easy to understand why Pep Guardiola's eyes light up whenever the conversation turns to De Bruyne and why there is a reasonable case that the midfielder deserves to hold on to his title as the Professional Footballers' Association player of the year.

What we saw in Paris, however, was a different kind of quality.

De Bruyne had already scored one goal and, with a nod of encouragement, he helped to create the other. An unorthodox assist but, for City, a brilliant one, all the same.

APRIL RESULTS

Premier League, April 3, 2021
Leicester City 0 Manchester City 2
Manchester City scorers: Mendy 58 Jesus 74

Champions League, quarter-final, first leg, April 6, 2021
Manchester City 2 Borussia Dortmund 1
Manchester City scorers: Du Bruyne 19 Foden 90

Premier League, April 10, 2021
Manchester City 1 Leeds United 2
Manchester City scorer: Torres 76

Champions League, April 14, 2021
B Dortmund 1 Manchester City 2
Manchester City scorers: Mahrez 55 Foden 75

FA Cup semi-final, April 17, 2021
Chelsea 1 Manchester City 0

Premier League, April 21, 2021
Aston Villa 1 Manchester City 2
Manchester City scorers: Foden 22 Rodri 40

Carabao Cup final, April 25, 2021
Manchester City 1 Tottenham Hotspur 0
Manchester City scorer: Laporte 82

Champions League, semi-final, first leg, April 28, 2021
Paris Saint-Germain 1 Manchester City 2
Manchester City scorers: De Bruyne 64 Mahrez 71

MAY

MANCHESTER CITY HAVE NOTHING LEFT TO FEAR IN THE CHAMPIONS LEAGUE

SAM LEE

MAY 5, 2021

All those one-sided Barcelona ties, the timid Real Madrid semi-final, Monaco, the Anfield collapse, Sergio Aguero's missed penalty, the VAR heartbreak, Raheem Sterling's sitter, Lyon. Bloody Lyon. All of those moments, all of the pain and ignominy, all banished by a Manchester City team that finally looks at home on the biggest stage following their 2-0 home win over Paris Saint-Germain in the Champions League semi-final second leg on Tuesday night (4-1 on aggregate).

Maybe not banished, actually. Maybe just put into context. This is Manchester City's journey to the Champions League final. These are experiences that money can't buy, the kind of things a club needs to go through before they can truly get a handle on this competition, one that magnifies and exploits any doubts.

Two years to get out of the group stages under Roberto Mancini, two years to get past the last 16 and then a farewell semi-final for Manuel Pellegrini, providing something of a foundation for Pep Guardiola's personal journey in the competition.

One that started off with the Catalan urging fans to show the Champions League some love, to embrace it as the European greats do. That year ended in Monaco, with City's players not quite buying into their manager's idea that the best way to defend a 5-3 aggregate lead was to go and add to it.

City's back-to-back Premier League titles, with 198 points over two seasons, were a sign that things had clicked, but whenever they took one step forward in Europe they took two back.

It's the competition they want to win, too, there is no doubt of that. When they won the domestic treble in 2018/19 the players did not hide the fact that they saw the Champions League as the next big challenge.

They beat Real Madrid 2-1 in both legs last year, a sign that things were changing. Then they lost to Lyon with a team set-up to stop counter-attacks, conceding three goals on the break, with two Ederson shockers and that scarcely believable Sterling miss at the back post. A bigger shambles you will not find. The atmosphere was "like a funeral" the next day, according to one source.

This is a different City now. Whatever happens in the final, when next season starts the conversation will not centre on quarter-final mental blocks or Guardiola's supposed overthinking. Fans will be looking forward to another semi-final, perhaps even another final. The narrative has changed and, in that sense at least, the battle has already been won. After seeing off Dortmund, Guardiola said they had "broken the bridge". They certainly have.

If their past undoings were a result of pressure, we can safely presume that that has not been an issue in recent months. City's 'problem' had always been that they could never quite replicate their domestic dominance on a European level, but they have done so now.

They have won their last seven Champions League games, a record for English teams in the competition. They have won 11 of their 12 matches this season. More than that, they have exuded confidence and there is now the same level of certainty no matter if they are playing at home or abroad.

They saw off Borussia Monchengladbach with little drama, which might not be the biggest achievement but they have made heavier weather of last-16 ties with Basel and Schalke, not to mention Monaco. Guardiola's strikerless system dominated their opponents, but he wasn't entirely convinced.

"Still I had the feeling when we finished the game against Gladbach that maybe it would not be enough to reach the final stages of the Champions League if we did not improve in some departments," he said a few days later.

The worry then was that Dortmund were set up to be another Lyon, that Erling Haaland et al would happily wait to exploit the spaces on the counter-attack that would surely open up over 180 minutes. Only they never really did.

City probably looked shakier in that first leg than in any other game but when Dortmund did score, and late on at that, Guardiola's men didn't lose their nerve, they didn't push forward to try to put things right and ended up making things worse, which has been the story of all their European woes. They kept it tight, they stuck to the plan and they got their goals. City caged Haaland.

"This is just the second time the club is in the semi-finals of the Champions League," Guardiola said. "We are not mature enough in the Champions League, but the players learned a lot in the last seasons. We are making steps forward for the next years."

They are making steps for now. Everything they have learned over those years, and in the past couple of months, saw them through against Paris Saint-Germain. We will never know how Kylian Mbappe would have changed the second leg but if the second half last week is anything to go by, he would not have made much difference in Manchester, no matter how good he is. Neymar was kept quiet, too, although it wasn't all smooth sailing.

"They must stick together in the bad moments and suffer together," Guardiola said before the game, and didn't they just.

He was expecting difficult moments and City had their share, especially in the first half. They let PSG get in behind their midfield, which was strange because it contained two men sitting deep, one of which was Fernandinho, who sees interceptions like Kevin De Bruyne sees passes. Sometimes they gave the ball away stupidly or didn't win it back quickly enough. Not often, but Guardiola raged on the sidelines more times than he would have liked.

They got lucky once, when Angel Di Maria shot wide after a rushed Ederson throw, but they were on hand to put out any other fires, the back four in particular. One Neymar run ended with a sliding block from Oleksandr Zinchenko, which earned him hugs from Ruben Dias and John Stones that genuinely rivalled a goal celebration.

All season, the two centre-backs have applauded each other's contributions and that camaraderie came to a head on Tuesday night, with both full-backs involved too. Walker and Zinchenko might have had their best games for the club. Stones was at his confident best, as he has been for most of the past six months, and Dias might have put in his most commanding performance yet, and that's saying something. "When the difficult times come, we step up," he said afterwards.

It seemed every shot PSG had ended up hitting some part of his anatomy, and when it was not him there was somebody else there to help out instead.

In that respect, this was perhaps more of an English-style win than Guardiola would have ever imagined. It was hardly kick and rush, far from it, but Dias was only a bandaged head and a bloodied shirt away from invoking some of the England national team's most famous nights, when putting your body on the line is more noteworthy than the football. In the first half, they sat back and played on the break, in a 4-4-2.

This has been a journey for Guardiola, too. While City's domestic success came after the players got to grip with his methods, Guardiola has had to make some concessions to get his team to a Champions League final for the first time in 10 years.

After all, he put City's Monaco failings down to not attacking enough. Two years later he tried to shut up shop at Tottenham. Last year he made too many concessions for Lyon, something which he may now admit.

"The closer you are to who you are, the more chance you have of going through," he said before the first leg in Paris last week. "Not when you are thinking about the opponent. It's about what you do. I want to be ourselves. That is my wish."

Now he has found the right balance, which is reflected by his consistent team selections. And this year, sources close to him say he is more than happy to keep games tight if that's what the situation dictates. The phrase "dark arts" has been used a few times by those familiar with his thinking.

Fernandinho, somewhat surprisingly, won his place back from Rodri after a somewhat shaky performance by the Spaniard in Paris. It looked like it might have backfired in the first half but after the break, the old warrior, who turned 36 on the day, helped shut PSG down and, perhaps more importantly, kept his team-mates on track.

Zinchenko was magnificent in possession, especially in the first half when the snowy pitch made conditions difficult, but he took exception to an Ander Herrera complaint late on and Fernandinho had to reprimand him, reminding him to keep his cool. A few moments later Guardiola and Walker had to stop Riyad Mahrez from getting involved because by this point PSG had lost their heads. Idrissa Gueye last week, Di Maria this. City were running rings around them and they resorted to crude fouls and quarrels.

City can handle that now, but they can still play a bit. Their goals were evidence of that, much more so than last week. Whether it's Ederson's fantastic contribution to the first goal or the one time they really exploited the space to settle the tie, they scored City goals, Guardiola goals.

Mahrez goals, more specifically. He got three of City's four over the two legs and if they do go on to win the Champions League then his contribution will be right up there.

So will De Bruyne, who played an inch-perfect pass in the build-up to the Algerian's second, just like the one he made against Dortmund. So will Phil Foden, who threatened to score a truly memorable goal in both legs and it would surprise nobody if he did so in the final.

The only other starters not singled out for a specific mention are Ilkay Gundogan and Bernardo Silva, who did as much as anybody to shut down PSG when they had the ball and to frustrate them when they didn't, showing them a glimpse and then spiriting it away.

City were in such control that the only question in the last 30 minutes was how many they would score (or how many PSG players would get sent off). They should probably have bagged a couple more given all the spaces that opened up but they had already proven their dominance, they had already made their point.

It's been a long time coming, but City have made a Champions League final and, most tellingly of all, they have nothing left to fear.

SLOWER ATTACKS AND A CODE OF HONOUR: INSIDE STORY OF HOW GUARDIOLA'S MANCHESTER CITY TOOK BACK CONTROL OF ENGLISH FOOTBALL

SAM LEE, TOM WORVILLE AND MARK CAREY

MAY 11, 2021

To understand Manchester City's Premier League title victory, we need to appreciate how they became Manchester City again. Because they had lost their way. Now, with a third title in four years, a fourth Carabao Cup on the spin and a Champions League final in place, it is easy to forget – and downright strange to remember – just how different things looked six months ago. There were even fans who wondered whether Pep Guardiola was the right man to take the team forward.

"If I did not feel we could do better I would not have extended my contract here, 100 per cent," he said. But when he put pen to paper in November he did not know exactly how he would put his City side back on top again, and it's fair to say there was some doubt about whether he could.

And the challenge was no mean feat: to become only the third manager – after Sir Alex Ferguson and Arsene Wenger – to rebuild a team and lead them to the title again. He has now done that and is, without any doubt whatsoever, up there with the very best to have ever coached in this country, and his team must be regarded as among the elite of English football history.

An end to the season like this seemed unimaginable even in the weeks after he had put pen to paper on that contract extension. Guardiola often seemed grumpy in press conferences, and more shockingly, City's football had become unrecognisable, even dull.

Guardiola has always set out to control football matches while in possession of the ball. Still, he had two problems: he had stuck to the relatively defensive tactics that he employed last season when City's high pressing dropped off and their midfield and defence were weakened by injury. The lack of a proper pre-season meant that the players were not fit enough to control a match for 90 minutes anyway.

City didn't look like City. They were defensively stable – helped by Ruben Dias' arrival after a harrowing 5-2 defeat against Leicester City – but they didn't create as much as they used to, and what they did create was thanks to Kevin De Bruyne, who sat in front of two deep-lying midfielders and carried much of the burden.

Heading into the November international break, City were 10th, but the club's top hierarchy was certain that Guardiola should stay for as long as possible. There was, in contrast to concern among the fanbase and the media, not a second of doubt.

They knew that they were the only club in world football to offer him complete freedom to make the decisions that he felt best and they were confident he would stay, but they didn't know for sure. Neither did Guardiola, really.

His wife and youngest daughter had moved back to Barcelona, and he had always said that he would want to see that his players were reacting to his messages if he were to stay beyond five years. Was that sustainable?

The final decision only came after conversations with Khaldoon Al Mubarak, the chairman, who reassured Guardiola that they were desperate for him to stay and to keep building. "The chairman now is a friend of mine, the sporting director and

CEO are friends of mine from Barcelona and that makes my life so easy," Guardiola said in March. "Because when we win we are happy and when we lose I don't feel, 'Why did we lose?' The question is, 'What can we do to get better?'"

But the new contract did not provide the answers overnight. In fact, they lost to Tottenham in the same way that they lost many games last season: mistakes were punished and spaces exploited, so it was no surprise, in mid-December, when City went to Old Trafford and shut up shop.

They kept the ball, of course, but they took few risks lest they open up gaps for Marcus Rashford or Anthony Martial to run into. As City fans called for late substitutions to take the game to a wounded United, freshly knocked out at the Champions League group stage, Guardiola was happy to stick rather than twist. It summed up their season to that point.

He did twist against West Bromwich Albion a few days later, asking both full-backs to attack and pushing De Bruyne right up alongside Phil Foden and Raheem Sterling, playing on their natural sides. They attacked, but the outcome did not match the intention and the 1-1 draw became a turning point.

"In that moment, we realised we were not brilliant," Guardiola has admitted. "Everything was heavy, it was not natural. We adjusted something, especially to put more players in front of the box. It was the day after the draw with West Brom, we could have won but after the game, I went to my staff and friends and said, 'The results don't matter . . . I don't recognise my team and the way we play . . . I don't like at all what I'm watching.'"

Guardiola pointed out that while managers and players often think they need to run more when things are going badly, he wanted his men to run less. "We ran too much," he says. "We were not in position, we ran too much, everyone moved right-left, left-right, moving without knowing exactly what we have to do with the ball.

"Our strength is that when we have the ball everybody knows exactly where their team-mates are on the pitch and that helps us to be calmer, use the process.

"Of course I think the team was always ready to fight without the ball, they always had energy, but with the ball, we were not good – just attack, attack, so quick, so quick. Everyone was so quick and in football we have to '*pausa*' and change the rhythm.

"If you play in a high rhythm, then after, you cannot surprise the opponent. We came back a little bit to what we have done in previous seasons, when David Silva was here, with 100 points, 98 points, our game was calmer, in one rhythm to change a little bit (to get faster) in the final third. We came back to those principles and the quality of the players made the rest."

'*Pausa*' is the ability to slow things down, to wait until just the right moment, and then release the ball. David Silva was City's one-man *pausa* machine, regulating the team's tempo, but his influence faded in his final season at the club. Ilkay Gundogan is his natural successor but Guardiola had used him in much deeper positions to help shield the defence since the autumn of the 2019/20 season.

What Guardiola needed to do was develop a way to get the control he had sought for the past 18 months, without sacrificing City's attacking threat. After a summit with director of football Txiki Begiristain, right-hand man Manel Estiarte, assistant coaches Rodolfo Borrell and Juanma Lillo, they established the blueprint that turned City's season around.

Gundogan was suddenly freed from the shackles, allowed to make forward runs – and the goals followed. Joao Cancelo, a regular creator of chances from left-back earlier in the season, became an inverted right-back, charged with moving through the lines and joining De Bruyne and Gundogan in advanced midfield positions. Suddenly the opposition had far more to worry about on the edge of their area, and the burden of creativity lifted from De Bruyne's shoulders.

Although Guardiola said in February that one of the key reasons for City's upturn in form was having "wingers high and wide" with Sterling having moved back to the right, Riyad Mahrez's performances have ensured that inverted wingers, one of the dreaded schemes from the autumn, are not entirely a thing of the past.

Oleksandr Zinchenko held the fort at the back alongside the already solid Dias-John Stones axis and helped Rodri in midfield by adding those extra passes that Guardiola craves, giving the team control. City had, almost immediately, re-established that *pausa* that is central to his entire football philosophy.

When Guardiola talks about slowing the game down, he was not lying: City's speed of attacks are slower, in terms of ball advancement towards goal in metres per second, than at any point in his reign, and indeed slower than any other Premier League team this season.

The sheer number of passes – over short spaces – organises the team, ensuring the players are in the right positions to attack and to defend against counterattacks. Faster passes, at the right moment, destabilise the opposition and open up spaces to exploit. If one word sums up City's reversal of fortunes it is patience, and if there is one fixture that sums up their resurgence it is Leicester.

In September, City lost 5-2 at home. In April, they won 2-0 away. "After leading 1-0 (at home), we became nervous, we wanted to score immediately, we wanted to attack quicker than we should attack," Guardiola reflected at the King Power. "We gave them the chance to let them run and after we conceded three penalties. In these kinds of games when the opponent decides to play deep and make the counter, you have to be patient. They are patient to make us impatient, and this is a big, big mistake."

Patience is also a word that sums up Foden's season. First, because he had to wait for his opportunities earlier in the season and is now one of the first names on the team sheet, but also because he is one of City's best players at changing the rhythm and capitalising on their methodical build-up.

Earlier in the campaign, he was trying to force the issue in a way that fans were crying out for given the generally stodgy performances. That wasn't what Guardiola wanted and Foden missed games against Liverpool and Manchester United. Now that everybody is on the same wavelength, the 20-year-old is a vital member of the team, often lighting up City's performances.

And yet, this is not quite the most sparkling of Guardiola's City teams, and the manager would not dispute that. In fact, that has been his intention. Although it is fair to say that their early-season performances and lack of a truly clinical finisher have hampered their 'goals for' column, Guardiola is much happier to sit on a 1-0 lead and then control the game carefully than perhaps at any point of his career, playing or managerial.

That much has been made especially clear in City's Champions League knockout ties against Borussia Dortmund and Paris Saint-Germain. In both away games, they fell behind but rallied without losing their composure. And once they had equalised in Dortmund, with an away goal in the bag that gave them a 3-2 aggregate lead, they played short, safe passes to feet, knowing they were in the ascendancy. At the right time, De Bruyne made a burst forward, won a corner, and Foden scored from the edge of the box.

Their crowning as Premier League champions was merely a formality, but they continue to evolve and at the end of May, they could achieve Champions League immortality. And although Guardiola has made any doubts about his ability look foolish, he will always direct praise towards his players and staff, without whom this latest triumph would not have been possible.

A

On the Wembley pitch, after City beat Tottenham in the Carabao Cup final, two of the most important men in City's season recorded a short video. "Look at this, Wembley with the captain, with my captain, my man."

At this point, Estiarte, Guardiola's long-term confidante, plants a kiss on the side of Fernandinho's head. He had been speaking in Spanish up until this point, but he switches to English to say, "I love you."

Fernandinho, every inch the City captain this season, joins in the Spanish. "We're making history here, eh?" he says. "We came to foreign lands to make history, and we'll never stop."

Estiarte has been described as City's 'gatekeeper', the man who stands between Guardiola's squad and the tidal wave of requests that come their way from the club's media and marketing departments. Described by CEO Ferran Soriano as "pretty inflexible", Estiarte's job is to preserve harmony in the dressing room and ensure the players are looked after as much as possible, and if that means others on the outside don't get their way, that's no problem.

It is no wonder, then, that Fernandinho has become so beloved by the management team. The Brazilian's importance over the years speaks for itself and his performances were fundamental to Guardiola's first successes at City. But this season, he has taken on huge responsibility off the pitch as club captain and has helped run a very tight ship.

"We have an incredible captain to guide and lead the rest of the players, he helps me to do a job I cannot do," Guardiola said in the midst of City's 21-game winning streak. "He does it for me, and that's why we can maintain this run."

The 35-year-old has started fewer games than in any of his eight seasons in Manchester, but his value in the dressing room has never been higher.

"If the manager misses something, if a player is upset, he'll see that in a player and he'll come and see how they're doing," Foden has said. "That's why he's the captain this year: because he's a great player and a great person."

His most famous intervention was the one that helped turn the team's entire season around, the mid-season meeting where he told his team-mates that they were not doing enough.

Around the time that Guardiola met with his trusted inner circle, City's first-team team delegate told the players before training one day that there would be a meeting. They expected to hear from the boss. Instead, it was Fernandinho.

There was a theory at the time that Fernandinho was simply passing on a message from Guardiola, perhaps because the squad would be more receptive to listening to one of their friends than the manager, whose dour mood earlier in the season had concerned a couple of players.

Fernandinho's recent article in *The Players' Tribune* lends credence to that idea. "Pep came and spoke to me as captain, as the leader of the team. He was blunt. He told me that not everyone was at 100 per cent. He was right. And he made it clear that the responsibility for keeping those standards rested with me."

Fernandinho told the players that their standards had slipped and that they needed to train hard if they were to play hard. "I told them what Pep had told me, that some things are inexcusable. I told them that what you do in training reflects back at you later on in the game.

"It was very frank, very honest. After me, all the others spoke their minds too. Everyone already knew we needed to change, but we needed to hear it said. We needed to be shaken. And it was important that we talked."

Guardiola also had fresh impetus. Lillo, his old mentor at the end of his playing days, arrived at City last summer and has proven invaluable since. Since losing Domenec Torrent and Mikel Arteta, Guardiola needed somebody who could spot things during matches that he could not, and to offer solutions. Lillo fits that brief, but he has also helped lift the Catalan's spirits, "especially in the bad moments", by reminding him of the team's virtues and providing him with new ideas. "Without him, being where we are in the table would have been impossible," Guardiola said in January, with City back on top of the league.

Along with a happier Guardiola and armed with tactical changes, the players' meeting has been held up as the turning point in a season that had been heading in a very different direction.

Some foundations were already in place, however. Fernandinho's influence had been noted well before City's form picked up – players were discussing it in November, very much during their slump – and the defence had already been shored up, with Dias helping to pull things together on and off the pitch.

Still just 23, Dias' role in the dressing room has also been vital. Upon arriving at City, he did not change the approach that made him one of Benfica's most vocal and commanding players, immediately imposing his personality on a new and more gilded group of players.

Guardiola has always been keen on bringing in motivational speakers to give the squad a boost, but with COVID-19 restrictions, that has been impossible. Dias cannot replicate the role of an external voice with an inspiring personal story, but he is continually trying to gee up his team-mates, encouraging them to stay together and work as a team.

"He's a central defender that leads the lines and leads the other ones. He helps the other ones take good decisions, and that is when you become an incredible central defender," Guardiola says of the defensive lynchpin. "There are incredible players who think just in their business, but he thinks about the business of the other ones, even the holding midfielders. He makes his partner better and this is so difficult to find in world football."

Dias and Stones have formed a close bond, working out together in the gym (as far as COVID-19 protocols allow) and that has been reflected in their on-pitch performances, with City recording 12 clean sheets in 18 games between Boxing Day and the end of February.

That relationship, with their on-pitch fist bumps, has summed up the unity that has formed within the squad as the season progressed and the wins racked up. When Zinchenko blocked a Neymar shot in the semi-final second leg, both central defenders converged on him to share the love – before breaking off to thwart a short corner.

"That relationship is a reflection of the relationship within City itself," Dias says. "It's that feeling of, 'No matter what you do, I'll be there for you'. You'll always have a guy next to you, ready to help you, ready to fight for you."

One particular Fernandinho implementation has had a hand in that, too. Always protective over even the most anodyne dressing-room secrets, the Brazilian has established something of a 'code of honour' this season, helping City to clamp down on leaks and ensuring that sensitive information stays in-house.

Certain information is always bound to filter out, of course (and it has done), but there has been a noticeable effort this season and even positive interactions between players are off-limits to anybody outside the group, often including the squad's friends and family. Instructions like that have helped foster a mentality in the team that has seen them pull away from all challengers domestically and, perhaps, in Europe too.

Guardiola has always tried to instil a collective mindset in his players – his insistence that players do not complain when they do not play is designed to maintain a happy, competitive group – and this season he has had Fernandinho enforcing that.

It has helped bring everybody together after a trying 2019/20 campaign and the early months of this season, in which pre-season only started 16 days after the bitter disappointment of Champions League elimination against Lyon.

Camaraderie, in the typical football sense, has not been easy to come by, though. COVID-19 restrictions mean players have had "very little interaction", according to one source. The City squad, for example, get changed into their kit at home, shower individually at the training ground (last year they had to shower at home) and take food away with them for the evening and breakfast the next day, as well as also taking kit to change into for the next session.

It had also been commonplace for players' friends and helpers to join them at the training ground, but that is now forbidden. Flights that players and Guardiola used to take to see friends and families overseas are also off-limits, thanks to COVID-19 but also the unrelenting calendar.

Other than team meetings, themselves split into smaller groups, and training sessions, the players cannot socialise how they did previously. Unlike at the start of the pandemic, team video calls no longer happen but between WhatsApp messages, travel, hotel stays and match days, the group has managed to stay close, and they have been almost swept along by the winning run that took off in the New Year.

Benjamin Mendy, a peripheral figure on the pitch, has been key for morale with his relentless quest to have fun and he has impressed coaches by continuing to be happy and supportive even when left out of the team, wishing his mates good luck and offering hugs and advice.

Not all of his team-mates have the same attitude and it would not be accurate to say that it has all been smooth sailing, however. Just like the last time City won the title in 2018/19 there have been bumps along the way. Back then, Mendy fell foul of Guardiola for not taking rehab seriously, while Leroy Sane and

Mahrez were left out of matchday squads for falling short of the manager's standards. Still, there was an overriding harmony within that squad that ensured those problems did not cause any major disruptions, even with De Bruyne out for much of the campaign.

This time around it has been a similar story. When Aymeric Laporte lost his place in the team in November, a meeting was held with the club and the upshot was that they started looking for a new centre-back, just in case one was needed. The Frenchman has steadily worked his way back into the reckoning and has recaptured something like his best form, although his reactions to being left out these days are hardly Mendy-esque.

Cancelo had a similar dip after being left out of the game against Dortmund in Germany, sources close to Aguero insist he is not entirely happy at how his exit from the club has been handled and then there's Sterling. The winger reacted angrily to losing his place in the team following defeat in March's Manchester derby, moving Guardiola to send a veiled message in a post-match interview and then leaving him out of the squad for an away game at Fulham. Sterling has lost his place to Foden but has continued to have opportunities when Guardiola has rotated his squad, although sources indicate that the relationship has been frosty ever since. Yet none of this has even come close to derailing City's season, no matter what happens in Europe.

Vincent Kompany and Fabian Delph always had big roles in rallying the team, even while not playing, and City missed that last season. This time around Fernandinho has picked up a lot of the slack, alongside Mendy. Dias has added fresh leadership while De Bruyne and Kyle Walker, who upped their game in this respect last season to limited success, have been joined by Stones and Zinchenko in offering words (and shouts!) of encouragement.

With Guardiola refreshed and the players together, the real Manchester City are back.

PEP GUARDIOLA WAS SUPPOSED TO COMPROMISE HIS PRINCIPLES, BUT HE CONQUERED THE PREMIER LEAGUE BY STAYING TRUE TO THEM

OLIVER KAY

MAY 12, 2021

Even now, there are people who will not be persuaded of Pep Guardiola's coaching talents until, like someone who has grown bored of world domination on Football Manager, he has resigned from his job at Manchester City and shown he can win titles with Burnley, Mainz or Real Valladolid.

It sounds rather like demanding that Michelangelo prove himself by painting a masterpiece on the ceiling of a village hall or for Martin Scorsese to demonstrate he can coax Oscar-winning performances out of a local amateur dramatics group.

True, it would be a fascinating experiment, finding out whether Guardiola could teach Burnley to play a possession-based game with no orthodox centre-forward and without the option of buying full-backs from Real Madrid, Monaco or Juventus at great expense if Matthew Lowton and Charlie Taylor didn't measure up to his requirements at full-back. But . . . we're back to Michelangelo, Scorsese and the sheer silliness of being unable to appreciate brilliance unless it is brought down from such heights and reproduced in an earthier, less rarefied environment.

That was meant to be the Premier League, wasn't it? They might tell you differently now, but there were a lot of people, sceptical of his achievements with Barcelona and Bayern Munich, who were convinced English football would expose his shortcomings. And now, after five seasons and three Premier League titles (plus one FA Cup, four League Cups and countless broken records, with a Champions League final to come later this month), they shrug their shoulders and ask why anyone should have expected any different when a manager has spent more than £880 million (more than £560 million net) on a squad that already included Fernandinho, David Silva, Kevin De Bruyne, Raheem Sterling and Sergio Aguero when he arrived in 2016.

There is something revisionist about all this, though. There were certainly a lot of doubts expressed about Guardiola when he first took over at City. It was widely agreed that, while his methods had worked to spectacular effect in La Liga and the Bundesliga, he was in for a shock when he came to the Premier League. There was no shortage of pundits, columnists and phone-in hosts peddling the 'cold Tuesday night in Stoke' theory back then. Even sages such as Arsene Wenger, Manuel Pellegrini and Jurgen Klopp suggested the former Barcelona and Bayern would find himself tested like never before.

Those doubts increased during a challenging first season in which Guardiola took a sledgehammer – actually no, make that a scalpel – to English football orthodoxy. He jettisoned England's goalkeeper, Joe Hart, because he wanted his last line of defence to be the first line of his attack. He left out Yaya Toure in order to play Kevin De Bruyne and David Silva alongside Fernandinho in midfield. In possession and in positioning, he made his defenders take risks far beyond anything they had done before. This was football, but not as we in England knew it.

A

Results in Guardiola's first season at Manchester City were disappointing. His team gained 12 more points than they had under Pellegrini the previous year, but they came a distant third, 15 points behind Antonio Conte's Chelsea. By mid-January they had lost five Premier League matches, including 4-2 at Leicester City and 4-0 at Everton, and there was much talk of how, unlike Conte at Chelsea and Jose Mourinho at Manchester United, he had misunderstood what was needed in English football.

There was an episode of Sky Sports' *Monday Night Football* show towards the end of that season when Gary Neville and Jamie Carragher made what seemed entirely reasonable points about what Guardiola's City team lacked. Claudio Bravo, who had replaced Hart in goal, was a concern. Carragher questioned whether De Bruyne and Silva, for all their obvious talent, had the power and strength to play in central midfield and whether perhaps a Toure type – or indeed Toure himself, who had struggled to win Guardiola's favour – might be needed.

Neville went through a long list of title-winning teams, from his own Manchester United side of the 1990s and 2000s to the great Arsenal, Chelsea and indeed City teams of the past, and pointed out how "every single team that has won the league, barring none, has had power and strength at the heart of them, that spine". To attempt to win the title without that physicality and resilience at the heart of the team "would defy Premier League logic," he said, "having to wade through those winter months and playing those horrible games that we know exist. Can you win a league playing that way?"

This was not an insular or isolated view. Guardiola himself had admitted to being taken aback by some aspects of English football. In one press conference he explained how he had been stunned while watching Swansea City beat Crystal Palace 5-4. "Nine goals, eight from set-pieces – corners, free-kicks, throw-ins," he said, shaking his head. "That is English football and I have to adapt because never before have I lived that."

Everyone expected Guardiola to compromise in year two: to invest in physical strength, as Conte and Mourinho had done from the start to widespread approval. Guardiola didn't do that. To a team that was felt to have a soft centre, he added Ederson, Kyle Walker, Danilo, Benjamin Mendy and Bernardo Silva, an outlay of more than £240 million in one summer – so yes, plenty of ammunition for the 'chequebook manager' crowd there – but one that still seemed, to use Neville's phrase, to "defy Premier League logic".

There was no compromise. For all the desperation to create a different narrative, nodding knowingly on those occasions whenever Ederson hit the ball long, City played an even lower proportion of long passes (six per cent) in Guardiola's second season than in his first (eight per cent) – and, needless to say, far lower than any other Premier League. From an average of 60.9 per cent possession per game in 2016/17, which was already the highest in the league, they recorded an average of 66.4 per cent in 2017/18. To put these figures in context, the average possession figures for the previous eight title-winning teams had ranged from a high of 56.9 per cent (Chelsea in 2009/10) to a low of 44.7 per cent (Leicester in 2015/16).

And then there was the football they played. In 2015/16, their final season under Pellegrini, they scored 71 goals in 38 Premier League games. In their first season under Guardiola, they scored 80. In his second campaign, they scored 106. It was a leap comparable to that at Barcelona (from 76 goals in La Liga the season before, under Frank Rijkaard, to 105 in Guardiola's first year in charge despite having offloaded Deco and Ronaldinho, two of the team's main creative forces).

Over City's back-to-back title-winning seasons of 2017/18 and 2018/19 – the first won by a landslide margin, the second involving an almighty tussle with Liverpool in which neither side seemed to give an inch – City won 64 Premier League games out of 76, taking 198 points from a possible 228. Prior to that, the best back-to-back figures in English football were Mourinho's Chelsea team, who recorded 58 wins and 186 points across the 2004/05 and 2005/06 seasons. Chelsea scored 144 goals in the process. City scored 201.

And then last season they regressed severely, left trailing in Liverpool's wake, unable to sustain the excellence of the previous two campaigns, and at last the nay-sayers were able to say, "We told you so." There were still times when they overwhelmed the opposition with their free-flowing football, as a record of 102 goals in 38 Premier League matches indicates, but nine defeats told a certain story. Losing several games while having more than 70 per cent of the possession (to United twice, Wolverhampton Wanderers and Southampton, as well as to Arsenal in the FA Cup semi-final and Lyon in an error-strewn Champions League quarter-final) led to suggestions that Guardiola had been 'found out'.

That argument persisted well into this season, as did the feeling that both Guardiola and City might be in need of a change. In February last year I wrote a column questioning whether, having seen his team's performance drop significantly in his fourth season in charge, he would have the motivation and the energy to oversee the next stage of City's development given that Vincent Kompany had left, David Silva was about to depart, Sergio Aguero and Fernandinho would not be far behind and there was a feeling, as in 2017, that the foundations of this team just didn't look strong enough.

Guardiola looked jaded and disillusioned, in need of the type of break that last summer simply did not allow. His contract was to expire at the end of this season and, after an alarmingly slow start to the new campaign, there were even City supporters and staff members who began to wonder whether a change might be in everyone's interests.

City were tenth in the Premier League last November, with 12 points and just 10 goals from their first seven matches, when the club announced that he had extended his deal to the end of the 2022/23 season. Two days later they were beaten 2-0 by Mourinho's Tottenham Hotspur, another of those games when City had so much of the ball but were picked off easily on the counter-attack. As *The Athletic*'s Sam Lee wrote after a 1-1 draw at home to West Bromwich Albion in mid-December, they hadn't looked like City – or at least not Guardiola's City – for months.

And yet here we are, less than five months later, congratulating them on their third Premier League title in four seasons. Would that outcome really have been so surprising back in December? Not really, given that the inconsistencies of others had ensured their deficit was a small one (and this before Liverpool's drastic loss of form after Christmas), but what really stands out is the scale of City's resurgence. Since mid-December they have played 23 Premier League games and won 20 of them. Extend that record to all competitions and it is 33 wins out of 37.

Clearly that enormous transfer budget is a highly significant factor. City might not generally buy at the very top end of the transfer market, but when a club's four central defenders have been signed for a combined total of £210 million, their three full-backs signed in deals valued at a combined £160 million and so on, it is hardly a feat of alchemy on the scale of, say, Brian Clough taking Nottingham Forest from the depths of the second tier and making them champions of England and then (twice) Europe.

Guardiola himself has suggested in press conferences that the main reason for their success is having "a lot of money to buy a lot of incredible players." When asked if he was being sarcastic or self-deprecating, he insisted not. "You can win one title with average players, but to win a lot of titles you need top, top, top players," he said in February. "And top players cost a lot of money. That was my reflection. So when Bayern Munich or Barcelona or Real Madrid or United or Juventus or AC Milan or Glasgow Celtic or Rangers win more titles, it is because they have more money than other clubs."

Guardiola makes it sound like he subscribes to the Soccernomics theory of football management. In their 2009 book, Stefan Szymanski and Simon Kuper argued that the influence of managers and coaches was "statistically insignificant" and that most of the variation in league performance could be explained by wage spending. Those managers that were acknowledged to be "statistically significant", which included Sir Alex Ferguson at United, only improved league performance by a small amount.

To some extent, that is true. The correlation between expenditure and success is clear, if not always as certain as *Soccernomics* suggests. But the theory seems flawed. United's expenditure in the eight years since Ferguson's retirement has not been far short of City's (£746 million net according to Transfermarkt) and far, far greater than when the Scot was in charge, yet they have not come close to challenging for a Premier League title over that time. Whether it relates to vision, authority, man-management, motivation, ability on the training pitch or strategic skill, the difference between the very best coaches and the rest can be enormous.

Much is said about the talent that Guardiola inherited at Barcelona (notably Xavi Hernandez, Andres Iniesta, Lionel Messi) but this was a team that came third in La Liga with 67 points under Frank Rijkaard in 2007/08. Guardiola came in, controversially ditched Deco and Ronaldinho and introduced a high-energy, high-risk style which saw them win La Liga with

87 points and 105 goals in his first season in charge as well as winning the Champions League. The season after that, it was 99 points. There was another league title and another Champions League the year after that. It didn't take them long in Spain to appreciate that this was a coach with an ability to liberate and elevate top-class players – and the football they played – to stratospheric levels.

You can suggest, as Syzmanski and Kuper might, that Barcelona's and Manchester City expenditure was such that they were expected to compete for and win the biggest prizes no matter which established coach they had in charge of their team. There is of course plenty of truth in that. But you can also look at the scale of the individual and collective improvement, as well as the daring, enterprising, innovative nature of their football, and suggest this was a coach doing far more than merely what was to be expected with a big squad full of great players.

As Matt Dickinson wrote in *The Times* this week, "Money buys you the world's best attacking goalkeeper, the defensive prowess of Ruben Dias, the ball-playing beauty of Kevin De Bruyne and Riyad Mahrez and the rest of the brilliant collective . . . but such wealth does not guarantee you singular creativity or the type of original thought that comes along so rarely, perhaps once in a generation. It does not automatically buy you relentless, almost insanely driven perfectionism."

That is what City got when they hired Guardiola. Pellegrini led them to a Premier League title, two League Cups and even a Champions League semi-final, but there was a feeling at the top of the club that, whereas the Chilean's team had been reliant on off-the-cuff brilliance, Guardiola would be transformative. Five years later, that appraisal has been more than vindicated.

There was no shortage of suggestions in the opening months of this season that the Guardiola effect had worn off, that he had stayed too long and run out of ideas. Could he re-energise this team? Did he have a new trick now that Plan A seemed to have stopped working? Could he organise a defence now that he no longer had Vincent Kompany to build around? Where were the goals going to come from? Did he have the patience and the vision to rebuild this team, given that John Stones, Joao Cancelo, Rodri and others didn't seem to be measuring up to the required standard?

He has answered all those questions, rehabilitating Stones in central defence alongside the formidable Dias, encouraging Cancelo to play with more creative freedom from full-back, integrating the capricious young talent of Foden, subtly changing De Bruyne's role from one game to the next and frequently operating without a recognised centre-forward. At a time when he was under pressure to come up with solutions and answer questions of a type he had never faced before, Guardiola has come up with the answers week after week after week.

And they are never the obvious answers. Much of the time they are counter-intuitive – or at least they were until his success made us far more open-minded to false-nines, inverted wingers and goalkeepers who are as comfortable with the ball at their feet as in their hands. Think of all those times he was warned he was going to have to adapt to the Premier League. Instead he has bent English football to his own vision and will.

Even in the Champions League, where he was frequently accused of overthinking as City kept falling short in his first four seasons in charge, Guardiola has succeeded by staying true to everything he believes in. Even when they were 1-0 down to Paris Saint-Germain at half-time in the semi-final first leg, having been comprehensively outplayed, he urged his players to stick to their principles and their "identity with and without the ball." They did that. Their second-half performance, which saw a notable tweak with the introduction of Oleksandr Zinchenko at left-back, was magnificent and they won 2-1.

In a recent interview with ESPN Brazil, Guardiola said that when he first arrived in the Premier League, "it was very direct, very box-to-box, a lot of challenges. We didn't try to do any of that. You can say, yes, that we did things our way. That is safe to say. We did it our way."

They have. If City's ongoing success has been a victory for a certain type of ownership model, it also represents another triumph for Guardiola over English football orthodoxy and thus another valuable lesson for a country that likes to give the impression it has forgotten more about the game than the rest of the world will ever know.

And yes of course it would be intriguing to see how he would cope with a lesser group of players. Would it frustrate him? Quite feasibly. Is he like the most brilliant university professor, better suited to working with high-fliers? Almost certainly. But when he keeps delivering results like this, he can afford to keep cherry-picking the best jobs.

As for whether he will ever tire of winning trophy after trophy and settle for a different type of challenge, rival supporters will certainly hope so. But in real life, rather than a computer simulation, it tends not to work like that.

RUBEN DIAS, PLAYER OF THE YEAR AND A MANCHESTER CITY CAPTAIN IN ALL BUT NAME

SAM LEE

MAY 20, 2021

We love a good narrative in the media so it's no surprise that Ruben Dias, the man who has had the most apparent impact on Manchester City's season, has won the Football Writers' Association Player of the Year award (to add to his *Athletic* award from earlier this week).

It is a prize that often goes to the league's standout entertainer, with previous deserved winners including Cristiano Ronaldo, Luis Suarez, Gareth Bale, Mohamed Salah, but there can be room for a general, for one of the warriors that we love in the English game. Like Scott Parker in 2011, famously, or Jordan Henderson last year, when the players themselves chose Bale and Kevin De Bruyne instead.

And it's that side to the 24-year-old's game that has seduced so many this season, the way he has galvanised a team that dropped below the required standard last year. He is almost a throwback, a centre-back that does prize clean sheets above clean shorts, somebody only too happy to get stuck in, to put his head in where the boots are flying.

We love a bit of that in this country, it's why we demand passion and energy from our England players while the Spaniards and the French are busy passing the ball to each other. The beauty of Pep Guardiola's City team is that they have both qualities, and it's Dias who has provided the steel.

Interestingly, De Bruyne was the favourite for this season's PFA award until very recently, and the fact he won it last year despite Liverpool's phenomenal season goes to show that sheer technical ability often wins the day, especially when the title-winning side does not have a standout player.

That is exactly the situation with City this year: their success has been built on a collective team effort, with no one player standing out far above the others, even De Bruyne. In fact, the Belgian isn't even among the three nominees for City's own player of the season award, which is quite something.

Ilkay Gundogan and Riyad Mahrez are the ones alongside Dias, which goes to show how many players have had outstanding seasons for the club (full disclosure, I would've voted for Gundogan had I been a member). Phil Foden, Bernardo Silva and John Stones could quite easily be added to that list as well.

And there were other eye-catching candidates elsewhere that could have denied Dias his recognition. It is a small sample size, but of five votes cast by *Evening Standard* journalists, two went to Dias, but two went to Harry Kane and one to Bruno Fernandes. Those other two players have carried their teams in the classic Roy of the Rovers style that we also seem to love on these shores.

It's not typically an award that City players win, either, as fans and players at the club have noticed. Raheem Sterling did win it in 2019, partly in recognition for speaking out against racial injustice, but in previous title-winning seasons the prizes went to Robin van Persie, Suarez and Salah.

Yet nobody could match Dias' compelling story this time around. The fact that City conceded five goals at home to

Leicester in the last game before he signed for the club sums it up quite nicely. They weren't great to watch for a couple of months after that, but they were more defensively solid at least. Then things clicked, they stormed to the Premier League title and now, with a more robust team than they have had under Guardiola, they could win the Champions League too.

They have gone from defensively naive to impenetrable, and a run of seven consecutive league clean sheets in January only backed that up. His impact has been likened to Virgil van Dijk's at Liverpool, although the towering Dutchman never won this particular award, surprising as that may be.

Stones looks like a new man, too, something else that Dias receives credit for, although it is impossible to know just how much. Stones himself clearly deserves praise for taking charge of his own situation, and similarly, Guardiola's role in turning around City cannot be ignored: his tactical changes made the team more potent and less susceptible to counter-attacks, so Dias has not been subjected to the same exposure as his predecessors last season.

But he has certainly looked more than comfortable when called into the old-fashioned defensive situations that not every City defender has relished in the past few years. When faced with a one-on-one situation, for example, he'll step back and manage the space behind him while holding up his adversary. He's certainly aggressive, though, and if there's an opportunity to jump in and win the ball back, he will, as Neymar found out in Paris. And for a defence that stays so compact when being attacked, his constant communicating is invaluable.

Guardiola talks about how Dias makes his team-mates play better, by ordering them around the pitch, constantly talking to them. Those who worked with him at Benfica were in no doubt that he would be exactly like this, despite it being his first season in a new country, in a different language, in a dressing room with bigger players and bigger goals, despite being 23 years old.

"He is a guy who lives 24 hours for his profession," Guardiola says. "Everything he does on and off the pitch – eating, sleeping, recovering – is to be perfect for the 95 minutes of the game."

It can be hard to appreciate the ins and outs of what that actually means, but perhaps City fans will get a glimpse on Sunday if they watch him in the warm-up before the game against Everton.

Before one high-profile game this season, while his team-mates were casually knocking the ball about between themselves, he was locked in discussions with Juanma Lillo, Guardiola's assistant, who was gesturing here there and everywhere with his hands, just like the Catalan does.

While the other players were doing their shooting drills, Dias stayed with Lorenzo Buenaventura doing all manner of exercises: staying on his toes in a jockeying position, sending half-volleyed passes back to Guardiola's trusted fitness coach first with his right foot and then his left, heading a ball that had bounced off the ground, heading a ball dropping out of the sky.

It only went on for one or two minutes but, by way of comparison, Stones used that time to help put out some cones. Dias then pinged the crossfield passes that he's been working on in training to Bernardo Silva, dropping them over the shooting drill, before taking part in the pre-match hugs.

Perhaps it was easy to buy into the leadership narrative but it certainly looked, on that day, that his grips were a bit tighter than the others. The whole squad do it, a sign of the unity among them, and Dias grasped Rodri, Gabriel Jesus, Stones and Joao Cancelo, giving them all a high-10 before walking off the pitch with his arm around Bernardo, whispering in his ear.

Not all of the senior City players are regarded as proper leaders in the mould of Vincent Kompany or, as this season has proven, Fernandinho, with players like De Bruyne and Kyle Walker sometimes providing vocal encouragement and/or criticism without the necessary inspiration, but Dias is regarded by his team-mates as a real captain.

They point to the simple things, like the fist bumps and pats on the back after tackles and blocks, little gestures that keep everybody on their toes and feeling motivated. Barking orders, dictating the line, calling out passes, dragging Oleksandr Zinchenko by the head. Those are the things that help make his team-mates better.

He arrived at City after the captains were voted in for the season, but he's regarded as a shoo-in for a place in the leadership group next year. Guardiola changed the voting system last summer and by opening it up to staff at the training ground, there was more variety in those who were put forward. But it is hard to imagine anybody, from players to chefs, overlooking Dias' role in the team.

It has been appreciated inside the club for a while and if any reminders were necessary his performance at the Etihad against Paris Saint-Germain, putting his body on the line as City made the final, provided one. It was also well-timed, coming just as votes were cast.

And now, with the recognition of the country's press, the narrative is firmly established: Ruben Dias is the best and most important player this season.

AGUERO IS HURT AT MANNER OF CITY EXIT BUT PUT IT ASIDE TO DO WHAT HE ALWAYS DOES – SCORE AND SMILE

SAM LEE

MAY 24, 2021

Twenty-five minutes, two goals, the man-of-the-match award, a typically humorous farewell speech and not a dry eye in the house. Even Pep Guardiola was welling up.

In many ways it was the perfect send-off for Sergio Aguero, the only frustration being that he couldn't get a hat-trick! That says a lot about the player he is, and everything he has done for Manchester City.

There's little else that can be said about him now, either – whether his quality or just how much he is revered by the City fans, but somehow Sunday's 5-0 win over Everton provided even more to talk about.

From the first minute, the fans sang his name, and when the time came to introduce him to the action just after the hour mark there was palpable irritation in the stands as Everton picked the most inopportune moment to keep the ball proficiently for the only time on the day.

The way that Riyad Mahrez immediately booted it out of play when City regained possession showed just how much everybody else in the ground wanted Aguero on the pitch.

If it were up to him, he would have another season's worth of days like this in City colours. For all the joy that his performance yesterday brought, for the fairytale goals that added to his legacy and the jubilant celebrations in front of fans once more, there is something of a sadness that accompanies his final weeks as a City player.

It is fair to say that Aguero has not had the happiest of goodbyes, although the situation has improved of late. His final weeks in Manchester have been strangely similar to his first months under Guardiola almost five years ago. If you were to only go by the official statements from those involved (which would be fair enough, really) you'd never know there was even a hint of trouble.

What really went on back then – Guardiola feeling Aguero wasn't the right fit, Aguero fearing he was being forced out – would only make a small footnote in the story of the striker's decade at City by now. And even then it would serve to show how committed he is to the club and to his profession, to put his ego to one side and to rebuild his game. Half of his decade at City has been shaped by what happened in that period. But history has repeated itself in recent weeks.

Going by all the public declarations and gestures, you would never know anything was awry, but several sources close to Aguero have all said that he is not happy with how his exit was handled or indeed the fact he has to make an exit this summer at all. They say that his problem has been with Guardiola, because it was he and he alone who decided there would be no new contract.

The official reason for Aguero not starting against Everton was that he chose to come on in the second half, because he's still not fit enough to play a full 90 minutes and would rather play the end of a game than the start.

Nobody has disputed that being the case, but there have been times in recent weeks, sources say, that Aguero hasn't played for

City despite being perfectly fit to do so, and that both he and the manager have been fine with that.

For a couple of weeks after his exit was confirmed in March, he and Guardiola were not speaking. Yet after he played and scored against Crystal Palace this month, the manager perhaps spoke more warmly about Aguero than he has about any player (except Lionel Messi).

"He is an absolutely top legend, extraordinary player, the most humble human being," Guardiola said. "That's why I love him as a man; another player in his situation could create conflict, a difficult situation, but he was completely the opposite."

Indeed, the 32-year-old has not done or said anything that would cause a problem publicly. He and Guardiola shared a very warm hug on the pitch on Sunday and the manager was emotional when discussing his striker as part of a fitting tribute, which was well received by people close to Aguero. And recent events clearly haven't taken any of the shine off this weekend's send-off.

Aguero was given his mosaic at the training ground, he posed in front of a mural in Manchester city centre and also with all the trophies he has won during his time at City – there might be another one come Saturday night, of course. And that was before his stunning two-goal farewell to the Etihad, which will live long in the memories of the 10,000 people here to witness it.

When addressing the fans on the pitch after the match was won and the latest trophy lifted, he didn't dwell on any low points for a single second. And why would he, when there were so many highs from the last decade that could not possibly be crammed into just five minutes? You could barely describe Sunday's spine-tingling cameo alone in that amount of time.

Not that he was especially lucid anyway. "I remember that day I played shit, I was so bad," he said of his most famous goal, against Queens Park Rangers to clinch the 2011/12 title in the final seconds of the season's final match. What his team-mates love about him most is that he always makes a joke, even in the bad moments.

So maybe none of this matters, other than leaving a bit of a sour taste for the player himself, but maybe it does if you consider that he probably would have stayed had he been given the opportunity, and maybe he could have given City another year of moments like this.

"I was lucky enough to see him on Wednesday," Sky Sports commentator Martin Tyler, he of "AGUEROOOOOO!" fame, said as the striker was given a guard of honour before kick-off. "He's sad to be leaving. I think he would've stayed but the word he used to me was, 'This is business, they want to bring in another striker.'"

Maybe that's why Guardiola was so emotional, because he made a 'cold' decision despite his feelings for the player he is moving on.

There is a possibility that this will all come out in the wash after the season has ended, that Aguero will criticise Guardiola, the greatest manager in the club's history. City figures are concerned he will speak to the Spanish press; Aguero confidantes suggested just last week that he may do.

No doubt, it would be better for everybody if it all blew over, and the way things panned out on Sunday might facilitate that. Another night of celebration in Porto after the Champions League final against Chelsea there next weekend would make things even sweeter.

Aguero wanted to stay at the club, so of course he is bitterly disappointed, and yet on Sunday everything ended just as it always has done with him. All smiles.

GUARDIOLA AND TUCHEL'S MEETINGS IN MUNICH BARS: "IT WAS LIKE WATCHING TWO GRANDMASTERS OF CHESS, LOCKED IN A BATTLE OF WITS"

RAPHAEL HONIGSTEIN

MAY 26, 2021

"At first, they were jabbing each other gently, checking each other out. But then the discussion quickly went to a whole new level. They were discussing moves and tactical changes from games that happened years ago. Pepper mills and wine glasses were being moved around, but most of the time, they were replaying entire games in their heads. I couldn't believe that they remembered the most minute detail. It was like, 'You know when you moved your full-backs inside against Real Madrid in 2009, the second half? Why was that?' and so on.

"It was like watching two grandmasters of chess, Fischer vs Spassky, locked in a battle of wits. Or Cicero and Socrates, discussing football philosophy."

Six years after sharing a table with Pep Guardiola and Thomas Tuchel in Schumann's Bar in central Munich, Michael Reschke still relishes talking about an evening that has become part of Bundesliga folklore. Guardiola, he says, hadn't planned on meeting the recently-departed Mainz coach over champagne and wine spritzers in the most famous bar in town that night. But it wasn't a chance encounter either.

"Pep and I had talked about Thomas shortly after I arrived to work as Bayern's sporting director in 2014," the 63-year-old tells *The Athletic.* "He asked me, 'Who is the most interesting young German coach?' I said, 'Tuchel.' Pep replied, 'Yes! We (Bayern) played against Mainz last season and they actually wanted to win against us! Many teams park the bus and are happy if they don't lose too big. But he really put us under pressure. With Mainz! I have huge respect for him.'"

With the exception of Jurgen Klopp's Borussia Dortmund, most Bundesliga sides had dug in deep in their own half to try to stymie Guardiola's possession game, much to the Catalan's frustration. "If I ever play like that, I'm finished as a coach," he told Reschke, only half in jest.

Against Tuchel's Mainz, though, it had been a different story. Yes, Bayern won both encounters, 4-1 and 2-0, in the previous 2013/14 campaign but did so with much more difficulty than the scorelines suggest.

In Munich, Mainz had led at half-time and shut out the champions' attack with a highly fluid 3-4-3 system that constantly kept adapting to disrupt Bayern's central build-up and create counter-attacking opportunities. (Guardiola responded by overloading the left side with David Alaba and Bastian Schweinsteiger, while Mario Gotze pinned backed defenders on the right). And in the return fixture five months later, Mainz had held their own until they finally conceded in the 82nd and 86th minutes. "It was fun today," Guardiola had said after the final whistle.

"Pep was already Pep, but it's worth remembering that Tuchel wasn't the coach he is today – a DFB Pokal (German Cup) winner with Dortmund, a Champions League finalist with Paris Saint-Germain and Chelsea," Reschke says. "He was a young guy who had coached Mainz for five years and was out of a job, on a sabbatical. But in those couple of games the year before, he had won Pep's attention. More than that, Pep admired him for having a go with a team of rather limited means, and for the precision of his game plan. 'Tuchel always has an answer', he said."

One day, Reschke told Guardiola in passing that he'd arranged to have drinks with Tuchel later on. He had been in contact with Tuchel for a few years, having looked at signing him for Bayer Leverkusen, where he had worked previously as sporting director. Guardiola spontaneously decided to join them at one of Schumann's corner tables that evening (anyone can enter the bar, but only frequent guests are given an actual seat). He was so keen on getting to know Tuchel that he even cancelled a couple of appointments.

The appreciation was mutual. During his time as Mainz coach, Tuchel had flown to Barcelona a couple of times to study Guardiola's team in the flesh. He had read all the Guardiola biographies as well. There was initially a 'master and apprentice' feel to their get-together, with Tuchel asking all the questions, and Guardiola replying in great depth. But after a while, the roles were reversed as they began to discuss their craft as equals.

"I like to talk about football myself quite a lot but I don't think I got a word in," says Reschke. "I was a mere spectator. They were speaking in a mixture of German and English, and didn't use any scientific terms at all, but it was still hard to keep up with them at times. They could recall dozens and dozens of specific situations from ages ago and talked through how things might have panned out differently if there had been any changes. It was all about actions and reactions.

"They were so wrapped up in their discussions that other people in the bar and even the waiters didn't dare approach them. They were in a bubble, for nearly four hours."

A few weeks later, the trio met for a second time, at Munich restaurant Brenner. This was a slightly more relaxed evening but just as intense in terms of the football debates, as a fourth attendee noted. Reschke had invited Peter Hermann, a Bayern assistant who had worked under former coach Jupp Heynckes, to join the party.

The hugely experienced now-69-year-old had been part of three Champions League finals (with Bayer Leverkusen in 2002 and in 2012 and 2013 with Bayern) but later confessed to Reschke that listening in on Guardiola and Tuchel felt like an epiphany. "He thanked me and said he called his wife to tell her that he was quitting football, the next morning," Reschke laughs. "Why? 'I always thought I knew a little bit about football,' he said. 'But I'm no longer so sure . . . These guys are in a different league.'"

Reschke had experienced a similar moment with Guardiola a few months earlier when the two of them had travelled to Italy to see Roma play ahead of a Champions League group game against Bayern. "It was crazy. Pep spoke of each team's strengths and weaknesses before kick-off and the match went exactly the way he had predicted. Later that week, he allowed me to sit in on the team meeting. Many of the moves and situations he had anticipated played out (when Bayern eventually played Roma), as if he had scripted it. It was incredible." Bayern annihilated Roma 7-1 in the Stadio Olimpico that night, in one of the most accomplished performances of Guardiola's three-year reign.

Guardiola and Tuchel share many similarities, Reschke believes. "They're both very demanding of their players and get on best with players who think as deeply about the game as they do," he says. "Those who simply want to play their own football tend to struggle. Tactically, both want to dominate. The starting point is always, 'How can we score a goal?' Thomas's way is slightly more technocratic, Pep's more arty."

Guardiola was so convinced of Tuchel's coaching qualities he urged Reschke to make him his successor in Munich. "He said, 'You have to bring him to Bayern!'"

Reschke, Tuchel and Bayern president Uli Hoeness did meet in Munich, but the timing wasn't right.

As for Saturday's Champions League final, Reschke predicts a "great battle" that will bring out the best of both of them. "Pep gets excited when there are games at a very high level, against special opponents or coaches, and Thomas has already shown that he can beat him this season. It's funny to think they will meet in Porto to contest the biggest trophy in club football after those fun nights in Munich. I'm pleased for them."

Maybe they'll find the time to toast the winner and console the loser after the final whistle.

IT'S GUARDIOLA'S NATURE TO TRY SOMETHING DIFFERENT IN A BIG CHAMPIONS LEAGUE GAME. HE JUST CAN'T HELP HIMSELF

SAM LEE

MAY 30, 2021

You know the fable about the frog and the scorpion, don't you? Long story short, the frog gives the scorpion a ride across the lake, and halfway through the scorpion stings him. "But scorpion," says the frog, "You promised you wouldn't sting me, now we're both going to drown." "Sorry," replied the scorpion, "but it is in my nature, dear frog."

And so it is Pep Guardiola's nature to try something different in a big Champions League game. He just cannot help himself, can he? From the first couple of defeats with Bayern Munich, to Monaco, Liverpool, Tottenham, Lyon (bloody Lyon!) and now Chelsea with Manchester City, there's always been something. And yet, in some of those games he has been unlucky, too – if not on Saturday night in Porto.

Guardiola, though, must feel he is damned if he does, and damned if he doesn't because, while he and Manchester City have got much, much closer, there's always something.

— **A** —

275

Perhaps one of the most intriguing things about Guardiola's history in this competition is that in the 10 years since he last guided a team to a European final, there are two defeats that affected him more than the others, and they couldn't be much further apart, chronologically. The first bad one was in his first season at Bayern Munich, when he famously abandoned his ideas in the semi-finals and adopted a more German, gung-ho approach. "A complete fuck up," he called it. "Such a dreadful defeat will stay with me forever, mentally and emotionally," he said at the time.

He was described as a "broken man", so affected by the 5-0 aggregate defeat at the hands of old foes Real Madrid in April 2014 – including 4-0 at home in the second leg – that the Bayern players wondered whether he would be OK, and chairman Karl-Heinz Rummenigge's wife was concerned for his well-being. Guardiola also felt the need to apologise to Philipp Lahm, his captain, during an hour-long heart-to-heart at the training ground.

The other one was last season after City lost 3-1 to Lyon in that pandemic-enforced one-off quarter-final. Far from gung-ho, he shut up shop. Three centre-backs and two holding midfielders. It hurt him so much, sources close to him say, because he recognised he had made a mistake in his selection. At least they created good chances, though.

"I cannot forget the big disappointment personally against Lyon, the support I had from my chairman," Guardiola said recently while praising Khaldoon Al Mubarak's role at City, letting slip his feelings about that game for the first time.

So one wonders how long Saturday night will stay with him. As he answered questions about his selection, the roar of the Chelsea fans could be heard as opposite number Thomas Tuchel lifted the trophy above his head. Brutal.

And if the 'overthinking' narrative was not firmly intertwined in the story of Guardiola's career after that crushing disappointment against Lyon last August, it will be now for eternity.

The idea that he overthinks the game is "absolute fucking nonsense!" according to Michael Reschke, Bayern's technical director when Guardiola was manager of the Bundesliga giants. Domenec Torrent, the Catalan's long-time trusted assistant, says he doesn't think too much about the big games, but about every game. "When we play a friendly – a friendly! – in pre-season, he does the same. He's incapable of going into a game, even a friendly, without watching and knowing how they play."

He probably overthought Bayern's 3-2 aggregate win over Benfica in the 2015/16 quarter-finals too, when he believed the Portuguese side to be so good that he hunched over his laptop for so long, analysing 10 of their previous matches, he put his back out. And not too much attention is paid now to that Sergio Aguero-Kevin De Bruyne switch in Madrid, with Gabriel Jesus operating as something of a left wing-back, because Guardiola's team won, 2-1. The false-nine system is the accepted winning formula now, too.

Even so, Thomas Muller's theory about his old Bayern boss, provided 18 months ago, does seem to have been given credence by what City have been through this season: the highs and, now, the lows.

"In knockout games, Pep pays a lot of attention to the opponents and their strengths," Bayern forward Muller told *The Athletic*. "He's always a little torn between paying extreme attention and respect to the strengths of the opposition – more so than against smaller teams – and sticking to his convictions and to a system he believes in, to go, 'We will play with that risk because that's who we are.'"

— **A** —

In this season's knockout ties, City strolled past Borussia Monchengladbach as you might expect, but then they did the same against Borussia Dortmund and Paris Saint-Germain, too.

They were patient and they were so confident in themselves they weren't too bothered by falling behind in two of those games, which has been a big problem in the past.

The only questions ahead of the final were Joao Cancelo or Oleksandr Zinchenko, Rodri or Fernandinho. Cancelo was too adventurous with his passes in the first leg against Dortmund on a night when City needed to be patient. Zinchenko was much more careful but also smooth; he helped City build their game better.

Both holding midfielders played in the away win over Crystal Palace at the beginning of this month and Guardiola decided during the game that, actually, he wanted Fernandinho for the second leg against PSG three days later. Rodri had given the ball away too many times in the first leg in Paris, he was rushing things. It wasn't the first time in the Champions League this season, which is odd (telling?) as he's been so assured in the league.

So it was all about keeping hold of the ball, really, and the only questions regarding the line-up related to which 11 players could keep the ball best. That had been the criteria for the quarter-final second leg in Dortmund – he said it himself. He stuck with it for PSG, because you would do, surely?

"The closer you are to who you are, the more chance you have of going through," Guardiola said before winning in the first leg, 2-1, in France. "Not when you are thinking about the opponent. It's about what you do. I want to be ourselves. That is my wish."

Why, then, pick a team for the final to abandon all of that? *All of it.* Not just changing some of the players (which begs plenty of questions in its own right) but the entire blueprint.

The thing is, Guardiola knows more about football than anybody reading this article, and that certainly includes this writer. He could sit us all down and explain to us what he really wanted, with all the little details that he spotted about Chelsea that he would never say publicly, and we would probably come away saying, "fair enough".

In his post-match press conference, he said that playing Ilkay Gundogan in a deep-lying role rather than Fernandinho or Rodri (who had, between them, featured in 59 of City's previous 60 games this season) was because he moves the ball quickly and can find other players in spaces.

But why were they just running really fast towards the Chelsea goal, then? After winning the Premier League title by being "patient", in Guardiola's words, by using the ball deliberately slowly and then striking at the right moment, they threw it all out of the window.

He said before the game that City are about "attack, attack, attack" and how beautiful it would have been, for the club and for him, had they tore through Chelsea to win their first Champions League with a performance that would have killed off the 'o' word forever.

But Guardiola also said in January that they're not a team to play by running up and down the pitch over 40 or 50 metres; that those days had gone when Leroy Sane left. Maybe De Bruyne and Raheem Sterling could do it, he said, but the counter-attacks were best left to Liverpool, Manchester United and Tottenham. Not so much Chelsea, back then. But we're in May now.

"I expected Fernandinho in the line-up," Tuchel said. The element of surprise clearly didn't work in City's favour.

"Gundogan played many years in this position, to have speed on the ball, find the small players, the brilliant players in between the lines and this was the decision," Guardiola explained.

Again, he could probably spell this out to us in great detail if he wanted to, and he says the players know what he wanted them to do (although they weren't too happy about the Lyon plan either) but why was that a better option than what had got City this far?

It's easy to sit at home or in the stands and question decisions after defeats, granted, but given Fernandinho had shone in recent weeks and earned his place for the semi-final second leg, why was he left out of the starting XI for the final?

But OK, if Gundogan needed to be moved away from the areas that have made him City's top scorer, or if City's best bet was to run through Chelsea at 100 miles per hour, why did Sterling have to be the one to come in? He's just not played well recently, it's as simple as that.

It must also be said that a lot of others didn't play well either. De Bruyne, who cruelly left the pitch in tears after being pole axed by Antonio Rudiger, had one of his worst nights, where nothing he tried came off. Riyad Mahrez, so decisive in recent weeks, barely got going.

As much as the game plan seemed incomprehensible, maybe there was some element of nervousness from the players on what was their first appearance on this stage. It's not as if the Chelsea players were around for their previous finals, but the sheer devastation of the City squad at full-time showed how much it meant to them. Zinchenko lay face down on the turf for minutes, ignoring his team-mates' attempts to cajole him up, before Ruben Dias hauled him to his feet.

"They played Champions League and cup finals as if they were friendlies," Guardiola said of his old team at Barcelona recently. "I was like, 'Fuck, lads we're playing a Champions League final, we're playing a cup final,' and they shrugged, they played them as if they were friendlies. There was the awareness, that assurance."

He then acknowledged that his City side are not quite there: "We're not so used to playing these 'friendlies'."

Individual performances are another part of the story, of course they are, but it must circle back to the team selection because, again, City's success has been built around getting their players to do what they're good at and shielding them from what they're not so good at. It sounds simple, but that's why they're so good. Rodri, for example, looked much better once the spaces either side of him closed up and he could focus on passing the ball instead of chasing after it.

So was it any surprise that Zinchenko, who has improved markedly off the ball, might have struggled when the entire team parted in front of him and left him hopelessly exposed at the back? They were on a hiding to nothing and it's just so difficult to work out why.

----------------------------- **A** -----------------------------

Guardiola must be asking himself all these questions – or at least some of them. He has got things right in the Champions League, victories that are airbrushed from history when we talk about overthinking. He's been hammered when his players have made mistakes, and he's been praised when his team have had lucky breaks. He points that out all the time.

And yet, no matter what we're talking about, no matter what his truth is, he knows he just can't get there (yet – because he surely will).

"It's like Barca-Chelsea (in the 2011/12 semi-final second leg) all over again," he said after his Bayern side battered Atletico Madrid in the 2015/16 semi-finals but went out anyway. "But this is worse."

Even when he had Lionel Messi, his supposed silver bullet, things went awry, and even when his teams have dominated, they've come up short. He tore his shirt to bits with his fingers after that Atletico game, exasperated.

"Pep took it the worst, and that's quite normal in the circumstances," City's chief executive Ferran Soriano says of the fall-out after their heartbreaking elimination at the hands of Tottenham two years ago. He had learned his lesson that season, tightening the team up for the first leg in London, only for Aguero to miss a penalty – like Messi against Chelsea, like Muller against Atleti.

The second leg of that quarter-final was much more dynamic, and it wasn't enough. He went ultra-defensive, by his standards, against Lyon in Lisbon nine months ago and now, 200 miles up the Portuguese coast, he went ultra-attacking. Same result. Same performance, really, only without the chances.

Why does it keep happening? Between bad luck and bad decisions, he might not know himself. It's just in his nature.

MANCHESTER CITY'S 2020/21: GREAT SEASON, TERRIBLE ENDING

SAM LEE

JUN 2, 2021

Is it still too soon? It might be a while before the pain fades but, without going fully 'York away' about it, Manchester City didn't have a bad old season, did they?

Expectations are much higher now than when City travelled to Bootham Crescent, and lost 2-1, as a mid-table third division side in December 1998; the players are some of the best in the world, the manager is a genius, so the argument that things were much worse in years gone isn't really applicable.

Losing Saturday's Champions League final to Chelsea, particularly in that manner, was galling. It's impossible to dismiss the feeling that this season could've been so much better. And with the Premier League title triumph so well analysed, celebrated so joyously the previous weekend and stored away in club history, it is hard to look past what happened in Porto less than 72 hours ago. It's still raw.

As one homebound fan at the airport afterwards put it, "I'm not angry, I'm just sad." The two trophies City won this season are little consolation when those emotions are in play. That's football.

And yet, it's also impossible to overlook all the factors that led to City playing 61 out of a possible 62 games this season,

283

coming closer to winning every trophy up for grabs than any English club has ever managed.

Pep Guardiola's reaction to the defeat has been similar: last season, when City were eliminated by Lyon, he didn't speak to the players at all, but at the weekend he went around the squad to congratulate them on a fine season, although the pain of how it ended was evident.

Maybe in a few days it will all be easier to digest. Rival fans will hold onto Porto forever but few clubs are ready to challenge City, as long as they make the necessary changes to their squad this summer. It was certainly the case over the duration of the season.

City are brilliant and while losing Saturday's final was crushing, it can't whitewash the previous six months of good work, the years before that, or the feeling they can go even further next season.

There is a new, traumatic chapter to City and Guardiola's Champions League story but the fact remains they got further in the competition than they had done previously, and they deserved to do so. They showed us things along their route to the final that were worth enjoying at the time and that bode well for the future.

It does sound a bit like loser talk but before this season, people wondered if they would ever get past a European quarter-final under Guardiola. Inevitably, that adds to the sense that the final was a big opportunity wasted (because it was), but it's still easy to see growth and huge potential.

All the positive stuff previously said about this team still applies. Their mid-season turnaround remains mightily impressive. If it weren't for that, they wouldn't have been playing Chelsea in Porto in the first place. If it weren't for that turnaround, Guardiola and City would have bigger problems to deal with this summer than they do. And if it weren't for Guardiola, City wouldn't have won so many trophies over the past five years.

He might infuriate with his selections once or twice per season, but it looks like that's just part of the deal with him. The rest of it is pretty sweet. There's nobody around who could do the job better.

It's like Kevin De Bruyne playing poorly in the final: you wouldn't swap him for anybody anyway, so you just have to accept it. It doesn't mean he's not a great player. Lionel Messi hasn't won a World Cup. The original Ronaldo never won the Champions League. Sometimes football works like this.

Yes, it's hard now, perhaps even pointless, to go back over the particulars of everything that led up to Saturday night. But City still won 21 games in a row in all competitions, City still had the Premier League's best defence and the best attack, City still kept the most clean sheets in the division, Guardiola still sat down with his inner circle and found a way, in the darkest moments of the season, to turn everything around in the blink of an eye; he defied expectations and took City back to the top of the Premier League and further than expected in Europe, finding a way to dominate games without a striker, to play attractive yet resilient football. Why didn't he just do it one more time in Porto?! Ah, that feeling will never go away.

But Phil Foden still scored that fine goal in a 4-1 win at Anfield, Ruben Dias still won the writers' Footballer of the Year award in his debut season, Bernardo Silva still enchanted fans with his industrious performances, Riyad Mahrez still showed his full potential, Ilkay Gundogan still reminded us why he's so important, John Stones still delighted fans with his comeback, Fernandinho still rolled back the years, Oleksandr Zinchenko and Rodri still shook off last season's doubts, there were still fans at Wembley to see City win the Carabao Cup for the fourth time in a row, there were even more of them at the Etihad to see City lift their third champions' trophy in four years, after a game where they still saw Sergio Aguero come on and score twice in his farewell Premier League appearance – one of the most special, emotional moments the stadium has ever witnessed.

That all happened. So did that disaster in Porto.

It was a great season, it was a disappointing season.

The two things will just have to live hand in hand.

MAY RESULTS

Premier League, May 1, 2021

Crystal Palace 0 Man City 2

Man City scorers: Aguero 57, Torres 59

Champions League, May 4, 2021

Man City 2 Paris Saint-Germain 0

Man City scorers: Mahrez 11, 63

Premier League, May 8, 2021

Man City 1 Chelsea 2

Man City scorers: Sterling 44

Premier League, May 14, 2021

Newcastle 3 Man City 4

Man City scorers: Cancelo 39, Torres 42, 64, 66

Premier League, May 18, 2021

Brighton 3 Man City 2

Man City scorers: Gundogan 2, Foden 48

Premier League, May 23, 2021

Man City 5 Everton 0

Man City scorers: De Bruyne 11, Jesus 14, Foden 53, Aguero 71, 76

Champions League, May 29, 2021

Man City 0 Chelsea 1

MANCHESTER CITY'S CHAMPIONS – BY THE COACHES WHO MOULDED THEM

SAM LEE, OLIVER KAY, JACK LANG, DANIEL TAYLOR,
CHARLOTTE HARPUR, ADAM CRAFTON AND PAUL TENORIO
MAY 29, 2021

These Manchester City players have won almost everything there is to be won over the past few years. They come from all over the world, thrown together by one of the most ambitious sporting projects in history and united by the footballing ideals of their brilliant coach, Pep Guardiola.

From Phil Foden to Sergio Aguero, Kevin De Bruyne to Ruben Dias, they each have their own stories.

To tell those stories, *The Athletic* has tracked down the coaches who shaped City's stars, the people who helped develop kids into players. These guys have come a long way, and this is their story . . .

EDERSON
Luiz Batista da Silva Junior, coach at Sao Paulo FC

I first saw Ederson play in an open trial we put on at a social club. I liked his sense of timing and his intelligence, which allowed him to learn all the fundamentals quickly. His character also stood out: he was determined and courageous on the pitch. Then there was his ability with the ball at his feet. He was always one of the standout players when we did possession games, and his friends used to insist that he could also play in defence.

The role model for every Sao Paulo goalkeeper at that time was Rogerio Ceni, who liked to pass out from the back, and even scored more than 100 goals from penalties and free-kicks. If you look at the goalkeepers who came through during those years, you will see that a lot of them have those characteristics. Ederson is no exception.

We had to iron out a few wrinkles in his game, particularly in terms of his movement. I worked him really hard, but Ederson never complained about anything. He kept quiet and accepted everything with a smile or a laugh. He was a hard trainer: often, when the other goalkeepers took part in practice matches, we'd do extra work on his positioning, diving saves and distribution.

He wasn't the first-choice goalkeeper in his age group because he had yet to fully develop, technically or physically. He was very skinny, very lightweight. I believed that he would develop further down the line and eventually break into the senior squad, but others were not convinced. At first, I managed to talk the academy bosses into giving him more time, but they eventually decided to let him go. I was annoyed at that decision.

I'm proud to have taught him the basics, which he still uses to perfection today. Ederson's nickname at Sao Paulo was Fatty – a silly joke because he was so thin. He's grown a lot since then. If I could give him a new nickname today, it would be The Wall.

KYLE WALKER

Paul Archer, his coach at Football Unites, Racism Divides

I was involved with a charity called Football Unites, Racism Divides, which is about using football to give opportunities and bring together people from different backgrounds.

We ran sessions once or twice a week and I remember a very young Kyle rocked up one day. I think he had been staying over at his cousin's. We were doing some skills in small groups, passing it backwards and forwards and doing some tricks on the ball. When he came back the next week, he said to me, "I've been practising that trick. Look at this."

He was a character, quite mischievous, but he always had a smile. He was from a tough area, not far from Bramall Lane, and he had to be able to look after himself. His parents helped him a lot. They were very supportive.

His enthusiasm and attitude really stood out. Also, he was very quick and skilful. After a couple of weeks, I looked at him and thought, "Wow. This kid isn't bad."

I also worked with Sheffield United's centre of excellence, so I got him involved there once he had reached the under-nines. He played as a winger there. He had great pace, a good shot, a trick or two up his sleeve. He wasn't necessarily the most talented in that team. There were others who he would probably say were technically better. But he had a fantastic attitude and work rate and he always wanted to improve.

He was still playing on the wing until he was in the under-15s, when he was picked at full-back for one game because they were playing against a team who had a very quick winger. To the surprise of a lot of people at the club, he did really well there and looked at home. He really blossomed at full-back, particularly after he had a growth spurt. He was probably 5ft 8in when he was 17, but then he got bigger and stronger, went on loan to

Northampton and did really well. Since then he has just gone from strength to strength.

RUBEN DIAS
Vitor Couto, Benfica under-12s and under-13s coach

In his first year, Ruben wasn't as physically developed as his team-mates. He was a tall guy, but he was just bones! But we knew that when he would improve his strength he would become an animal.

In the early years, he wasn't the most technical defender that we had. He didn't need to defend too much because at Benfica, we have the best players in the country and the games are 80-90 per cent attacking. Defending was something he had to improve in the biggest games at under-18 and under-19 level; and he made some mistakes because it was not something that he had to do a lot of. It was the same for David Luiz.

I think he started to catch his team-mates' attention at 16. Their performances were top-level, so if the guy is not good in the small details and he talks, they won't listen. But if he makes a difference he is somebody to follow, and Ruben was like that from 16 years old. It was the Ruben we see now.

Some players communicate only because we tell them to, but the way Ruben communicates is out of the ordinary. He tells his team-mates to press the opponents… sometimes he pressed the referees, too. The work he did in his early year shows that he works hard and listens – another indicator that he would be a top player.

Inside one month he was the boss at Manchester City! He talks to everybody, puts everybody in position. That was Ruben when he was 12.

AYMERIC LAPORTE
Jose Maria Amorrortu, academy director at Athletic

He is very extroverted and very confident. I always used to say that he was like a joker in a pack of cards – he could just get you out of difficult situations. When he was younger he could play in any position on the pitch. He wasn't just a defender, he could bring it out from the back and arrive in other positions. He had a lot of confidence in what he could do and that allowed him to make decisions without any fear. Sometimes he had problems with his concentration because he was so confident in himself that it could lead to a mistake. As he matured he got better and much more consistent.

He always needed more demanding challenges to be motivated because he could do the simpler ones. In his first year at Athletic, his dad wanted us to push him even more, to put him up an age group. I remember a conversation with him and Aymeric, telling them that we had a lot of confidence in him as a player but that we had plans and that they should be patient and have faith in us. A year later, he played in the first team.

I remember a conversation I had with Marcelo Bielsa when Aymeric started to train with the first team. He said to me, "This kid gives me a lot of confidence because he's very natural and he doesn't get nervous when training with the older players, he's just another player."

He had a lot of offers to leave, but he rejected them because although he always wanted to improve, he wanted Athletic to improve too. That's important. When he did move to Manchester City, he was very grateful to the club and to us.

JOHN STONES
Mark Smith, coach at Penistone Church

Two of us, Albert Rennison and myself, were doing coaching sessions for kids and this little lad came along one day. He was only five years old and he was so quiet. We had the kids doing little drills – right foot, left foot, bring the ball across your body, step across the ball – and immediately he did it to a tee. Everything you showed him, he carried it out perfectly.

From a very early age, John looked like he could be a footballer. But I also felt that he could have become a top athlete. He was tall and leggy and he had a great stride. He could run all day. He was such a natural athlete.

He used to play in defence, as the last man. Knowing he could play a bit, I would say to him, "If you're on the ball and you've got time, make them think you're going to lump it forward, but instead just roll your foot across the ball. Then have a look at who's moved, where the space is appearing. Take your time." He always took that on board. I think that's one of his great strengths to this day.

He went to Barnsley when he was eight, joining their centre of excellence. It wasn't always easy for him, but his quality and his attitude took him through.

He was a model pupil, a well-behaved kid from a lovely family. And he hasn't changed. He's still the nice, soft-natured lad he was back then – which is the way people in Penistone tend to be.

But I remember him playing for me in the Barnsley schools team a few years later, up against this tough lad, and John put his foot on the ball and I heard him say, "You want this ball? Come and get it . . . well, you can't have it. It's mine." And he went away with the ball.

That was the moment I knew he was going on a long journey as a footballer. I hadn't seen that in him before. He needed to develop that little bit of arrogance on the pitch.

NATHAN AKE
Harry de Jong, coach at VV Wilhelmus

Nathan was six when I first worked with him. He had a good left foot, he was powerful and he really enjoyed football. You could see the talent and he was more advanced than the other kids, although he was a little bit shy.

I have also worked in professional football but I was surprised to see a boy so good at that level. I told Nathan's father that if he carried on in this way he could go far in football. His parents are a little shy too, like Nathan, so they said, "Well that would be great, we'll see." Very calm! But I felt a responsibility to help him fulfil his potential

He then went to a professional club, ADO Den Haag, from eight to 11, then from 11 to 16, he was at Feyenoord. Wilhelmus is a feeder club for ADO, so they had a lot of scouts at our games. They asked me questions about him – what he was like as a person? Was his family background stable? How does he behave on and off the pitch? Of course, the answers were good, he was a pleasant boy, he always wanted to train. He's one of the guys you want on your team.

What stands out most is just his general character, his personality. He still keeps in touch with his friends, he remembers his roots. He still invites me to games in England – I went to Chelsea and Bournemouth games and Nathan's parents are still involved in Wilhelmus. He was just an all-round good kid, and a good player.

BENJAMIN MENDY
Mohamed Sall, coach at Le Havre from 1992 to 2015

The first time I saw him was when he came from Paris accompanied by his parents, sister and brother to sign for Le Havre at the age of 13. He was polite, kind, a very respectful boy. Average height, quite slim, not very tall or strong.

When he arrived, he played as an attacker, but he wasn't made for it. He had a difficult start. He missed his family. I thought he just needed time. I did two exercises: a 10-metre speed test, one from a standing start and one from a running start. He was the slowest from a standing start but the quickest from the running one so I knew that he had to be a defender. It's not difficult. A player who needs to be rolling should be put in defence.

If you watch him today, when he collects the ball, controls it and runs from a standstill, he can't beat a player. But when he plays off the shoulder, then he's interesting.

I explained this to him but he was adamant he wanted to stay up front. During one training session – he was also in the same training group as Paul Pogba – it wasn't going well. We put him in midfield, back up front, then in defence and he was strong there. "You see?" I said but he didn't budge. He was like that until the last game of the season, he didn't give up on it. We had a cup final against ALM Evreux, Steve Mandanda's former club, and Benjamin started up front but after 25 minutes we were trailing 1-0. We had to do something. "Benjamin, you play on the left," I shouted. He looked at me. He wasn't happy. I said, "Benjamin, you play on the left or you come off."

He went to the left and at half-time we were leading 2-1 thanks to him. He stayed there, made decisive passes, scored a goal and we won the game 6-1 against a very good team.

Benjamin came to see me.

"Momo, momo," he called.

"What's up?" I said.

"I found my position," he said.

"Ah, bon? What is it, up front?"

"No, no, no, it's not up front."

"Which position then?"

"It's left-back!"

The next season, he went up a category, he shone as a left-back and was called up by the French national youth team.

OLEKSANDR ZINCHENKO
Viktor Karpeta, coach at FC Monolit Illichivsk

Alex was 11 when he joined our football academy, but he trained with the under-13s. The team was doing some physical tests and they were running long distances. They had to run three kilometres in 12 minutes. Alex was among the leading group after the first half of the distance, but with a few laps remaining, he began to complain that he couldn't run any more. I said to him, "It's OK, you can stop, you already did very well," but he kept on running and finished with the leading group. His determination and desire to be the best has helped him to be so successful.

JOAO CANCELO
Rodrigo Magalhaes, Benfica technical
coordinator up to under-15 level

If we can give Cancelo a nickname it would probably be 'Fast and Dangerous'. That was Cancelo at that age. He was very, very competitive, very aggressive, the way he wanted to recover the ball. Then with the ball, he always wanted to make the other team suffer. We love those kinds of players. If we started a small exercise, Cancelo wanted to win and be the best in every situation.

In the under-19 national championship, we played a tough game at Rio Ave, a good team with their own crowd, and Cancelo said, "OK, we need a hero so I'm here, I'll be man of the match, I'll score." He scored two goals and I think one of them was straight from a corner. We needed a guy with character, personality, to step up, to say, "There's no chance we're losing the championship." His personality led everybody to success.

When he was in the B team, sometimes he would come to our under-19s training. Cancelo got involved in the sessions and we had two or three trialists in there. It started with a *rondo* and after 30 seconds, he made two or three hard tackles on the trialists and they started complaining a little. Imagine, two or three guys rubbing their hands about being at Benfica, then the session starts and Cancelo tells them, "Put the ball here, receive it like that." When they fail once or twice he goes 'boom, boom, boom' and makes two or three tackles . . . they were in a panic! He was saying, "What the fuck is this, they don't have any chance to play here, get rid of these guys!"

RODRI

Jose Maria Amorrortu, academy director at Atletico Madrid

We brought him into the club in the 'infantil' (12 or 13 years old) category. He was very young and he stood out because of his vision, his insight, because he had great knowledge of the game and he anticipated different situations. When it came to decision making there are things that a lot of players find difficult, but he did them easily, very naturally. He anticipated what could happen in the game and he played in a very simple way.

Rodri is very tall and strong now but as a kid, he was a little delayed in his physical development. He was very thin, but we knew we had to have patience with him, to delay the developmental work a little. He had things in his head that he wanted to do, but because of his physicality he couldn't do them. When he grew up and became stronger he could do everything.

He made the game tick, he was a playmaker. He didn't need to run much to play well. He was like a sheikh, a pharaoh that led the others to play well. He was a kid that had great vision, a 360-degree view, which is rare, and every time he got the ball he did something that benefited the other players. In Spain, we have always valued this type of player.

ILKAY GUNDOGAN
Michael Oenning, his coach at Bochum and Nurnberg

In the first training session, I asked him to hit some long balls with top-spin and lots of different kinds of crosses. He did it immediately with both feet. It was like a game for him and I said, "You will be a professional player." He didn't believe it.

He was born in a Turkish community in Germany (in Gelsenkirchen), so nothing was easy for him. He learned to survive, but in the beginning, was really shy. He hid a little bit. He always had some doubts about himself. He was interested in his team-mates and always looking after others. If you really wanted to know what was going on in his head, you had to ask him.

He was a complete footballer at 17, two footed. The first touch was always good. In the beginning, he dribbled all the time and then turned. What you saw this season, when he goes into the box and is able to score, that ability was always there but he forgot it because the coaches always told him to play with one or two touches.

He was a No. 10, nothing else. He was able to score but also to give these assists, these key passes high up the pitch. I never expected him to become a defensive midfielder, never ever.

I always thought he would lose something if he played deeper but the last 10 years showed something different. I know that his great favourites were Andres Iniesta and Xavi, especially Xavi, and he tried to copy him. His biggest dream was to play in Spain, but of course, now he has a Spanish coach, so Spain has come to England.

FERNANDINHO

Leandro Niehues, Fernandinho's coach for two-and-a-half years at Parana Soccer Technical Center (PSTC)

I first met Fernando when he was 13. He was a slender kid, but so physically strong. A lot of lightweight players suffer on the pitch, but not him. He was explosive and fast, so he could close down opponents very quickly – and he could play as well. He also read the game really well: he always understood where to move, what to do next. He was training with the under-18s at 14 or 15, so I never doubted he would go far. He was a prodigy.

One of his best characteristics was his versatility. He was good defensively and going forward, so I made sure he played in different positions. With me, Fernando played as a defensive midfielder, as a right wing-back, as a playmaker and even as a second striker. I used him as a wing-back fairly often. He could cover the ground on the right flank and had the quality to come inside as well. That versatility opened a lot of doors for him at Athletico Paranaense. A lot of his first opportunities in the first team came at right wing-back.

He always had that knack for avoiding yellow cards. He was an aggressive marker and committed plenty of fouls, but he was always close to his man, so it never seemed like he was arriving late to a tackle. Fernando's personality also helped: he was a nice guy and charismatic, which often meant he avoided bookings.

The best players in youth football aren't always the most popular with their team-mates, but everyone liked Fernando. He wasn't the most talkative and he wasn't the ringleader when the kids were messing about; he was a bit more reserved. But he had a good heart.

Kleberson, who played for Manchester United, also started at PSTC, and people always wanted to judge Fernando against him. I always told people that in footballing terms, I expected Fernando to get to a higher level. Yes, Kleberson won the World Cup, but Fernando's career speaks for itself.

BERNARDO SILVA
Rodrigo Magalhaes, Benfica technical
coordinator up to under-15 level

At seven-a-side, Bernardo was amazing with the ball. It was an extension of his body and he had a magic left foot. With his game knowledge and decision-making, he was different to the others. But in the long-term development process, we saw some difficulties. Under-15 to under-18 was difficult for Bernardo because he had matured at a different age from his colleagues.

At 15, he had a biological age of 13 or 14 but it was not a problem. Sometimes we have under-15s playing in the under-14s. It's not just physical, it affects the mind, the body, the nervous system, the speed that you can think and act.

For example, Bernardo sometimes looked to do a long-distance pass and it wasn't successful, but we asked him what he wanted to do and he said, "Mister, I saw the line between the centre-back and the right-back and I tried to put the ball in this space," and everybody said, "OK, Bernardo, that's good, keep trying to do it, you don't have the strength now but maybe in one or two seasons that pass will work. Believe in yourself."

Bernardo was a cerebral player, he had a 360-degree view of the game. I remember when he was in the under-12s, we started to explain an exercise and Bernardo gave us three or four new solutions to succeed in the drill. The coach said to me, "What the fuck is this? I need to throw this training session in the bin, this kid is giving all the answers!"

Another example was a game in Spain a year later. Normally in Portugal, we play seven-a-side in a 2-3-1 structure, but in Spain, we played against 3-1-2 or 3-2-1. During the first or second game, Bernardo started talking to his team-mates, explaining to them how to defend against those systems. It was amazing how a kid of 12 or 13 years old could have that kind of game comprehension, the ability to adapt to overcome a different system. Nobody expected us to get far in the tournament. The club only paid for us to have a local guide for the group stage, but we got to the final.

When he had the ball it was like a kid with candy, because of the smile on his face. That's a good characteristic because sometimes we saw players who, after a few years of football, were not happy any more. Bernardo always tried to do different things and it was contagious for the other players.

PHIL FODEN
Joe Makin, football development officer for Foden's junior team, Reddish Vulcans. Also works in recruitment for Manchester City's academy

Phil came to see me a while back and, at one point, he just looked at me and said, "You can be honest with me, did you really think I was going to make it?"

I told him that, in 2008, I put a little piece on the front page of the Reddish Vulcans website. He was seven at the time. The words were, "Remember the name of Phil Foden – a left foot to die for."

And Phil said, "My mum's got that framed!"

Phil was spotted on a schools programme that involved a coach from City going into every primary school in Greater Manchester to offer the five and six-year-olds a 45-minute sport and leisure session.

Phil was obviously very talented. And he had balance. The doubters always ask, "How can you tell at such an early age?" And the others ask, "What do you look for in someone that young?" In my experience the only thing I really look for is balance. Phil had it. And he was blessed with that left foot – which, for some strange reason, always looks more graceful than a right foot.

He got fast-tracked to City's academy at Platt Lane and started going down there twice a week. I got talking to his dad, Phil senior, and found out he wasn't registered to a junior football club. We encourage grassroots football at that age because you can't beat having that competitive edge. So I invited him to Vulcans.

I remember one time we were playing at Curzon Ashton. Phil scored a couple of goals in the first two or three minutes. I was standing on the touchline and heard one of the parents from the opposition saying, "You would pay to watch this, wouldn't you?"

It had quickly become obvious he was pretty special. On the first or second time he came down for training with the under-sevens, a dad came over to me and said, "That little boy with the left foot, the new boy, where has he come from?"

I put my hands together in a praying motion, looked up to the sky and said, "Heaven."

KEVIN DE BRUYNE
Rudy Schelstraete, coach at KVV Drongen

Kevin stood out first of all because he was a tiny boy with a red face and blond hair, which was almost white. But when he started playing, he stood out because of his football.

He was very special. He was playing above his age group and he could do things with the ball that the other boys in the team couldn't. He was quick, he could dribble, he had a powerful shot and he could make beautiful passes and crosses that other players couldn't. He was only six years old but he was playing like an adult.

The other thing was that he was a winner. He was always desperate to win. I remember once when we were losing a game, Kevin walked off the pitch crying and went straight to the changing room. His father, who was coaching with me, went after him and told him to come back. Kevin said, "We're losing. I don't want to lose any more." His father said to him, "You have to go back. You don't leave your team-mates during a match."

Kevin went back out there and it was like there was steam coming out of his nose. I'm sure he scored a goal. That was the thing with Kevin. Whenever we were losing, the other players would give him the ball. Usually, he would go straight through the opposition and score a goal.

He was exceptional. Everybody could see it. Not just me, but the other coaches in the other teams. The coach from KAA Gent came to watch him and asked if he wanted to play with the team there. Kevin went along and when he came back he said the training was better there! I didn't take it personally. Kevin was so serious about football and he knew what he was doing. And look at him now.

RIYAD MAHREZ
Franck Satougle coached Mahrez
at AAS Sarcelles from 2002 to 2004

His dad is his motivation. Unfortunately, he passed away when Riyad was a teenager, but they were always together. His dad loved football, took him to training, travelled everywhere with him. When his father died it gave him the strength to succeed and do what he's doing now.

The first time I saw Riyad was when his dad brought him to the club. He was a small, skinny boy. We didn't think, 'Wow, watch this kid'. He needed to be quicker, more physical and grow a bit but from a technical point of view, he was way above the rest. He was a bit shy but very confident in his ability. He knew what he wanted. He just needed time to develop physically.

Riyad always had a football tucked under his arm, whether it was 8am or at lunchtime. If he had a spare five minutes, he'd practise his skills on his own just to perfect his technique. The whole town knew Riyad. He would go from playing in one neighbourhood to the next.

He wasn't ashamed to say he loved football. Some people mocked him and told him not to make a fool of himself but it didn't bother Riyad because he knew he'd get to the top. There are players who have that natural talent. He was a very good dribbler. It was as if he was playing with a hand instead of a foot.

Ever since he was a boy, he would convince you that he's going to shoot with his left only to fake it. You think he's going one way, then he skips past. When he was younger, he never used his right foot. I've noticed that since he's arrived in England, he's worked a lot on that.

When his friends moved on to play for Bordeaux and Parisian clubs, he suffered a bit. He was frustrated because he knew technically he was just as good as them. Up until he was 17 years old, he stayed in the same physical shape. He went to St Mirren in Scotland for a month and when he came back, it was as if he had metamorphosed. He was a completely different player, he did everything quicker, he was tougher, that was a turning point for him.

I'll never forget the first round of the Coupe de France at the end of the year. He played with the adults. We were losing 3-0, Riyad came on at half-time and we won 5-3. I swear to you, he did everything, he made the difference. From that day on, I thought he had something. He couldn't stay with us.

He's a simple guy who likes to joke around. He hasn't changed. After the Champions League game against Paris Saint-Germain, we were laughing on the phone just as if he was still at AAS Sarcelles.

FERRAN TORRES
Raul Munoz, coach at the Valencia academy

Even when he was six years old, he struck me as a remarkably ambitious kid. He always wanted to play more, to win more, to train more, to listen more and be the best player. He had those defining characteristics. He is a humble kid and he remembers where he came from. He stays in touch with the coaches who guided him as a child and continues to talk to us. He is introverted and quiet but on the pitch, he competes as well as anybody.

He was part of the gifted generation of 2000 that was very strong at Valencia and a handful have gone on to be professionals, such as Abel Ruiz at Braga, Victor Chust at Real Madrid and Hugo Guillamon at Valencia. It is obviously very difficult to forecast who will become a star player. We knew he had talent but so many things have to go your way to reach the top. There are players who had the talent and competitive spirit, perhaps even greater than Ferran's at the time, who have not made it.

One of his defining qualities as a player was always his ability to use the ball with both feet. When we played in local leagues in Valencia, there was always quite a big difference in quality between our academy teams and those who played against us. As such, we set the players individual challenges, beyond winning the match. In the case of Ferran, if he was playing on the right wing, we challenged him to try and score with his left foot or with a header. He began to work very hard on his left foot and scored a high number of goals with his left, even when he was seven or eight years old.

He was playing as an up-and-down right winger in the younger age groups, although he did have a year as a centre-forward when he was 12 years old and we made the transition from eight-a-side games to eleven-a-side games. This is because he was struggling with his physical co-ordination. He had grown very tall very quickly and it took a bit of time for him to adapt to that in his physical movements. Of course, we continued to believe in him and bet on him as a player. But we moved him to centre-forward because he was looking a little awkward on the wing. It was only for a few months but helped rebuild his confidence during the growth spurt.

By the time he was 14 or 15, his physical condition really took shape and his body became fully formed. After that, there were far less doubts about him. But his qualities as a six-year-old are visible today. He ran harder and further than the other kids and seemed resilient physically. It was as though he never became tired. From a technical point of view, he was very composed in tight spaces, his one-on-one finishing was clinical and he became a very good crosser of the ball. I am very proud of him.

RAHEEM STERLING

*Clive Ellington is a coach for Alpha and Omega FC in Kingsbury,
north-west London, and a mentor for children in the Brent district*

He was eight when I saw him. He was in the school playground
and he stood out straight away. I asked him who he played for
and he said he didn't have a club. So we took him to Alpha and,
at his first training session, all the coaches stood in awe. We
knew straight away we had someone special on our hands, even
if he didn't recognise it himself.

The things he was doing with a ball, you'd normally see from
a 14 or 15-year-old who had been coached at a high level. It
just came naturally to him. He was small for his age, with a low
centre of gravity. His agility and ability, on and off the ball, was
good. Talent, technique. And he had a passion for football. It
was his first love.

We knew we had a lot more to do with, and for, him. He
had to understand the mechanics of teamwork and discipline.
Knowing how to win gracefully, how to lose humbly. From
eight to 12, he just grew and grew and grew. At times, you'd
think it was a one-man team. But the memory that really
stands out is when he joined QPR's youth set-up and a game
against Arsenal.

I remember Arsenal's coach asking their substitutes, "Who
wants to get on?" Everyone was reluctant to go on because
Raheem was running the show. The only way to stop him
back then was to kick him. He was getting kicked left, right
and centre and, in the end, he called the referee a cheat. The
referee said to the manager, "Look, take him off before I send
him off." So they took him off to calm down. The minute he
went off, the Arsenal coach asked again, "Right, who wants to
go on?" And it was a very different response that time – "I do!
I do! I do!"

There were some scouts at that match who had come down to watch the other players and, afterwards, Raheem was the talk of the town. Everyone was talking in the canteen, all asking the same thing: "Who's that kid?"

GABRIEL JESUS
Jose Mamede, coach at Pequeninos do Meio Ambiente

Gabriel was eight when he arrived at the club. He first turned up with two friends and asked how they could join the team. I told them they just had to come along to training with their boots . . . but if they didn't have any, we could work something out.

I knew there was something different about him from the first day. He had '*ginga*' – that innate swing that the best Brazilian players have. He dribbled well, he was intelligent. I looked at him and saw another Ronaldo Fenomeno, particularly in his speed and his explosiveness.

He also had this real desire to score goals – and he scored hatfuls at Pequeninos. That was his biggest strength. I kept following his progress after he moved to Palmeiras, and he scored a lot for their youth sides. But when he reached the first team, he wasn't playing in his true position. For me, Gabriel is a No. 9 – a natural-born striker. He loves scoring goals. He was always the top scorer in his age group. He'd average three or four goals a match.

He was very committed: he never missed a training session and always gave everything. Sometimes, he would get agitated on the pitch. He used to get kicked a lot and the referees didn't always protect him properly. He would get really wound up, to the point where I often had to shout: "Gabriel, keep your head! They're trying to get a reaction from you!" Everyone in the local league knew about him and knew he had that side to him.

He left when he was 14 because we didn't have teams for under-15s and above. We always thought he would go far. I remember telling him exactly that at our Christmas party one year. I was certain that he would turn professional. There was simply no way it wasn't going to happen. He was a really focused kid: he clearly knew what he wanted. And he was just so much better than the rest.

He has returned to the club two or three times in the last few years. He donated some boots to the kids, things like that. Our club has a social function. We play in the grounds of a military prison and we give out lots of food baskets: we used to give food to Gabriel's family back when he was here. I remember one occasion when he made a surprise visit, on the day of a tournament we run at the club. Even I didn't know he was coming. Gabriel handed out the medals and you can just imagine what that was like for the little kids. It was unforgettable.

I have followed every step of his journey. I remember looking for his name in the newspaper when it was rumoured that he was about to get his senior debut for Palmeiras. To see him playing, then scoring, then becoming this phenomenon in Brazil, then moving to Europe . . . it has been amazing.

I'm a card-carrying member of the Gabriel fan club. I'm always cheering for him.

SERGIO AGUERO
*Jorge Ariza, who spotted Aguero on local pitches
and took him to first his first club, Primero de Mayo*

He was a short, stocky five or six-year-old with a good physique. He gave these instructions, "run here", "play it there", and if he knew how to give those instructions it's because he had the intelligence to read the game. I thought to myself that he had to be a good player, but I must admit that when I saw him play properly, he exceeded all my expectations.

Already, at only five years old, he had that something extra that sets the chosen ones apart. He was touched by a magic wand. It wasn't just talent. It was intelligence, the shrewdness to analyse what was happening on the field of play. He saw things one step ahead of the others, and that made the difference. And when you sometimes thought that he had faded out from a game, he would pop up all of a sudden and win it by himself. He would drop deep and demand the ball on the floor from the goalkeeper, then jink his way past everyone. And they'd be kicking lumps out of him! But he would carry on without complaining and would end up teeing up a free team-mate for a goal, or just score himself. They couldn't stop him, it was a complete riot.

When I arrived (to collect him), he used to ask me to hold on a few minutes, He was always playing games or penalty shootouts with bigger boys, 12 or 13 years old. He would play them for loose change and would always win. Then with the money, he would buy these little juices they sold in the neighbourhood. The same image invariably pops into my head: Sergio running after the car with that prize in his hand.

"El Correntino" Ramirez, coach at
Primero de Mayo and Loma Alegre

It was a great team, with Kun as its talisman. As well as pure ability, he struck the ball so powerfully. A free-kick was almost as good as a goal. For his age, you could already see he was different. He went everywhere with Cristian Formiga, with whom he dovetailed so well on the field of play, whether they were playing on concrete or earth pitches. They had a telepathic understanding. Cristian was the goalscorer, but it was 'Kun' who really stood out. He was the playmaker on concrete surfaces, and more of a finisher on earth pitches.

*The Aguero passages were taken from his book *Born to Rise, My Story*